LIFE LESSONS

Effective Strategies for Living the Victories

Hong Yang
50/50

All scriptural quotations are taken from the Holy Bible,
New International Version (NIV) (1978) by New York
International Bible Society, and New King James Version
(NKJV) (1982) by Thomas Nelson, Inc.

ISBN: 978-1-59684-791-0
Copyright 2013
by Hong Y. Yang

Printed by Derek Press
1080 Montgomery Ave
Cleveland TN 37311
U.S.A.

Cover design: Esther Yang
Cover painting: Lucinda Yang
Text layout: Carmen Davis

Table of Contents

Prologue

There is a very interesting and intriguing observation by the wise man King Solomon in Ecclesiastes 3:11 that has always fascinated me. The Creator God "has made everything beautiful in its time. He has also set eternity in the hearts of men; yet they can not fathom what God has done from beginning to end." We are all travelers, voyagers and sojourners in the journey of life towards eternity. There are always plenty of things to do, various people to meet, many places to go, and lots of decisions to make. We must daily choose whether to embrace life actively, positively, heartily and fully, or to face life passively, pessimistically, negatively and half-heartedly. The choice for your life is yours, and yours alone to make. Success is here for you to take. All you have to do is to start living your life like it matters because your life does matter! This of necessity must start with careful and prayerful examination, for as Socrates proclaimed over two thousand years ago, "An unexamined life is not worth living," and as Viktor Frankl in his logotherapy (healing through meaning) confirmed, "an unexamined life leads to spiritual neurosis." In order to live a life of victory, success, prosperity, and abundance here and now, and a life that really matters also there and then eternally, one needs to ponder upon four of the most essential and fundamental issues of life. They are, namely, the origin, the identity, the purpose, and the destiny of one's personal life on earth.

The question of one's origin: Where did I come from anyway? In order to find meaning and make sense of the present, and prepare hopefully for the future, one needs to know his past and learn from the past.

The question of one's identity: Who am I? And Whose am I? One's identity is intimately and intricately related with one's origin. In order to know who we are, we need to know whose we are, for no one is an island unto himself.

The question of one's purpose: What in the world am I here for? What is the meaning of life? Identify your mission and your role within the big picture of the divine design. Ask yourself the key questions, "Why am I here?" and "What am I meant to be and to do with my life?" Life is very fulfilling to those who have found the purpose of living.

The question of one's destiny: Is this all there is to life? Where am I going? What does the future hold for me? Destiny deals with that which must take place. We are all designed with the destiny for eternity, everlasting life in heaven or in hell.

Thankfully, God's Word offers us the wonderful answers to all these questions in the form of powerful spiritual principles, and these principles in turn give us, according to Dr. John Maxwell (p.768), three crucial tools for a prosperous and victorious life to anyone who will put them into their daily practice:

> They are a guide; they help us stay on the right path.
> They are a guard; they keep our hearts and bodies protected.
> They are a gauge; they enable us to evaluate where we are.

Additionally, these solid and sound principles, tried and true throughout the ages by the tests of human experiences and even empirically proven in research, "build our character, direct our decisions, and correct our lifestyles." When used properly according to the Basic Instructions Before Leaving Earth (the BIBLE), these life lessons will bring us much love, joy, peace, contentment and fulfillment in this life, and bright hope for the things to come in the next. A person equipped and empowered by these valuable principles and victorious lessons will doubtlessly live his or her life actively, positively and optimistically. I have observed that a life's pessimist only sees all the adversities in the midst of an obvious opportunity, but an optimist of life can see all the opportunities in spite of an adversity. Many times in our lives, your adversity is your university! Don't shun it; attend it seriously. I have also noticed that the losers of life always want to feel good before they will do the right thing, but the winners of life always do the right thing and then they feel good as a result of doing it. So always do the right things for the right reason no matter whether you feel it or not, or feel like it or not. Set the bar high, do it with excellence. Don't try to be perfect as you can not, not in this world at least, but be professional with what you do, and do it with excellence.

Victorious and successful people, like lasting leadership that leaves a legacy, do not merely react to the happenings in their culture or across cultures; they base their life and leadership on a set of tested, proven, timeless and universal principles. They match or marry their cultural context to the basic powerful and practical principles they hold dear. Their lives are principle-centered, and not at all pleasure-driven. To live a purpose-driven life victoriously and abundantly, one must consume the Word of God daily and draw life lessons in the form of powerful principles for personal application and practice. This volume intends to share some of these most dynamic lessons I have thus learned in the past fifty years of my life, with the sincere hope and earnest prayers that they will bless you by adding special values and promoting precious virtues to you, enabling you with the effective strategies for living the victories. do it with excellence. Don't try to be perfect as you can not, not in this world at least, but be professional with what you do, and do it with excellence.

Victorious and successful people, like lasting leadership that leaves a legacy, do not merely react to the happenings in their culture or across cultures; they base their life and leadership on a set of tested, proven, timeless and universal principles. They match or marry their cultural context to the basic powerful and practical principles they hold dear. Their lives are principle-centered, and not at all pleasure-driven. To live a purpose-driven life victoriously and abundantly, one must consume the Word of God daily and draw life lessons in the form of powerful principles for personal application and practice. This volume intends to share some of these most dynamic lessons I have thus learned in the past fifty years of my life, with the sincere hope and earnest prayers that they will bless you by adding special values and promoting precious virtues to you, enabling you with the effective strategies for living the victories.

Chapter 1
Random Thoughts on
Gratitude, Passion and Hope

It is imperative that a godly person be a person of gratitude for the blessings of the Lord in the past, a person of passion for the opportunities to serve at the present, and a person of hope for bigger, better and brighter dreams for the future. A healthy heart is a grateful heart; a healthy heart is a passionate heart and a healthy heart is a hopeful heart. Here are a few of my thoughts in balance among gratitude, passion and hope in juxtaposition with the past, the present and the future.

Gratitude: Be truly thankful to God for Whom He is in your life and what the Lord has done for you and through you in all the years of the past!

I Thessalonians 5:18: Give thanks in all circumstances, for this is God's will for you in Christ Jesus.

Phil 4: 6-7: Be anxious for nothing, but in everything by prayer and supplication, with thanksgiving, let your request be made know to God; and the peace of God which surpasses all understanding, will guard your hearts and minds through Christ Jesus.

Gratitude is a duty which ought to be paid, but which none has a right to expect—Rousseau (Henry. p.113).

Count Your Blessings
Amid the conflicts whether big or small,
Do not be disheartened, God is over all;
Count your man blessing angels will attend,
Help and comfort give you to your journey's end.

Count your blessings, name them one by one,
Count your blessings, see what God hath done!
Count your blessings, name them one by one,
And it will surprise you what the Lord hath done.
(Johnson Oatman, Jr.)

Gratitude unlocks the fullness of life.
It turns what we have into enough, and more.
It turns denial into acceptance, chaos into order, confusion into clarity.

It turns a meal into a feast, a house into a home, a stranger into a friend.

Gratitude makes sense of our past, brings peace for today, and creates a vision for tomorrow!
(Melody Beattie)

One of the many lasting life lessons I have learned is the great value of thanksgiving, thanking God for my Lord Jesus, thanking the Lord for His church, and thanking thousands of others all over the world for the numerous benefits and blessings that have been bountifully showered upon me and my family. Psalm 103:2 wholeheartedly declares, "Praise the Lord, O my soul, and forget not all His benefits." Here is a worthy life lesson to remember and apply: don't forget any of the favors that others have done for you; and don't remember any of the favors you have done for others. This attitude of genuine gratitude has brought me more altitude of life and greater fortitude in ministries to others! Thank you Lord for all that You are and all that You have done and will do!

The Bible teaches us to give thanks "in all circumstances," not necessary for all things, but in all things we thank God as He channels us to His eternal purpose in Christ Jesus. I thank God for the sunshine, thank God for the rain, thank God for the water, thank God for the air, thank God for the clothes we wear, thank God for the bike I ride, for the car I drive, for the house I live in, for the foods to eat, for the favors I enjoy, for the faith that strengthens me, and my family and the friends I have and I love. I also thank God for the trials and adversities, for without trials, there would be no triumphs, and without adversities, we would not have the universities to learn life lessons from. God has a purpose in all things, and all things work together for the good of those who love God and who are called according to His purpose so that we can become more and more like Jesus the Son of God (Rom 8:28-29). If we will trust Him and pray, look up to Him and obey, the Lord will turn our dark night into a bright day. He can and he will transform your misery and tragedy into His melody and glory! Praise the Lord and thank Him in all things. Do not take things for granted, big or small.

When one is grateful for what the Lord has done for him in life, he will no longer be griping or grumbling. This grateful person is normally so filled with contentment with God provision that he will has no time in life or room in his heart to criticize or to complain. Philippines 2:14-15 instructs us to do everything without arguing or complaining so that we will become blameless and pure children of God in this crooked and depraved generation. Instead we will be shining for Jesus like stars in the universe as we hold out the Word of life. While legitimate complaints due to negligence or injustice have their proper place in the work places, spiritually speaking however, complaining against God is a very dangerous thing because (1). It is a manifestation of our insubordination to His divine authority; (2). It is revelation of our dissatisfaction with His provision; and (3). It is a sure killer of the spirit of contentment.

The attitude of gratitude to God and significant and relevant others is a small thing that makes a big difference. When we give thanks to God with a grateful heart, gratitude will:

1. give our heart a greater measure of joy, peace, love and contentment;

2. guard our heart from becoming greedy or calloused;

3. govern our actions toward more generosity to godly causes;

4. guide our future with confidence and hope.

Passion: Be genuinely enthused, excited and exuberant for what the Lord is enabling you to do for His glory at the present!

The opposite of love is not hate; it is indifference;
The opposite of art is not ugliness; it is indifference;
The opposite of faith is not heresy; it is indifference;
The opposite of life is not death; it is indifference!
—Ellie Wiesel (*www.Jewish-wisdom.com*)

The most powerful weapon on earth is the human soul on fire— Ferdinand Foch (*www.leadershipquotes.com*)

When you set yourself on fire, people love to come and see you burn —John Wesley (*www.leadershipquotes.com*)

Only passions, great passions, can elevate the soul to great things --- Denis Diderot (*www.quotationspage.com*)

Nothing great in the world has been accomplished with passion --- George Wilhelm (*www.quotationspage.com*)

John 2:16-17: To those who sold doves, He said, "Get these out of here! How dare you turn my Father's house into a market!" His disciples remembered that it is written: "Zeal for your house will consume me."

Romans 12:11: Never be lacking in zeal, but keep your spiritual fervor, serving the Lord.

Gal 4:18: It is fine to be zealous, provided that the purpose is good, and to be so always, and not just when I am with you.

Just from the analysis of this particular verse above, we can see the three major dimensions of passion, especially a passion for Christ and His cause:

(1). Our passion for life must be pure. Like fire that can both bless and curse, and like a double-edged sword that can both kill and heal, passion must be handled with prayerfully and careful. Passion without purity in intention and motivation can become perversion and pollution to self and others because passion is very contagious and infectious; but a passion with purity is positive, powerful, persuasive and productive!

(2). Our passion for life must be purposeful. Life must have passion in order to be exciting and exuberant. Life must also have purpose so that the passion can be properly and effectively channel as constructive energy toward some worthwhile life goal. He or she who is both purposeful and passionate gets things done successfully and lives a live of abundant victories in all areas.

(3). Our passion for life must be persistent. Paul says that our fine zeal for a good purpose should be always the same, perpetual and permanent in order to accomplish major feats for the Lord and make key strides for His Kingdom on earth. A Passionate life with pure purpose and persistent perseverance is totally pleasing unto the Lord.

Hope: Be expectant and anticipate the greater things the Lord will do in you and through you for the years to come, for He always saves the best for the last. Don't grow wear and never lose heart, for the best is yet to come! God always saves the best for the last.

I Corinthians 15:19: If in this life only we have hope in Christ, we are of all men the most pitiable.

Romans 15:13: May the God of Hope fill you with all joy and peace as you trust in Him, so that you may overflow with hope by the power of the Holy Spirit.

As long as there is a God, there will always be hope.

Your failures are never fatal or final with God.

Your future shall be as bright as the promises of your God!

I more I live, the more I am convinced that life must have meaning,

4

and that life must have hope, for hope deferred makes our heart sick, but when the desire comes, it is a tree of life (Prov 13:12). He who has no hope in life has no life at all. The ones who have stopped hoping have actually stopped living! But praise the Lord that Jesus Christ came to offer us life, new life, abundant life and victorious life, the life that the devil and his demons have tried to steal, kill and destroy (John 10:10). The Bible is a book of faith, hope and love. If Hebrews chapter 11 is the faith chapter, and I Corinthians 13 is the love chapter, then Romans chapter15 is the hope chapter. Let us look at the source of our hope, the security of our hope, strength of our hope and the sign of our hope briefly.

1. The source of our hope: the Holy Scripture. Everything that was written in the past was written to teach us, so that through the endurance and the encouragement of the Scriptures, we might have hope (Rom 15:4). The Holy Bible, the Word of God is not able to save us and fill us with the blessed hope in Jesus Christ and in the life to come, it also sustains us with plenty of encouragements; it enables us to endure to the very end without growing weary or ever lose heart! And he or she who endures to the end shall be saved and victorious!

2. The security of our Hope: the Lord Christ Jesus. In the last days, God has chosen to make known to the Gentiles, the glorious riches of this mystery, which is "Christ in you, the hope of glory." (Col 1:27). Christ is our source and sustenance and salvation and all the Scriptures from Genesis to Revelations point to none other than Jesus Himself (Luke 24:27). Our security is not found in our political or financial or educational or even religious systems. Our security is found only in Christ Jesus our Lord! And upon Christ Jesus this solid rock I stand, all other ground is but sinking sand!

3. The strength and Seal of our hope: the presence of the Holy Spirit. If we trust in the Lord Jesus, the Bible promises us that the God of hope will so fill us all that we will overflow with hope by the power of the Holy Spirit (Rom 15:13). Furthermore, we can rejoice in the hope of His glory and this hope does not disappoint us, for God has poured out His love into our hearts by the Holy Spirit, Whom he has given us (Rom 5:3, 5). Just as hope deferred makes the heart sick, so a heart full of hope rejoices and is made glad by the Holy Spirit!

4. The sign and signal of our hope: "all joy and peace" as you trust in Jesus. Romans 15:13 guarantees us that if we keep our trust in Jesus the Lord and are filled by the Holy Spirit, which is not a suggestion but a strong command (Eph 5:18), we will have the life manifestation and

daily demonstration and natural spiritual extension of joy and peace in spite of all the distresses and hardships of our temporary hostile circumstances. Peace and joy are the clearest signs and signals of a Spirit-filled, Spirit-empowered and Spirit-led Christian life. It is a life with joy unspeakable and full of glory; and it is a life of peace from the prince of Peace, a peace with God and a peace from God. And peace of God which transcends all understanding will guard your hearts and your minds in Christ Jesus (Phil 4:7).

Chapter 2
World Missions:
The Very Heartthrob of the Lord

The Preeminence of the Great Commission
for Global Evangelization

Having had the privilege and honor to follow the Lord wholeheartedly and serve the Lord willingly, gladly, passionately and enthusiastically over the past 30 years, I am now more convinced in my mind and more convicted in my heart than ever before, that the whole Bible from the very beginning of Genesis 1:1 to the very end of Revelations 22:21 carries only two main themes, the first is the story and necessity of our personal redemption through faith in Jesus Christ as Savior and Lord; and the second which seems to have been lost to many churches today, is God's last command and our first and concern and call to carry out and to finish the Great Commission by the evangelization of the all the nations! This indeed is also the last of the four essential components of the prayer of our High Priest Jesus in the Gospel of John Chapter 17, namely, glorification of the Son, unification of the apostles, sanctification of the believers by the Word of Truth, and evangelization of the nations.

The more evangelization on our part, the more glorification and exaltation on the Lord's part; the more evangelization of the nations, the more effective and efficient edification of the church of Christ our Lord; the faster we carry out world evangelization, the quicker will be the second coming of the King of Kings, for as the Scripture powerfully and prophetically proclaims through the mouth of our Lord: "And this gospel of the kingdom will be preached in all the world as a witness to all the nations, and then the end will come" (Matt 24:14). Jesus did not die on the cross just so we could have personal redemption alone. He died to pay for the sins of the world and to provide salvation for whosoever that will believe! Likewise, the Lord has not blessed us all just so that we can be happy; He has blessed us for the purpose of becoming a blessing unto all the nations as the Abrahamic promise teaches us in Gen 12:2-3 . . . "I will bless you . . . and in you all the families of the earth shall be blessed." Blessed to be a blessing, for nothing is greater for a child of God than being abundantly blessed and mightily used of the Lord at His pleasure and for His Eternal Kingdom purpose!

In order to make it clear and important, our Lord Jesus issues the Great Commission as His divine mandate for world missions at least five times on different occasion in all the Gospels and the Book of Acts. This was so because of the famous hermeneutical principle which declares that what is clear is always important, and what is important is always clear! Indeed the Great Commission the Lord Jesus gives is not an option or suggestion to be considered, but a non-negotiable command to be obeyed! Let us therefore pay close attention to them with a careful and prayerful examination with the full intention and strong determination for its implementation and completion.

Two Seas in Israel — A Poem by Helen Steiner Rice

Once is a sparkling sapphire jewel,
Its waters are clear, clean and cool.
Along its shores the children play,
And travelers seek it on their way.
And water gives so lavishly
her choicest gems to the Galilee...
But unto the south the Jordan flows,
into a sea where noting grows.
No splash of fish, no singing of bird,
no children's laughter is ever heard.
The air hangs heavy all around,
and nature shuns this barren ground.
Both seas receives the Jordan's flow,
the water is just the same as we know.
But one of the seas, like liquid sun,
can warm the heart of everyone.
While further south another sea,
is dead, dark and miserly.
It takes each drop the Jordan brings,
and to each drop it fiercely clings.
It hoards and holds the Jordan's waves,
until like shackled, captured slaves.
The fresh clean Jordan turns to salt,
and dies within the Dead Sea's vault.
But the Jordan flows on rapturously,
as it enters and leaves the Galilee.
For every drop that Jordan gives,
becomes a laughing wave that lives.

For the Galilee gives back each drop,
and its waters flow and never stop.
And in this living and laughing sea,
that takes and gives so generously,
we find the key to life and living,
it is not in keeping, but in giving.
Yes, there are two Israeli seas,
And we are fashioned after these!

We as followers and servants of the Lord Jesus Christ must be always reminded to look outward, onward, forward and particularly upward, and never to retreat too much inward, backward, or downward, for the Kingdom of God and the Promised Land are not behind us; they are before us! If we become insular, we will become self-centered and self-righteous and self-serving and selfish, and then die, just like the Dead Sea. We would be constantly holding, hoarding and hiding, and dying, just like the Dead Sea in Israel.

According to the well-known author of Asia Harvest, Paul Hattaway (p.3), the Dead Sea provides for all of us a great spiritual lesson from the natural. Nothing lives in the Dead Sea except bacteria and other organisms. Yet there are well over 150 rivers and streams of fresh water that daily flow into it, among which is the vibrant Jordan River. The reason why all the fresh and living water flows into it and dies is because the Dead Sea does not have a single outlet, and the life-giving water has absolutely nowhere to go. This is the spiritual life lesson for every Christian, every church, every movement and every denomination: that "without an active and effective outlet for our faith, you too will become stagnant and die"! What a timely warning and what a real challenge for us all! On the other hand, just like the Sea of Galilee, if we will consciously develop and daily exercise our faith (see Luke 9:23 for instance), then we will grow to be forceful and fruitful, powerful and productive for the Master's purpose! Only when we are willing to give away our lives and sacrifice our lives to Jesus by risk-taking for His cause and kingdom, then we will find the true life, gain peace and fulfillments from life, and achieve many successes in life.

Therefore, let us heed the Words of our Lord as found in Luke 6:38, "Give, and it will be given to you. A good measure, pressed down, shaken together, and running over, will be poured into your lap." As the most famous Christian verse of the Holy Bible teaches us in John 3:16, for God so loved the world that He gave . . . indeed one can give without loving(out of pity or pride); but no one can truly love without giving! What a life lesson to learn from the Lord of light and life in whom there is no darkness, not even a shadow of turning with Him! Care and share are inseparably interlocked together. When we care we will share, and only we share, we show beyond the shadow of a doubt that we truly care. If we care deeply about someone or some cause, we will share generously and sacrificially toward it, because care and share work in proportion to each other. And this is true with the Great Commission.

The Great Commission is our mission, our reason for being. It is our vision for it provides clear direction as to where we must go from here. It was forcefully set forth by the Lord Himself and recorded emphatically five times for emphasis in the gospels of Matthew, Mark, Luke, and John, and the Book of Acts of the Apostles. What is important is always made clear, and what has been made clear is always important. It is our absolute priority: first thing first. The Great Commissions is unambiguously the closest thing to the heart of God. As a matter of fact, I totally believe that the Great Commission is the very heartbeat, the very heartthrob of the Lord Himself. Since the Great Commissions has to do with soul winning and disciple making in all the nations among all the ethnic people groups, the supreme task for the church of Jesus Christ both now and in the future, has to be the evangelization of the whole world with the Holy Word in the power of the Holy Spirit!

Let us now take a look at the five recorded versions of the Great Commission all proceeded from the very mouth of the Lord in the New Testament.

Matthew 28:18-20: Then Jesus came to them and said, "All authority in heaven and on earth has been given to me. Therefore go and make disciples of all nations, baptizing them in the name of the Father and of the Son and of the Holy Spirit, and teaching them to obey everything (all things whatsoever) I have commanded you. And surely I will be with you always, to the very end of the age.

Mark 16:15: He said to them, "Go into all the world and preach the good news to all creation."

Luke 24:47: And repentance and forgiveness of sins will be preached in His name to all nations, beginning at Jerusalem.

John 20:21: Again Jesus said, "Peace be with you! As the Father has sent Me, I am sending you."

Acts 1:8: But you will receive power when the Holy Spirit comes on you; and you will be My witnesses in Jerusalem, and in all Judea and

Samaria, and to the ends of the earth."

The Four Major Reasons for Global Missions

1. A Command from Above (Matt 28:18-20)

Commands from the Lord of Lords are absolutely non-negotiable and must be obeyed fully. This is a non-negotiable command from the risen Lord of glory. Notice the 4 times the little powerful word "all" is used in these three verses Matt 28. All authority, all nations, all things, and always! Jesus has imparted to us all His authority to overcome all the obstacles of the enemy and win and live the promised victories (Luke 10:19). He commands us to take up His authority and use it for in His name and for His glory. He commands us to go into all the ethnic people groups, particularly those still unreached by the Gospel of Christ. He commands us to win souls and to make disciples by teaching them to obey the commandments as we live a life of obedience before them. And if we do all of these premises, He has this blessed promise for us that He will be with us all the time, never leaving us alone or forsaking us as orphans.

2. A Cry from Beneath (Luke 16:19-31)

This is a very moving passage from the teachings of the Lord Jesus. It is not a parable, but a divine vision He imparts to us from heaven. We learn so much from this passage about hell which is just as real and eternal as heaven itself. Not only is hell real, death on earth is certain for all of us, then comes the divine judgment (Heb 9:27). What is most touching here is the man's hearty cry from hell with 7 specific wishes:

A. He wished that he had paid any attention to the Word of God (vv.29-30), but he did not because he was too self-absorbed in his own pleasures to study the Word, although he obviously had access to it;

B. He wished that he had paid attention to the suffering, the needy and the poor and powerful around him. But he did not (vv.19-21);

C. He wished that he had done something good to alleviate the suffering of the poor, but he did not (vv. 19-20);

D.   He wished that he could go to the other side to be in the loving comforting presence of father Abraham (vv.24-26);

E. He wished that somehow Lazarus could be sent to him with just a little water to cool his burning tongue because he was terribly tormented in that place (v.24);

F. He wished for divine mercy from Father Abraham, a type of God the heavenly Father (v.24). But it was impossible. He had passed the point of no return and it was too late. Even the Father of compassion and God of mercies will not do anything once we pass the point of eternal separation between heaven and hell. That's why the Lord admonishes us to seize the day to work for Him and not to waste any time or opportunity to respond to Him and His call because when night comes, no one can work. It will be too late.

G. He wished finally that his five brothers in his father's house could have some gospel witnesses to them (vv.27-28). If it is to be, it is up you me, as they say! This is the last wish and actually the only wish he had that we can still do something about: go and share with them about the saving grace of the Lord Jesus. This evangelization of his brothers' souls will not be based on emotional and sensational resurrection of Lazarus, as this man incorrectly assumed and erroneously supposed, but on the power of the Gospel of Christ itself, the Word of God (vv.29-31). So then faith comes by hearing, and hearing by the Word of God (Rom 10:17).

3. A Call from Without (Acts 16:6-10)

This is unquestionably a vision from heaven, revealed to Paul by the Holy Spirit, specifically, by the Spirit of Jesus (v.7). In the vision, the man was literally begging Paul to "Come over to Macedonia and help us." In this encounter, there are a number of life lessons and spiritual principles we can and must learn from the missionary Apostle Paul and his companions. Vision provides ministry direction; Mission must follow the vision in order to see the final fruition; Missions work is team work for one person can not accomplish the Great Commission; Obedience is the key link between received vision and the projected mission; Spiritual humility and sensitivity are crucial elements in the life of the kingdom servants; Action must be taken decisively and without delay, with a sense of urgency and in His full authority. "After Paul had seen the vision, we got ready at once to leave for Macedonia . . . " (v.10). Let us pray to the Lord to always stay humble in heart and remain spiritually sensitive to heed to His voice and do His bidding in life.

4. A Conviction from Within (I Cor 9:19-27)

This passion-packed and purpose-driven passage speaks volumes to our lives. It uses the powerful three-letter word "all" several times to express the Pauline purpose, passion, plan and power. It provides us with eight effective strategies to win and live the victories in life whether you are in your own country or serving in other foreign nations: These strategies, simply put, are humility, sensitivity, principled flexibility, adjustability and adaptability, connectivity, unity, urgency, and intentionality with devotion, dedication, disciplines and determination. What a heroic apostle Paul for us all! Let us, as he personally invites us to two chapters later, imitate and emulate him from the inside out, just as Paul imitates and emulates Christ (I Cor 11:1). The only way we can lead others fruitfully is to first of all follow Christ and His Apostle Paul here faithfully, for effective leadership comes from faithful Followership. This is a very valuable lesson for life, a living example for all.

The Seven Mega Trends in World Missions:

1. From being a mission field to becoming a mission force: Former missions fields have now become missions force. Examples of this shift can be observed everywhere, especially in the nations of South Korea, the Philippines, Guatemala, Brazil and Argentina.

2. From the West to the rest and the best: Missionaries and missions leadership used to come primarily and predominantly from the West, but now they are beginning to come from al the rest of the world as God is selecting and anointing and using the very best for His soon-coming Kingdom.

3. From confrontation to infiltration: in most of the hostile nations dominated by Islam, Communism, Hinduism and Buddhism, more effective are the strategy of infiltration like salt, with love, to carry out life style and friendship evangelism over long periods of time. This takes time and patience and wisdom and absolute integrity for those involved to win the hearts of hostility and even hatred to the Lord Jesus. This is difficult and at times can be quite life threatening, for with God and faith in God, all things are possible and nothing shall be impossible to Him who can convert the hearts of stone into the heart of tender flesh and set in on fire for His purpose!

4. From Religion to relation: God hates the sins arrogance, sloth and divorce, and perhaps religion due to all the negative connotations. He loves souls, all peoples of all places, fellowship and intimate relationship

with His creation. More and more emphases are now being rightly placed on relational approach to missions. To be missional is to be relational, and the Holy Trinity is holy relationship among the Father, the Son and the Spirit, united in purpose and perfect in harmony. Humans are made in His image and likeness for meaningful and significant relationships.

5. From temple to tabernacle: This shift has caused the rise of many thousands of house churches in the U.S. and elsewhere in the world (see Kreider & McClung's book, *Starting A House Church: A New Model for Living Out Your Faith*). This entirely biblical model (especially in the New Testament and in nations where the believers face persecutions) stresses the tabernacle mentality (read Act 15:16-17 – God will rebuild the tabernacle of David) which is characterized by flexibility, cost-efficiency, relational intimacy, stronger accountability, more emphasis on effective discipleship, and more dynamic as a movement, among other benefits, as opposed to the organized religion perceived to be too formal, ceremonial, ritualistic, expensive, and impersonal, with a mentality like a dead monument which requires constant maintenance.

6. From small denominational mind to big Kingdom heart: Without little doubt, denominational loyalty is about to become history. Younger generations of followers of Jesus have gotten their priority right, first thing first: Seek first the kingdom of God and His righteousness and then all the other needs we have will be provided for us (Matt 6:33). This is a healthy change as we emphasize networking, for the kingdom of God is like a net. We need to work together as partners to complete each other; we do not need to compete with each other out of a narrow-minded denominational label or ego which has confused, divided and even paralyzed so many good and godly people. Let us be complementary to each other and not contradictory to one another. We need each other as the Body of Christ to put forth concerted efforts of personnel and resources to finish His work once and for all. This requires a lot of humility of heart and wisdom of the Spirit and a big vision of the Kingdom of heaven.

7. From dunamis (power) to marturis (martyr) with radical and reckless abandon—Acts 1:8 has been fulfilled and Acts 8:1 has become or will become a new reality in many parts of the world. A theology of the cross is emphasized to pay the prize for the cause of Christ, as Jesus did. The costs of discipleship will includes self denial, self sacrifices, self death, sufferings and martyrdom, are to be expected as we live in the last days. The Good News is that along with the increase of persecution

and tribulation, there will also be more outpouring of the Spirit and power to overcome the forces of darkness and evil. We have nothing to worry about, and we shall be victorious by faith in the name of Jesus simply because greater is He who lives in us than he who lives in the world (I John 4:4, 5:4).

Chapter 3
The Soul of Discipleship: Reach, Teach and Dispatch (Discover, Develop and Deploy)

Reach the Lost at Any Cost

I Corinthians 9:22: I have become all things to all men that by all means I may save some.

I Thessalonians 1: 2-8: We always thank God for all of you, mentioning you in our prayers. We continually remember before our God and Father your work produced by faith, your labor prompt by love, and your endurance inspired by hope in our Lord Jesus Christ. Brothers loved by God, we know that He has chosen you, because our gospel came to you not simply in words, but also with power, with the Holy Spirit and with deep conviction. You know how we lived among you for your sake. You became imitators of us and of the Lord; in spite of severe suffering, you welcomed the message with joy given by the Holy Spirit. And so you became a model for all the believers in Macedonia and Achaia. The Lord's message rang out from you… and your faith in God has become known everywhere.

It is no secret that no one can reap a harvest if he does not reach the lost. There is no reaping with joy if we do not sow the seed with tears. In order to have a bumper harvest, we must diligent and intentionally plant the seed. This is the law of sowing and reaping in the agricultural as well as in the spiritual. This Thessalonians passage above quoted holds some wonderful and powerful principles as to how the apostle Paul reached them and how they in turn reached the lost around them with the Gospel of faith, hope and love (v.3, I Cor 13:13). The supreme task of the church is the evangelization of the whole world with the whole Gospel for the whole man, reaching one soul at a time, until all have heard!

1. In order to reach the lost, we ourselves must be filled by the Holy Spirit (vv.5-6). Ephesians 5:18 commands us to seek and be filled by, and remain full in the Holy Spirit. Act 8:26-40 tells us the amazingly effective apostle, Philip the Evangelist in reaching the Ethiopian eunuch with the Gospel of Jesus Christ. He started out being guided and directed by the Holy Spirit to reach this soul and he ended with great rejoicing as the Holy Spirit once again directed to other places for evangelistic purpose.

2. In order to reach the lost, we must be filled with power from on High (v.5). The Bible promises us that we will receive this supernatural

power for successful witnesses for Jesus when the Holy Spirit has come down upon us both in this verse five and in Acts 1:8 and Acts 10:38. This same dynamic relationship of the Holy Spirit and power both in Jesus life and the disciples' ministries existed then and still exist among us who desire to reach souls for Jesus. The outpouring of the Holy Spirit (Joel 2 and Acts 2) is the outpouring of power, of plans. Of purposes for our lives! The coming of the Holy Spirit is the coming of wisdom, holiness, truth and anointing, not only to enable us to live the victorious lives, but also to empower us for the service in His Kingdom, among which is the reaching, winning and saving of human souls who are lost in sin and Satan and dying of hopeless despair.

3. In order to reach the lost, we must be filled with joy given by the Holy Spirit (v.6). Joy is contagious and people will notice your smiling face and be touched by your joyful life. Be joyful always and again I say rejoice! In His presence is there the fullness of joy (Psalm 16:11), and the joy of the Lord is your strength (Neh 8:10). I still remember the time when I was saved through a miraculous encounter with the Lord late Oct 1983 in Kaifeng China. Ever since then, He has turned all my miseries into His divine melodies all because of His great faithfulness, and abundant mercies which are new to me every morning (Lam 3:22-23). I was filled and am still being frequently refilled by His joy unspeakable and full of glory! This joy in my personal life has indeed touched tens of thousands of people who know me in life and ministries all over the world. That's not all, for the best is yet to come and the Lord always saves the best for the last for His faithful, flourishing and fruitful followers!

4. In order to reach the lost, we must spend plenty of time preparing ourselves with the Lord in prayers (v.2). No prayer, no power; and more prayer, more power! In prayers we get close with the Lord and feel His very desires. His desires become our very own desires as we delight in Him (Psalm 37:4). In prayers we feel the burden of the Lord for souls and let this same burden and passion and compassion to reach and win souls touch and burden and break our own hearts for the Lord! In prayers we will have the same mind and attitude too as they are in Christ Jesus the Lord (Phil 2:5).

5. In order to reach the lost, we must live authentic lives as examples and models unto us (vv.6-7). The law of the picture tells us that not only monkeys do what monkeys see, human beings by and large also do what they see other do. Therefore, seeing is believing, as mere words or talks are really cheap. Let our light of holiness and integrity and kindness so

shine before men that they will see our good deeds and give glory to our Heavenly Father (Matt 5:16). As one famous theologian once said to his disciples, by all means we must preach the Word, and if necessary, use words. Most of the vital things in life are not taught but caught! We are who we are by how we live our lives daily among the people.

6. In order to reach the lost, we also must clearly present the gospel with personal words of deep conviction (v.5), words that ordinary people can understand and relate to, and words can touch hearts and connect souls and ignite passion. Passionate words of communication always do the hearty connection, not just mental clarification. While walking the Christian walk is important, talking the talk is also important. In some sense, talk is indeed cheap; but in other sense, talk is not cheap at all, for words carry weight. Once spoken out, you can not take your words back. Demonstration is great, but declaration also does send out a force as words are ideas planted in the mind that can result in acts, both they positive, negative, constructive, destructive or suggestive. Indeed we must reach the lost with faithful representation of the Gospel though our lives. Neither should neglect the effective presentation of the Good News with anointed preaching and teaching. Paul refers to the gospel in verse 5 as "our gospel" and "my gospel" in other places to illustrate the principle of soul winning: in order to be effective, one has to be deep in personal conviction and personal testimonies! The power of one's personal life transformed by the gospel of God's grace is beyond estimation as it touches and influences millions of people for ages to come!

7. In order to reach the lost, we must be willing to pay the cost (v.6). The Lord Jesus prophesied in Luke 21:16-18 that we will be hated of men because of Him and His message, betrayed even by families and some of us will be even put to death, as He was. Severe persecutions and oppositions from the enemy out of the permissive will of God do not weaken or damp the spirit of evangelism or church growth, they toughen and strengthen our determination to preach the Word and reach souls. The devil is an evil devil, obviously as his name suggests; but the devil is also a dumb devil. Praise the Lord that to this day, he still has a hard time understanding that the more the church is persecuted, the fasted the gospel is spread al over the places. The church of Christ, paradoxically, has thrived under adverse circumstances, and she has become lukewarm and dispassionate in times of comforts and affluence.

8. In order to reach the lost, we must work hard by faith and not by sight (v.3). The righteous of the Lord must learn to live by faith, for

without faith, it is impossible to please the Lord, and with faith, all things are possible! Our faith in the Lord pleases Him and in turn the Lord prospers the faithful with all kinds of favors, among them the winning of new converts to Jesus. Those who have patience will acquire wisdom. He that wins souls is wise!

9. In order to reach the lost, we must carry our ministries as labor of love (v.3), with hands ready for labor and hearts full of love. The only pure motivation for evangelization is the love of God so full and strong in our hearts that we must share it with all others, especially those who are unlovable and loveless. Jesus asked peter three times if he truly loved Him in John 21, and Paul declares that it is the love of Christ that compels us to go and communicate Christ to the world (II Cor 5:14) because people desperately need the Lord for their aimless and meaningless existence, for their lives that do not know peace or purpose just like mine and millions of others like mines before.

10. In order to reach the lost, we must endure to the very end ourselves and inspire others with the hope that the Lord has given us (v.3). Just as the Lord endured the Cross (Heb 12:2), we must endure to the end and endure hardship like soldiers of the cross. If we do not endure the bad days and bad years, we will not live to see and enjoy the good days and years that the Lord has prepared for His faithful. We can endure with patience because our hearts are filled by the power of Christ in us, the hope of His glory (Col 1:27), and this hope in us will inspire others to receive the gospel and follow Jesus.

Teach Them to Obey

Matt 28:19-20: Therefore go and make disciples of all nations, baptizing them in the name of ... and teaching them to obey everything I have commanded you. And surely I will be with you always, to the very end of the age.

Psalm 90:12: Teach us to number our days aright, that we may gain a heart of wisdom.

Psalm 143:10: Teach me to do your will, for you are my God; may your good Spirit lead me on level ground.

John 14: 26: But the Counselor, the Holy Spirit, whom the Father will send in My name, will teach you all things and will remind you of everything I have said to you.

Romans 2:21: You then, who teach others, do you not teach yourself?

Titus 2:1, 7-8, 15: You must teach what is in accord with sound doctrine . . . In everything, set them an example by doing what is good. In your teaching, show integrity, seriousness and soundness of speech that can not be condemned, so that those who oppose you may be ashamed because they have nothing bad to say about us… These then, are the things you should teach. Encourage and rebuke with all authority. Do not let anyone despise you.

James 3:1: Not many of you should presume to be teachers, my brothers, because you know that we who teach will be judged more strictly.

Here are several of the most basic elements that have come to my mind as a Christian educator of 25 years or so in our attempt to teach those who have been reached by the gospel of God's grace and called of the Lord to ministries. These elements are knowing, growing, glowing, showing and going to get the job done in spirit and in truth, with authentic humility and networking cooperation with others of like passions and vision. Let us examine them one by one:

1. To teach is to know. In order to teach others, we must through the Holy Scriptures, the Holy Spirit, the holy saints of wisdom, knowledge and experience, be thoroughly taught ourselves, for one can not give what he or she does not have. That is a life lesson worthy of our learning! Let us learn diligently to show ourselves approved of God and qualified to teach others.

2. To teach is to grow. In order to cause others to grow spiritually and academically, we must keep growing in His grace and wisdom ourselves (II Pet 3:18). We must imitate the Lord Jesus in Luke 2:52, to grow in all the vital aspects of life, in wisdom, in stature, in favor with God and with people! Anything that's alive and healthy is always growing. This is a law of life both physically and spiritually. When our mentors see our growth, they will be proud of us; and when our mentees see our growth and maturity and wisdom, they will be eager to learn from us.

3. To teach is to glow. Jesus is the light of the world (John 8:12). When he imparted this blessed gospel light unto us, we then are the light of the world too as His ambassadors on earth (Matt 5:14). This means that you do have the light inside of you, it will shine out through you for all to see and to glorify us (Matt 5:16)! You can not hide the light, at least not for too long. Glow with the favor and glory of the Lord, glow for Jesus. Be prosperous and successful and multiply to bless others for the cause of Christ!

4. To teach is to show. One may declare his belief by what he says, but the Bible commands us to "show our faith by what we do." (James 2:18). Show what you know! When the disciples doubted the Jesus of resurrection as men of little faith who were hiding for the fear of the Jews and Romans, Jesus the Lord appeared to them and "showed them His hands and feet." (Luke 24:40). This is the power of examples which are not just the main means to teach and train others, for they are the only really effective ways to teach and train others! The Lord Jesus not only commanded us in the Great Commission to teacher others to obey everything He taught, He also demonstrated personal and total obedience to the will of the Father (Phil 2:8, Heb 5:8) right in front of the disciples. Jesus showed us the way as He is the way, first being and then doing; first mend ourselves and then mend others. In order to successfully teach others to obey the Lord, we must obey the Lord in everything ourselves first. Nothing is more ineffective in our teaching than a life of pretense and hypocrisy, falsehood and fakery. Nothing is more detrimental for us and for our followers than saying one thing and doing another. On the other hand, nothing is more powerful than a real life story for God's glory. We best influence and impact others not simply by wise words of our preaching, but by the authentic practice of what we preach in everyday living.

5. To teach is to go. Faith is a verb. It is an action verb! How did Jesus teach most of the time? Jesus went to all the towns and villages (Matt 9:35); Jesus sent the seventy two workers to every town and place to minister (Luke 10:1); and Jesus commanded His disciples then and still is commanding us now to "go and do likewise" (Luke 10:37). Jesus was no hypocrite for he did not ask us to go in to all the nations without Himself going as our example. We can not "do" if we are not willing to "go" first. The turtle is going nowhere until it sticks its little lazy head out!

Go, and take your disciples or students with you as you go! Many of the precious things in your data base, so to speak, will not be taught. They will be caught, caught in your attitudes and action, not accidentally but providentially, and caught in real life experience. That was how the disciples remembered Jesus' passionate love for the house of God, and his jealous and zealous ways of proclamation and protection in the temple with a big old whip in His hand, turning over tables of the money changers and chasing them out, with all kinds of doves and lambs flying and running all over the places (John 2:12-16). Just imagine the situation with you in the midst of it! What an unforgettable object lesson to learn for life! Therefore, don't waste your life any more idling around for the world and being seduced every which way by the devil; go boldly and risk necessarily your life for Jesus and His cause, and then you will find the true purpose and passion of life only when you are willing to lose it (John 12:24).

This is "what to know before you go," and this the challenge after you know, in the mighty name of Jesus, "Go!" No more human disappointment as you know that you live under and with a divine appointment! You have an appointment with eternity. Go in peace, go with His prayers and blessings, go in His name and in the power of the Holy Spirit! Go to prosper and go to win the victory. Now here the infallible and inerrant Word of the Lord Jesus Christ, with both its premises and promise as always in John 15:16, "You did not choose Me, but I chose you to go and bear fruit --- fruit that will last. Then the Father will give you whatever you ask in my name."

Dispatch Them Out Speedily to Finish the Task Well

John 20:21: Again Jesus said, "Peace Be with you! As the Father has sent me, I am sending you."

The Lord Jesus not only declared with His lips that He was to send out His disciples as He was sent down from the heavenly Father, He also demonstrated some key methods in His sending out the twelve and even seventy-two others to complete the Great Commission after his thorough teaching and training them. Let us take a careful look at Luke 10:1-24, and see how the Lord Jesus sends out the workers to the harvest.

1. Jesus sends out the workers by Divine Appointments (v.1) and with His own Kingdom authority (vv.16, 18). Many of us have experience plenty of disappointments for a variety of reasons, but more often than not, I have discovered our human disappointments are His Divine Appointments. Jesus personally appointed them only after much spiritual preparations of teaching them the Word, praying with them, living and serving humbly and faithfully as an example before them and using all kinds of situations and experiences as object lessons to let them practice what they have learned.

2. Jesus sends out the workers two by two, always in pairs, with a team approach and in the team spirit of kingdom cooperation (v.1), not individualistic ambition to make a name for themselves. "Two are better than one, because they have a good return for their work: If one falls down, his friend can help him up! Also if two lie down together, they

will keep warm. But how can one keep warm alone? Though one may be overpowered, two can defend themselves. A cord of three strands is not quickly broken" (Eccl 4:9-12). One famous proverb says it well this way: if one wants to travel fast, let him travel alone; but if one wants to travel far, let us travel together. How true this is!

Noted theologian Dr. Henri Nouwen (1994, pp.98-99) has this honest and insight observation on the Jesus strategy of dispatching workers in pairs to the harvest fields:

> Traveling is seldom good for the spiritual life, especially traveling alone. It's all too much, too sensual and distracting to keep our hearts and minds focused on God . . . Jesus does not want us to travel alone. He sends us two by two. Traveling together radically shifted the significance of my trips. Instead of lecture trips they became missions, instead of situations full of temptations they became spiritual adventures, instead of times of loneliness they became opportunities for community.

> The words of Jesus, "Where two or three are gathered in my name I am in their midst," have become very real for me. Together we are well protected against the seductive powers surrounding us and together we can reveal something of God that none of us is able to reveal on our own. Together indeed, we can be as cunning as snakes and as innocent as doves.

3. Jesus sends out the workers by praying for them with a sense of urgency and importance for the task ahead of them (v.2).

4. Jesus sends out the workers by warning them of the hardness of hearts among the people, of the dangers in ministries such as snares, attacks, rejection, opposition and even persecution (vv. 3, 11, 16).

5. Jesus sends out the workers by giving them specific instructions about how to enter houses and towns, how to behave and how to deal with inhospitality (vv.4-15).

6. Jesus sends out the workers with a specific emphasis on the message they are to preach: not religious sectarianism, but the soon-coming Kingdom of God (vv.9, 11).

7. Jesus sends out the workers by teaching them to stress the necessity of repentance and renunciation of sin (v. 13) as a preparation for the coming kingdom of Christ. Repent, for the Kingdom of God is at hand!

8. Jesus not only sends out the workers, He also requires them to come back periodically to report on their missions experiences (v.17).

This is a crucial part of the Christian leadership, not only the confident delegation of His authority to them, but also the spiritual supervision of real life and ministries. Upon hearing their victorious accounts of overcoming demonic forces, Jesus gives them reinforcements with great visions and the blessed assurance of eternal rewards in heaven (vv.18-20).

Jesus publicly and full of joy, praises the heavenly Father for the revelation of the kingdom power to the disciples (vv.21-22); Then wisely and privately (vv.24), Jesus calls the workers unto Himself to inspire more spiritual desire with more fresh kingdom fire to go out into all the world and spread the Word of Messianic hope, and speed the light of His love!

Chapter 4
Communicating Christ Cross-culturally

Luke 17: 15-18: One of them, when he saw he was healed, came back, praising God in a loud voice. He threw himself at Jesus' feet and thanked Him—and he was a Samaritan. Jesus asked, "Were not all ten cleansed? Where are the other nine? Was no one found to return and give praise to God except this foreigner?"

The compassionate ministries of Jesus were not only intra-cultural among His own Jewish people; they were also inter-cultural and trans-cultural. In order to be like Jesus, we must also communicate Christ cross-culturally and compassionately.

In the Luke 17 passage above cited, the Lord Jesus was pleased with the humility and gratitude of the one man out of ten who alone came to Jesus and thanked Him for the healing of his leprosy. This man was a foreigner and a Samaritan, normally despised by the Jews of that time as half-bred and inferior people. In this chapter, we are going to look at two of the most significant chapters of the Bible which serves as model for us to do cross-cultural services. Both of these chapters (Luke 10 and John 4) deal with Jesus' concern, care and compassion for all of the down-trodden and oppressed peoples of the world, especially in the cultural context of the Samaritans. Let us draw some life lessons from them.

The Parable of the Good Samaritan (Luke 10: 25-37)

In order to understand the text correctly, one needs to know the context clearly. This famous parable was given by Jesus on an occasion when an expert of the law was "inquiring" of Him the Teacher as to what he must do to inherit eternal life and who his neighbor might be. In both inquires, the expert of the law had the ulterior motive of wanting to really "test Jesus" (v.25) and "justify himself" (v.29). When we deal with people, we need to be prayerful and discernible about their motives, for the motive is more important than the motion, just as character is always much more important than charisma, and attitude is always more essential than activities.

In reply to his questions, Jesus lifted us the heart of the law of God who is none other than the Law of Love, for God is Love (I John 4:8). The more we love God and each other, the more we are God like! This expert obviously knew the law well as Jesus affirmed him for answering correctly: the three-dimensionality of love, like forgiveness and blessings

—upward with God, inward with the self, and outward with all others. This also reminds us the Golden Rule of the Bible that "in everything, do to others what you would have them do to you, for this sums up the Law and the Prophets." (Matt 7:12). This agape love of God includes also the command to "love your enemies, do good to them, and lend to them without expecting to get anything back. Then your reward will be great and you will be called the sons of the Most High." (Luke 6:35). Talking about tough love here! Emphasizing the importance of knowing the law clearly and answering the questions correctly, and the greater challenge of doing it here, especially at the end of the parable of the Good Samaritan (Luke 10:28 & 37)! Indeed the greatest challenge of life is the love challenge, and that is why Peter the closest apostle to Jesus, had to be challenged repeatedly three times in John 21:15, 16, 17. We are daily challenged by the Lord of the Scriptures and the Spirit of conviction to love, not in words alone, but in deeds for authentic faith is an action verb! Now that you have answered correctly, then go ahead, "do it and you will live." (Luke 10:28). Now that you know who your neighbor is through the example of this special Samaritan, "Go and do likewise." (Luke 10:37). Model for someone, we must first model after someone. In this parable, the Good Samaritan models after the Lord Jesus and in turns he also models for us all to follow suit.

There are three kinds of people mentioned and involved in Jesus' parable of the Good Samaritan, with three distinctly different philosophies about life and sharing life's resources, namely the robbers, the religious and the Samaritan which the Lord highly lifted for us all to model after. Let us take a quick look at these disparities:

1. The life philosophy of the robbers: What is yours is mine and I am going to take it, by force if necessary;

2. The life philosophy of the religious: What is mine is mine, I worked hard to get what is mine, and I am going to keep it.

3. The life philosophy of the Good Samaritan: What is mine is yours and let us share it!

Since this parable is about genuine love for neighbors, what are the characteristics of true love that the Lord Jesus emphasizes and teaches in Luke 10? Here are 8 of them:

1. True love notices (v.33). The Samaritan paid attention and saw the wounded. Lamentations 3:51 points out an intimate connection between the eyes and the heart as also many times in the life of the Lord: my eyes have affected my soul or my

heart. What we see does affect, positively or negatively, how we feel! That's why exposures and experiences in life are so vitally important for learning and growth and maturity. As it has often been said, that the eyes are a better pupil than the ears or the tongue, and that seeing is believing. Experience is the best teacher in that it is not what has happened to you or with you, but rather what you have made out of what has just happened.

2. True love initiates (v. 34). The Samaritan did not pass by on the other side of the road as the priest and the Levite did. He not only saw the man, but being moved with compassion in his heart, he also decisively went to where the man was to see what he could possibly do about the tragic situation.

3. True love risks (v.30). Courage is a necessity and risk-taking is a necessary ministry leadership trait. The Samaritan did all he did in spite of the potential danger of being robbed and beaten half dead. If we truly love someone, we will dare to risk our life for him or her, no question or hesitation whatsoever, like a mother to her child. In our spiritual and ministerial endeavors for the glory of the Lord, the life lesson is this: don't waste your life for the world; risk your life for Jesus!

4. True love hurts (v.30). Some times, those you love the most can hurt you the worst.

5. True love transcends (v.38). It transcends all racial colors, human cultures, socio-economic classes, and man-made categories.

6. True love shares (v.35). If you care, then you will share; and only when we tangibly share, we show that we truly care.

7. True love costs (v.34). King David famously declared that "I insist on paying the full price. I will not take for the Lord what is yours, or sacrifice a burnt offering that costs me nothing." (I Chron 21:24). It is a law of life that one can not give what he does not have. And what do we have that we did not receive as gifts from the gracious Father above? Cross-cultural compassion is very costly, but not nearly as costly as the cost of the cross Jesus paid in full for us! He instructed us in Luke 14 to intelligently estimate the expenses of going to wars or building a house way before we even think about starting. Prayerful and careful calculation of the costs of discipleship is a necessity and it demonstrates wisdom, responsibility and

maturity to win and live the victory!

8. True love remembers, returns and reimburses (v.35). This Good Samaritan, who is a typology of our compassionate Lord Jesus, does not forget the wounded in the inn, but promises to return and reimburse any further expenses that may incur. We may be beaten and even "dismembered" by the enemy, but the Lord our loving healer will return and "remember" us His Body! He knows all our pains not just as facts, but has feelings of our infirmities because He sympathizes and empathizes with us always (Heb 4:15). Therefore come boldly and confidently to the throne of His grace to obtain mercies in times of our needs. Likewise, when we really love someone, we think of them constantly. We long to look for the opportunity to return to be with them and do something special for them As a result of the heart of compassion, miracles happen and both sides get comforted and blessed both in this life and in the age to come (Mark 10:29-30)! Here is leadership in a nutshell: Carry the sack, lead the pack, keep coming back! True love remembers, returns and generously reimburses! Love never fails!

The violent and cruel robbers in the parable committed the Sin of Commission; the selfish and indifferent religious folks like the priest and the Levite committed the Sin of Omission in that they knew the things they ought to do and willfully did not do it (James 4:17). But the Good Samaritan exemplifies six valuable virtues we can discover, develop and deploy in our lives to be a blessing to many others in many cultures around the world. They all happen to start with the same letter "A" for alliteration as we already have four All's in just one verse Luke 10:27:

1. Attention—The Good Samaritan was attentive to his environment.

2. Awareness— He who pays attention becomes aware of what is going on around him.

3. Availability of the heart—A heart full of compassion is always available to the people in need. Be a person who is approachable be others and then they will open accesses for you and become your assets.

4. Ability of the hand—No one would have really remembered the Good Samaritan were it not for his purse. And neither could he have done what he did were it not for his financial abilities and economic resources. I am convinced that money always follows ministries, and not the other way round. I also have numerous experiences to verify

and authenticate the infallible truth that when God sees our heart pure and available for the Master's purpose, He will enable and empower us with the right resources to do the job. The Good Samaritan was blessed and was willing to be a blessing. As a result of this, greater shall be his reward in the future.

5. Action—Normal sentences usually contains one verb to denote action. Yet Luke 10: 34 is a brief sentence with six dynamic action verbs as a manifestation of the dynamics of faith. "He went to him and bandaged his wounds, pouring on oil and wine. Then he put the man on his own donkey, took him to the inn and took care of him." What a man of faith and man of action! True faith is pure love in action with good intention. No more, no less! Period!

6. Award—This is the promised eternal blessing guaranteed for the people of the Good Samaritan kind. The apostle Paul at the end of his earthly life and mission, concluded that he was like a drink offering being poured out and that the time for his departure to the Lord has come. "I have fought the good fight, I have finished the race, I have kept the faith. Now there is in store for me the crown of righteousness, which the Lord the righteous Judge, will award to me on that day—and not only to me but also to all who have longed for His appearing." (II Tim 4:7-8). What an amazing life and an inspiring testimony! The same will be true of the Good Samaritan who will also be awarded the crown of eternal life in glory with the Lord! Be encouraged and inspired to be a Samaritan's Purse to reach and rescue many others who have been robbed of joy and peace and beaten half dead by the demons. One of my very favorite passages as a living reminder for me daily has to be Colossians 3:23-24, for they provide me with the correct perspective of the kingdom, and the top priority of the King Jesus in everything I say and do. These verses both admonish and assure us that "Whatever you do, work at it with all your heart, as working for the Lord, not for men, since you know you will receive an inheritance from the Lord as a reward. It is the Lord Christ you are serving." Keep on keeping on, for the best is yet to come and the Lord always saves the best for the last, to those who will endure for Him and with Him until the very end! Let us all "go and do likewise" for the praises and honors of our Lord!

Jesus the Lord and the Woman of Samaria (John 4:4-42)

In addition to the well-know parable of the Good Samaritan taught by Jesus, there is also the famous encounter of the Lord with the sinful and isolated Samaritan woman in John 4. What life lessons can we learn from Jesus Himself in this real life episode of cross-cultural communication to assist us for more effectiveness? How can we communicate Christ cross-culturally? I do not believe there is anything better or more effective we can grasp on how to communicate Christ than how Christ Himself communicated with the Samaritan woman. There are at least 10 vital principles:

1. The Christ-centered cross-cultural communicator must begin with the end in mind (vv.39-42). Jesus is our greatest example in this area of vision and visualization, especially in Luke 10:18 and the entire book of Revelation. In this particular case, the Lord began ministering to this Samaritan lady with a clear vision of her potential of becoming a great and influential evangelist and discipler of her community and town. It is this vision that always drives Jesus with purposeful passion and mighty mission!

To begin with the end in mind literally means to start your design with a clear understanding of your final destiny. It means to know at all times where you are now and where you are going, "so that the steps you take are always in the right direction." (Covey, p.98). Many people in the world act without any or much understanding, go on a path without knowing where it leads, and forming habits without knowledge of their impacts or consequences. We must always ask ourselves the crucial questions with the end in mind: What are we trying to accomplish? What are the outcomes we hope to achieve (Davis, 2009, p.55). This focused vision with consistent action will bring your end eventually into fruition.

2. The Christ-centered cross-cultural communicator must become a diligent student of historical hostilities and current tensions across the cultures and ethnicities (vv.5-9).

3. The Christ-centered cross-cultural communicator must become keenly aware of the existing differences in cultural contexts, conflicts and confrontations across cultures (vv.5-9).

4. The Christ-centered cross-cultural communicator must always fix attention at all times on the person of Jesus, His purpose, passion, power and presence in communicating Christ to others (vv. 10, 26, 34). This comes out as a result of one's spiritual intimacy and personal relationship with Jesus through constantly abiding in Him (John 15).

5. The Christ-centered cross-cultural communicator must understand and know the process and stages of faith development (vv. 9, 19, 29, 42).

6. The Christ-centered cross-cultural communicator ought to learn to

utilize the relevant geographies, stories and artifacts to contextualize and indigenize his or her message on Christ (vv.4-6, 19-20), using the simple and ordinary daily things of life to illustrate the deep life principles of the Kingdom of God.

7. The Christ-centered cross-cultural communicator must confront caringly the audience with challenge, choice and change for the better! (v.16). Choices should be provided along with the challenges, just as remedies should be provided after rebukes, as the Lord Jesus did in His dealing with the Laodicean church in Revelation 3:14-19. Since cross cultural communication must carry with it the heart of compassion and since the Lord always disciplines those He loves (Heb 12), the cross-cultural communicator cares enough to confront and dares enough to challenge and discipline, lovingly of course, with the provision of alternatives and choices, and the proven promises of blessings due to wise choices and decisions on the part of the listening and watching audience.

8. The Christ-centered cross-cultural communicator must be a motivator, mobilizer and multiplier by precepts and example so that people will want to follow with action of their own (vv.4, 28, 39-42) to drive greater impact.

9. The Christ-centered cross-cultural communicator concentrates his or her cross-cultural communication of Christ on the word, will, work and ways of God. This communication task is to be carried out resolutely and finished effectively with vision, authority, energy, and urgency (vv.34-35).

10. The Christ-centered cross-cultural communicator should put in place a concrete plan of evaluation to measure the result of the work and its progress towards goal achievement (v.42). Treatment without assessment becomes punishment. This is true medically as well as in all areas of life. Accurate assessments and sound appraisals prevent all sorts of confusions and distractions. They also provide insights as to what to delete, what to continue, and what to insert for current actions and future directions.

Chapter 5
Back to Jerusalem: The Vision and Passion of the Underground House Church Movements in China

The past several months have been significantly and permanently marked in my missions ministry to the northwestern part of China, the part of China with 4 key provinces Qing-hai, Gan-su, Ning-xia and the huge Xin-jiang which is one sixth of the entire China and which alone borders six Muslim countries, namely from the N to the S: Kazakhstan, Kyrgyzstan, Uzbekistan, Tajikistan, Afghanistan, and Pakistan, which needless to say, are all Muslim nations that desperately need to hear and receive the glorious Gospel of our Lord Jesus Christ, the Gospel of love, joy, peace, reconciliation, healing and hope instead of the Koran messages of bitterness, hate and revenge.

As a matter of fact, geographically, there are some 30 countries between China and Israel that are entirely Islamic states that need our urgent prayers and ministries. This section of the world is also the very heart of the so-called 10/40 Window, the highest concentration of the most unreached people groups (UPG) (such as over one billion Chinese, one billion Indians and two billion Muslims). Although the underground house churches in China have been frequently persecuted for the past 60 some years under atheistic communism to varying degrees (warnings and threats with loss of jobs and confiscation of property, violent arrests, heavy fines, physical torture, labor camp, and even martyrdom), yet these precious and passionate Chinese disciples of the Lord are determined to go westward to reach the Hindus and Muslims with the love of Jesus all the way till they eventually reach Jerusalem, Israel where the Gospel originally started.

"The Back to Jerusalem" concept for the Chinese Christians actually originated in the 1940's when they leaders read Isaiah 49:11-12 which prophetically proclaims that in the last days, our God will do mighty miracles by converting the mountains (which represent barriers and obstacles and impassable blocks etc) into High highways, and that people from far-away places will be coming to bless Jerusalem, from the North, and the South and the West, and even from "the Land of Sinim". To this very day, many old Jewish Rabbis in Israel can confirm and still refer to the ancient nation of China as "Sinim". Not only so, the word "Sinim," according to many serious Hebrew and Biblical scholars, indeed refers to China, hence, China studies is known as "sinology," and the China-US relations is called the Sino-American relations, and to make someone or something Chinese is to "sinocize" him or it. Isaiah 49:12 is believed by the millions of Chinese Christians on fire for the Lord as the only reference to China and the Chinese in the whole Bible, depicting the vital role of the Christians in China in finishing the Great Commission of the Lord Jesus Christ!

But in order to go back to Jerusalem and be a blessing to His chosen people, the Christians in China must move westward, and of necessity, must evangelize the Muslims with the good news of the love of Jesus Christ by following the Silk Road. The Silk Road had been well traveled by caravans for centuries through the Gobi Desert, including the famous Marco Polo from Venice Italy! Today, the various underground house movements for the first time ever, has come together to make a joint thrust into the missions field west of China with the vision of eventually sending out 100,000 Chinese missionaries to the Muslim world, a tithe of 10% of the approximate 100 million believers in China today! China is not going to remain as the Largest Missions Field forever; it is becoming and will be the Largest Missions Force in the world ever since our Lord set His feet on it! This is the vision and it is already translated into faithful and fruitful action!

A number of missionary training schools have been started underground in China, and a few openly and legally operating both long and short terms overseas such as Manila the Philippians, Thailand, USA, and the Siberian Russia among the Chinese Christians who can operate openly without persecution. Thousands of them have moved to the northwest of China and revival is taking place with explosive evangelism, with some 30,000 souls coming to faith in Christ daily in the past years till now. Hundreds have put their lives on the line and boldly crossed the borders by various means to the Muslim world with some astounding results of soul winning by signs, wonders and dreams and visions!

Recently, I invited several of our Leaders back from the northwestern part of China and a few from Pakistan and one from Iran for leadership development, a time of reporting and recharging, and I was utterly amazed at what a mighty God we serve. He is doing mighty things in the end times for His glory among the Muslims by using the suffering and persecuted Christian saints in China. The Chinese Christians are certainly called and seem to be uniquely qualified and particularly enthused for such a task of Muslim evangelism for the following reasons:

1. These Christians can not stay long in one location being wanted

gospel fugitives by the authorities in their provinces and country. They are forced to be on the move to escape arrests and are therefore scattered abroad for the Lord's use! You see, the devil is not just an evil devil, but also a dumb devil. One Chinese missionary told me that persecution is God's blessing in disguise. Years of hard-labor prison for his faith and ministries were a blessing because the communist prison "became my best Bible school, my faith-building ground!"

2. The Chinese Christians are used to atheistic and communistic hardships, persecutions, and have paid the high and heavy price of sufferings for their faith through prison labor camps and martyrdom. They are both able and willing to endure everything for their Lord!

3. The Muslims look at the Chinese with much more trust and friendship, and generally do not view the Chinese with suspicion as a threat or an object of hate, as they would a typical Westerner from the U.S, Europe and Australia. The historical Silk Road helps to enhance this aspect, and millions of Muslims settled in northwest of China historically. (There are over 30 million of them in the 4 provinces NW of China mentioned above).

4. They know they are called and commissioned to go by the inspiration of the Holy Spirit, and by the great Commissions of the Lord (Matthew 28) and by Acts 1:8.

5. They are willing, in fact eager to pay the heavy price of Muslim outreach, even at the cost of their own lives. I have often heard them say with their lives to back up what they have said, that "we consider our lives worth nothing to us if only we may finish the race and complete the task the Lord has given us!" Their intense desire is to hear from the Master at the end: Well done, my good and faithful servants! Enter Ye into the joy of your Lord!" (Matthew 25).

As a matter of fact, they sang me a song with five stanzas that moved and touched my heart and soul deeply as they cried in tears to the Lord. It is entitled "To Be A Martyr for the Lord" (Wei Zhu Xuen Dao). The first four stanzas were a review and summary of what has happened to the disciples of Christ, starting from Christ Himself who died on the Cross for us, through Stephen stoned to death, Matthew beheaded, Luke hanged, Philip and Peter crucified, Bartholomew skinned alive and Jude pierced through to death by many arrows, etc. Here is the last stanza and the chorus that accompanies each of the five stanzas:

"I, too, Lord, am willing to pay such a price! Whether insults or persecution, false accusations and abandonment by family, friends and the workplace, I am ready to leave everything behind, and follow You, Lord!"

Chorus: To be a martyr, Oh, to be a martyr, I am well
prepared, Lord, to be a martyr for You today!

I felt so unworthy to "train" them with my empty jargon of westernized theology from the ivory towers of many of our western cemeteries (Oh, sorry, I mean, seminaries)! Lord, please help me to endure hardship like a soldier for Jesus, and be a passionate minister and visionary missionary on fire for you today like my Chinese brothers and sisters who really have really forsaken all they have, living by faith alone, and who stand ready to be counted for the faith in Jesus, no matter the cost! I know that the greatest challenge to the Great Commission is not the rising radical Islam, but a sleepy, lazy, and lukewarm Christianity of complacency! How about you, my brother or sister, who is reading this challenging chapter? Are you challenged and inspired yet? Are you ready for action?

The heart of the Lord Jesus is missions and missions and more missions until all have heard the Gospel of God's grace. The work of world missions is on the cutting edge in this aspect. As we all know, no one can truly be living on the cutting edge of any ministry without shedding some blood once awhile (a song our brothers and sisters in the Chinese underground house churches often sing says that for the cause of Christ, we are willing to shed sweat, shed tears and shed blood!). No one can receive the promised prize without paying the necessary price! We started out by partnering and supporting 29 Chinese Christians to the NW the year before last, 31 last yr along with the starting of our first Bible school in that hard and hostile region, and this year at least 50 new Chinese missionaries to the NW of China with a new Bible school to produce harvester exclusively for the Uighur Muslims) and beyond.

By now, several of them have entered into the Muslim nations by doing some tent-making work and starting little Chinese restaurants by which the Gospel is being spread out. One of our missionaries told me that he let a whole family of former Muslims to Christ who made it easy for him. When he was led by the Spirit to go to this particular household, they were eagerly waiting for him and ready to listen and receive Jesus as their Lord because they saw in their dreams the night before Jesus revealing Himself to them as their Savior! Praise God! With signs and wonders, the Gospel of Jesus Christ is being preached among the

Muslims. Nothing shall be impossible with God, and to him who trust the Lord, all things are possible to Him who believe (Mark 9:23)!

The Chinese Christian missionaries sincerely believe that the Gospel since the beginning in Jerusalem has been spreading always westward to Rome, England and Spain, the Americas, the Far East with the great revivals taking place in Korea, Indonesia, and especially China now. They are convinced and completely convicted of the truth and fact that they are to be the last baton of the Gospel Fire moving further westward to blanket the Middle East with the Gospel and bring it back to where it all started. Thus fulfilling the promise and purpose by His presence and power the Book of Acts 1:8, and then the end will come (Matt 24:14) because by then, the Gospel will have been preached to all the nations, having encircled the entire globe! What a powerful vision and passion to rise up for God! Let us all partner and network with them in different ways to fulfill this God-given vision with kingdom passion!

Chapter 6
The Heart of All Issues
and the Issue of the Heart

Isaiah 29:13 & Matthew 15:8: The Lord says, "These people come near to me with their mouth and honor me with their lips, but their hearts are far from me. Their worship of me is made up only of rules taught by men.

Jeremiah 17:9-10: The heart is deceitful above all things and beyond cure. Who can understand it? I the Lord search the heart, and examine the mind, to reward a man according to his conduct, according to what his deeds deserve.

Proverbs 4:23: Above all else, guard your heart, for it is the wellspring of life (another version says it this way: for it will affect everything you do).

Proverbs 15:13: A happy heart makes the face cheerful.

I Samuel 16:7: But the Lord said to Samuel, "Do not consider his appearance or his height, for I have rejected him. The Lord does not look at the things man looks at. Man looks at the outward appearance, but the Lord looks at the heart."

Matthew 5:28: But I tell you that anyone who looks at a woman lustfully has already committed adultery with her in his heart.

Matthew 23:27-28: Woe to you teachers of the law and Pharisees, you hypocrites! You are like whitewashed tombs, which look beautiful on the outside but on the inside are full of … In the same way, on the outside you appear to people as righteous but on the inside you are full of hypocrisy and wickedness.

Mark 7:21-23: For from within, out of men's heart, come evil thoughts, sexual immorality, theft, murder, adultery, greed, malice, deceit, lewdness, envy, slander, arrogance and folly. All these evils come from inside and make a man 'unclean.'

Matthew 5:8: Blessed are the pure in heart, for they will see God.

Hebrews 12:14: Make every effort to live in peace with all men and to be holy; without holiness no one will see the Lord.

Rev 2:23: I am He who searches the hearts and minds, and will repay each of you according to their deeds.

Hearts are stronger than swords—Wendell Philips (Henry, p.119).

Without any doubt whatsoever, the single most difficult challenge for all human kind regardless of time and space, colors and cultures, has not been what lies before us or behind. It is what lies within us. It is what is going on in the heart that affects and determines everything a person does. At the heart of every issue is always first and foremost, the issue of the heart. If the heart is right, eventually everything will work out well sooner or later; but if the heart is wrong, nothing will be right in the final analysis. The heart is the absolute center of human life, with compassion, tenderness, kindness, forgiveness, generosity and selfless sacrifices. Simultaneously, the heart is also the fountainhead of covetousness, doubt and unbelief, and all sorts of evil as is seen in Mark 7:21-23 above quoted. That is why we must guard our heart above all things. And that is why the Lord does not look and judge by the outward appearances, but He examines and judges according to the intents and motives of our hearts.

We are strongly admonished throughout the Bible to keep our eyes centrally focused on Jesus, the Author and the Finisher of our faith (Heb 12:2), so that we will not grow weary and will never lose heart (Heb 12:3, II Cor 4:1, 16). You may lose your money, lose your face, and even lose your health eventually, as all of us will, but never ever lose heart! Always keep up the courage! In my office at the Pentecostal Theological Seminary here in Cleveland TN USA, hanging on the wall are two proverbial axioms in Chinese written with brush stroke on bamboo sheets. They are very deeply meaningful to me over the past 20 years serving as an adjunct professor of Christian education and inter-cultural counseling (1993-2013), because they contain great wisdom from my native land of China. They touch the "heart" of what I am going to share in this chapter: the heart of the most significant issues of life is none other than the issue of the heart! These saying serve as a constant reminder for me to self-examine my own heart condition with brutal honesty and cross-examine my heart by the authoritative Word of God so that I can make sure that I will not be living with any pride or greed, or in self-illusion, delusion or self-deception, lest I lose heart. Here is what these Chinese proverbs say:

A heart of determination is strength;
A heart full of faith is already success;
A discouraged heart is a weak heart;
A heart in despair is death!

Definition of the Heart

Biologically and medically speaking, the heart refers to the human organ inside the person's chest which maintains the flow of blood through the body by regular contractions. Biblically speaking, however, the heart signifies specifically the center of an individual and the well spring of one's life (Luke 6:45, Prov 4:23). According to the Full Life Study Bible (pp.906-907), the human heart contains the totality of that person:

1. The heart is the center of human intellect. Many actions that actually take place in the heart are primary issues involving the mind. Humans can doubt and question in their heart (Mk 11:23), believe in their heart (Rom 10:9), think and ponder in their heart (Prov 23:7, Mk 2:8, Lk 2:19), meditate in their heart (Ps1:2), and devise plans in their heart (Ps 140:2).

2. The heart is the center of human emotions. There are so many identifiable and powerful emotions that go on in the human hearts. These emotions include the glad heart (Ex 4:14), the loving heart (Deut 6:5), the fearful heart (Jos 5:1), the courageous heart (Ps 27:14), the repentant, refreshed and revived heart (Ps 51:17, Phm 7, Isa 57:15), the anxious and anguished and angry heart (Prov 12:25, Rom 9:2, Prov 19:3), the delighted heart (Jer 15:16), the grieving heart (La 2:18), the excited heart (Lk 24:32), the troubled heart (Jn 14:1), and the humble heart (Mt 11:29). All of these actions within the human hearts are primarily emotional in nature.

3. The heart is the center of human volition, the activation of the power of the will. The Scripture talks about the heart that has a strong volitional side to see the Lord. "You will seek me and you will find me when you seek me with all your heart." (Jer 29:13). Our heart can be hardened and thus refuses to do what God clearly and strongly commands (Ex 4:21). There are the hearts that desire to receive from the Lord (Ps 21:1-2), and the hearts that sincerely want to do something (Rom 10:1).

The Desires of the Human Hearts

Isaiah 55:11: So is my Word that goes out of my mouth: It will not return to me empty, but will accomplish what I desire and achieve the purpose for which I sent it.

Psalm 51: 6: Surely You desire truth in the inner parts; You teach me wisdom in the inmost place.

Psalm 1:2: But His delight is in the law of the Lord, and on His law, he meditates day and night.

Psalm 37:4: Delight yourself in the Lord, and He will give you the desires of your heart.

As the seat and center of the human personality, the heart, without a question, is capable of all kinds of desires, some are pure, holy and lofty, while others are selfish, wicked, evil and even satanic. In order to properly identify and handle them, one must have a core or a center. For us, it has to be the Word of God and the biblically standards set forth by God Himself. The Bible instructs us on the divine desires, what God really wants from His creatures like us: truth, holiness, righteous, compassion, faith and obedience, among others. In light of the biblical truths and principles, we can then evaluate and assess our own human desires and align our own to that which is His. In order to acquire the fresh holy fire, we must align ourselves with His divine desires. Moreover, we are obligated to expose, teach, show and warn others with both precepts and examples, to the very best of our abilities, and as much as possible, as did the pious Ezra. "For Ezra had devoted himself to the study and observance of the law of God, and to teaching its decrees and laws in Israel." (Ezra 7:10).

The Motives and the Man are all in the heart (Prov 27:19, I Cor 4:5). We can not really know the man until we know his motives. While we can observe his outward motions and actions, it takes time and dealings to know his real inner motive, the heart condition.

Our heart determines our character (Prov 23:7, Matt 15:8). Therefore, we must watch our hearts carefully and prayerfully above all other things and make sure it is pure and not polluted so as to develop sound moral and ethical character which is above all charisma.

Our heart decides our destiny (Eccl 3:11, Prov 4:23). Most people throughout human history, especially the rich and powerful (sometimes the poor and the powerless too), do not wish to die. They want to live for ever to enjoy the pleasures and the good fortunes they have. They desire longevity and even eternity for their lives. But if our hearts are not right in accordance with the Holy Word of God, our longevity will be our long misery, and the ultimate destiny will be eternity in hell without the presence of the Lord our Maker.

Set your hearts on things above where Christ is seated at the right hand of God (Col 3:1). When we have the right focus, we will be granted the force and favor to live in His glorious freedom and bear much lasting spiritual fruit for Him.

How About Your Heart Now?
The Heart Conditions without God

Apart from God and His regenerative Holy Spirit work, the human heart is indeed the source of evil and wickedness (Mark 7:21-23, Mt 15:18). People who are apart from God are senseless, faithless and heartless (Rom 1:31, Lm 4:3). The Full Life Study Bible says it well (P.906):

> When Adam and Eve chose to follow the serpent's temptation to eat from the tree of knowledge of good and evil, their decision drastically affected the human heart—it became filled with evil, at present therefore, according to Jeremiah's testimony, "The heart is deceitful above all things and beyond cure. Who can understand it?" (Jer 17:9). Jesus confirmed Jeremiah's diagnosis when he said that what makes a man unclean before God is not the failure to follow some ceremonial law, but the willingness to listen to wicked inclinations ledged in one's heart such as "evil thoughts, sexual immorality, theft, murder, adultery, greed, malice, deceit, lewdness, envy, slander, arrogance and folly" (Mk 7:21-22). Jesus taught about the seriousness of sin in the heart (Mt 5:27-28, see Ex 20:14).

> Hearts that are committed to doing evil run the grave risk of becoming hardened. Those who persistently refuse to listen to God's Word and to obey what He commands, and instead following the wicked desire of their hearts, will find that God will eventually harden their hearts so that they loose all sensitivity to His Word and to the desires of the Holy Spirit (Ex 7:3, Heb 3:8).

Give your heart completely to the Lord (Prov 3:5-6). Since our heart is the very fountain of our life, and the Lord is the way, the Truth and the Life itself, we must unreservedly and willingly give our heart to the Lord our Maker and allow Him to do all the necessary regular maintenance and even radical surgery if needed so that we can become more sensitive to Him and become more and more like Him from within.

Guard your heart carefully against the devil (Prov 4:23). While we are willing to give our heart to Jesus for His use and purpose, it is also our duty to watch out against the subtle devil of pride and greed and lusts of all kinds. You do not have to look for him. He will come to you secretly and subtly, particularly when you are Hungry, Angry, Lonely and Tired (HALT!) with all his seductions and temptations. Be careful and prayerful not to fall under his feet. Submit yourself to God with all the great spiritual disciplines and take up the weapon of spiritual warfare outlined and prepared for you in Ephesians chapter 6. Fight the good fight of faith! The Lord will help you win the battles mentally, emotionally, relationally and financially, and live the victories in all these and other areas!

How About Your Heart Now? The Heart Conditions with God

Regeneration is God's answer to the sinfulness of the human hearts. Regeneration is a matter of the heart, and it comes to all who will sincerely repent of their sins, turn to God and place their faith in Jesus Christ as Savior and Lord. A person who has been regenerated with new birth by faith in Jesus receives a new heart from God Himself (Psalm 51:10, Eze 11:19), and this regenerated heart is the source of faith (Rom 10:9-10) and the source of goodness (Luke 6:45). According to the sound teaching of the *Full Life Study Bible* (p. 907):

> Within the heart of those who experience spiritual birth, God creates a desire to love Him and obey Him . . . Such love for and obedience to God cannot be separated from obedience to His law (Ps 119:34, 69, 112); Jesus taught that love for God with the whole heart and love for one's neighbor summarize God's entire Law (Mt 22:37-40). Love from the heart is the essential ingredient in obedience . . . Outward obedience without an inner desire to serve God is hypocrisy and is severely condemned by our Lord (Lk 21:1-4).

A heart regenerated and growing in the grace of God is one that trusts in God (Prov 3:5), sings to God (Col 3:16), seeks God (Ps 119:2, 10), cry out to God (Ps 84:2) and praises God all the time (Ps 91). This kind of heart is sensitive and responsive (II King 22:19), full of discernments (I King 3:9,12), pure, (Ps 24:451:10, Mt 5:8)), steadfast and undivided (Ps 86:11, 108:1), sincere (Col 3:22), fully committed (I King 8:61), peaceful and grateful (Col 3:15-16). May God who alone knows and regenerates with conviction and faith in our heart continue to humble us and purify us from the inside out, so that our heart can be close to that of Jesus. This is the kind of heart that our Lord will for sure bless and use!

The Lord & the Heart: God alone knows the hearts of all people (I Kings 8:39, II Chro 6:30).

He alone can search the human heart, touch and move the human heart, and convert the human heart by the mighty power of His Holy Word and the convicting presence of His Holy Spirit. Yes the operation of God demands the cooperation of man. In order for the Holy Spirit to powerfully operate in our lives and ministries, we must yield to His prompting and leading with humility, trust and obedience to fully cooperate with Him! Let us humble and purify ourselves before God and beg Him to help us with a heart broken and pleasing for the Master's purpose. And we de truly delight ourselves in the Lord, He then will certainly give us the desires of our heart which will be more passionately burning within us for His glory and praises (Ps 37:4).

The Lord & the Heart: God is greater than our hearts
(I John 3:20).

While this is a clear assertion about God's omnipotence and sovereignty, it also implies the necessity of our obedience! As a natural law, creatures (people or animals) respect, admire and obey those who are better, stronger and greater than themselves. Spiritually, the law of life also applies well. I John 4:4 and 5:4 do remind us and declare to us that as children of God and by faith in this Almighty God, we can and we shall overcome oppositions and live in victory, simply "because the One who is in you is greater than the one who is in the world." Amen!

A Life Lesson from A Story of China's Great Wall

Several years ago, I received an anonymous Email devotional from a close friend based on an ancient story of the Great Wall while I was leading a mission team evangelizing on the Wall outside Beijing China. It has illustrated well the heart issue which determines the character formation: A heart of greed is the root of character corruption which eventually leads to personal and even national destruction. Here goes this good and pointed devotional:

The words of Proverbs 14:34 could be chiseled on the tombstone of many civilizations: "Righteousness exalts a nation, but sin is a reproach to any people." We think we can build a nation on the gross national product or defend it with armaments, but God says that countries are built on the character of their people.

The people of ancient China sought security from the barbaric hordes that swept down from the north, so they erected the Great Wall of China. The massive wall stretched for 1,500 miles. It was 12 to 40 feet wide and 20 to 50 feet high. The wall was too high for the enemy to scale, too thick to tear down, and too long to go around.

Yet during the first 100 years of the wall's existence, China was invaded three times. How was the security breached? The enemies simply bribed a gatekeeper and then marched easily through a gate. The fatal flaw in China's defense laid in spending its wealth to build a wall but paying much less to build the character of the gatekeepers.

A bigger defense system won't ultimately protect our nation. But we can contribute to her security by being "blameless and harmless . . . without fault in the midst of a crooked and perverse generation" (Phil. 2:15).

Protection of a nation's land does not come only from its mighty hand; It comes from more from the purity of the devoted and dedicated heart. Security is just a fraud unless the people trust in God. A nation is only as strong as the character of its citizens. (Source: *Our Daily Bread*, Devotional Feb 1, 1997)

Chapter 7
Sustenance, Sufficiency and Superiority: Random Thoughts on Five Life Stages

Ecclesiastes 3:1,2,7: There is a time for everything, and a season for every activity under heaven: a time to be born and a time to die, a time to plant and a time to uproot, a time to tear and a time to mend, a time to be silent and a time to speak.

Generally speaking, we as humans all go through some similar life stages in the pursuit of the meaning, purpose, and the fulfillments of life. All of us have the right and even the constitutional guarantee (if you live in the United States, that is) to life, liberty and the "pursuit" of happiness. You are guaranteed the right to pursue happiness, but you not guaranteed to automatically possess it. You are the one who will have to be discernible, disciplined, determined, and responsible enough to "catch" it. Through my personal participation with and careful observations of saints and sinners, friends and foes alike, I believe that I have reached and caught the conclusions with the following five life stages, namely, struggle, survival, success, significance and surrender. Let me explain them to you now, brief but to the point.

I. Struggle

John 16:33: In this world, you will have trouble—Jesus

Life is a struggle, at times very intense and painful struggle. Life is full of struggles, physical struggle, mental struggle, financial struggles, emotional struggle, relational struggle, military struggle, political struggle, to mention just a few. There is no life on earth that I know of that is devoid of any struggles. This is part and parcel of the human existence and the human experience whether you experiment with it or not. It will naturally and normally come to you before you look for it. All of us in this world live with some form of disequilibrium and imbalance in some areas. One has to learn to understand it, adapt and adjust to it, and cope with it on a daily basis with the right perspective which gives power, and with the proper attitude which gives the altitude. Yes, inevitable struggle along, nevertheless!

II. Survival

In spite of the painful struggles which result in many types of human sufferings, most people amazingly continue to live. As the famous American author Robert Frost once said, "I can summarize everything I have learned in life with only three words: it goes on!" How true and realistic, simple and profound his statement is! Humans, made in the image of the Almighty God, are endowed by their Creator with one special characteristic: resilience. We are surprisingly able to readily recover from all kinds of hurts, damages and misfortunes, and even come out of them stronger, wiser, and more mature in life than ever before. The experiences of survival from disasters and calamities teach us many valuable life lessons that we can not learn otherwise from fine lectures and excellent books. Experiences, as they say, are the best teachers, and they have experienced it do not need to overly explain it. This is like knowing God.

III. Success

Nothing succeeds like success—Dumas (Henry, p.271).

All you need in this life is ignorance and confidence, and then success is sure—Mark Twain (Henry, p.271)

Survivors surprise others with successes and surpass many others due to the extremes and excesses they have experienced. There are no successes without some excesses, for success requires the person to put up excessive efforts and endeavors. Success demands substantial sacrifices of time, talents and treasures. No sacrifices, no successes. In order to go up, one must learn to give up. Once a person has played by the rules and paid the necessary price, he or she will be paid with precious prize, be it economic, academic, social or political.

IV. Significance

Extrinsic successes such as money, status and the maintenance of certain image do not guarantee or offer meaning or purpose to life. Success without significance is indeed meaningless. This has been the sincere reflection of hundreds of my "successful friends". People try so desperately hard, at the cost of their health and marriages and families in an attempt to catch success, and once they have caught it, they find that it is all empty and that they have lost themselves in the process. It is particularly true in the study of the psychology of human happiness. Repeated and reputable researches have been extensively done to show that most of the factors that determine one's happiness come from one's genetic dispositions and intrinsic values, and only a small percentage

(10% by most estimations) of our happiness actually come from the financial security and prosperity (money) and the social status which most people so eagerly covet and crave for. Only the intrinsic values of life such as compassion, higher spiritual cause and purpose, faith and hope in a divine center can provide the individual with a sense of significance.

V. Surrender

Matthew 10:39: "Whoever finds his life will lose it, and whoever loses his life for my sake will find it."—Jesus of Nazareth

The greatest of man's power is the measure of his surrender—William Booth.

Blessed are those whose lives are completely surrendered to God, for only in such a surrender are God's abundant blessings realized—anonymous.

To surrender is to submit, to yield to the will, the authority and or the power of another; to surrender is to give up control over something or someone or some place; to surrender is to give oneself up; and finally to surrender is to agree willing and gladly, to obey the recognized authority. One's surrender or submission, knowingly and willingly, to the higher authority of the divine Lord initiate a positive relations, and enables him or her for intimate fellowship. When we who have experienced certain measures of success and significance only after many trials, toils and dangerous snares of struggles and survivals, are willing and obedient to surrender and submit ourselves, our own agendas and ambitions and authorities to the ultimate authority, the King Jesus, we begin to experience life to the fullest. So many of the things that have been so possessive of our lives, suddenly become no long that important to us in the light of Him and His Kingdom perspective, priority and purpose. Surrender or submission to the Lordship of Christ Jesus is the highest stage of life with the most fulfillments both on earth here and now and in heaven eternally there and then! I have found this to be a truth absolutely trustworthy.

Chapter 8
Why We Never Lose Heart:
A Study on II Corinthians 4 & II Samuel 12

II Corinthians 4:1, 16: Therefore, since through God's mercy we have this ministry, we do not lose heart . . . Therefore, we do not lose heart.

Hebrews: Therefore . . . let us lay aside every weight, and the sin which so easily ensnares us, and let us run with endurance the race that is set before us. Looking us Jesus, the author and finisher of our faith who...endured the cross, despising the shame...Consider Him who endured such opposition from sinful men, so that you will not grow weary and lose heart.

The man who can not endure the bad, will not live to see the good—Jewish Proverb (*www.quotationspage.com*)

A Study of II Corinthians 4

It has been rightly articulated that if you have lost money, you really have lost nothing because money comes and money goes; if you have lost your health, you have as a believer lost perhaps 50 percent; but you have lost hope in life, then you have lost it all, 100 percent! Hope deferred makes the human heart sick (Prov 13:12). On the one hand, there is no real living without hope, for he who has stopped hoping has actually stopped living! On the other hand, those who have hope in the Lord can endure anything and everything. They can mount up with wings as eagles! And all that was written in Bible in the past was written to teach us, so that through the endurance and encouragement from the Scriptures, we might have hope for "the God of Hope" (Rom 15:4, 13,) who is Christ in you, "the hope of glory" (Col 1:27).

Unquestionably, one of my favorite chapters among others (Heb 11, Rom 12 and I Cor 13) is II Corinthians 4. It starts with us "not losing heart" (verse 1) and ends with us "not losing heart" (verse 16). In this brief but powerful chapter of only 18 verses, the great apostle Paul of the Christian faith definitively delineates for us 10 major reasons as to why we will never lose heart. Here is the list for our careful examination.

We do not lose heart because:

1. Our ministry does not depend on man's might, but on God's mercy which makes us steadfast with determination (v.1, also Lam 3:23);

2. We have renounced secret and shameful ways of deception and distortion (v.2)—holiness;

3. We live by the plain truth of God's Word (v.2)—truthfulness;

4. We commend ourselves to every man's conscience in the sight of God (v.2)—transparency;

5. We preach and live out Jesus as servants of the Lord (vv.5-6), showing His life, sharing His love and shining His light with humility, Christo-centrality and influence;

6. We have this treasure in earthen vessels or in jars of clay to manifest the power of God through the orthodoxy and the orthopraxis of Christ's cross of life and death (vv.7-12);

7. We believe and speak with the spirit of faith (v. 13);

8. We live with the certainty and glory of Christ's resurrection, and the confidence and hope of our own resurrection (vv.14-15);

9. We focus our vision and concentrate our full attention, not on the brevity of life and its many afflictions, but on Christ and the eternal glory of being with Him (vv.17-18);

10. We operate our life and ministry with endurance and effectiveness, daily renewing our spirits with the great expectancy of the glorious soon-coming Kingdom of God (v.16).

A Study of II Samuel 12

One of the most dramatic and moving chapters in the whole Bible has to be the vivid confrontation of Prophet Nathan against the sinful King David in II Samuel 12. Because what David did in secret (lies, murder, deception and adulterous relation with Bathsheba) greatly displease God (2 Sam 11), the rebukes then were quite severe and the consequences of sins were very hard, harsh, extremely costly and even deadly in both spiritual and physical areas! And because David despised the word of the Lord by doing what was evil in His eyes (v.9), The divine punishments included 3 major things: the sword of violence would not leave David's home (v.10); the secret sins would be exposed in broad day light before all Israel (v.12), and the death of the child Bathsheba born to David (v.18).

The very first verse of II Samuel 11 seems to reveal the key to our understanding of the causes of David's sin against God. In the spring when all the kings at the time went off to war for territorial claims and sovereignty, David sent Joab out with the Israelite army, "but David remained in Jerusalem," idling around and enjoying the leisure and pleasure of his luxurious palace life. This indeed was the beginning of trouble for Kingdom and the Davidian kingdom. The morale of this verse is rather simple and clear, in that when we do not do what we are supposed to do (as all the Kings went to war in the spring, David, being a king, should have gone to war instead of jus sending someone else off on his behalf), we will end up doing what we are not supposed to do. Verse versa, if we and our resources (time, talents and treasures) are fully occupied with doing the right thing out of the pure motive, for sure we will not have the desire or the energy to do the wrong thing. Indeed, idleness is the devil's workshop, and if you give him an inch, he will take a mile. We are not unaware of his satanic schemes of delusion, disillusion, deception, distraction and destruction!

The Lord is always true to His promises and even to His pronouncements of the three major curses on David and his household. He not only promises, but He also delivers—performs His promises according to His perfect will and in His own sovereign time, be they good or bad! Because what David did had made the enemies of the Lord show utter contempt and despise the chosen children of God, "the son born to you will die" (v.14). in the following few verses (vv.15, 18), "the Lord struck the child" and "the child died" in spite of King David's sincere and earnest confession, repentance(v.13) and urgent pleading with the Lord day and night lying on the ground with prayers and fasting (vv.16-17). The morale of this incident is that even though the Father of compassion and Lord of mercy does forgive us of our sins when we confess and repent, yet the sinner has to bear the reproaches of his sin and suffer the costly consequences thereof (vv.13-14). In other words, God forgives the sinner, but he does not remove the penalty of the sin caused either by commission or omission.

What can we learn from the example of David, the man after God's own heart, in dealing with grief and the loss of life as a result of sin?

1. Confessions and repentance are necessary as they are commanded of God. Confession brings conviction, and repentance brings revival and renewal (v.13). Psalm 51 is the heartbreaking and heartwarming confession and repentance of David; Psalm 32 is an excellent description and wonderful example of confession and conviction, help and healing as a result. The Word of the Lord instructs us that if we claim to be without sin, and the truth of God is not in us. But if we confess our sins, our God is faithful and just, and will not only forgive us ours sins, but also purify us from all of our unrighteousness (I John 1:8-9). Praise the Lord for the

wonderful promises if only will we fulfill our part of the premise, that is, sincere confession and true repentance before the Lord!

2. In spite of our confession and repentance, we must be willing to pay the price for our sins, with whatever costs and consequences the Lord sees fit to render upon us. The wage of sin is death, and this death can be spiritual, psychological, financial, relational and even physical as in the case of the beloved first child between David and Bathsheba (vv. 10, 11, 14). No complaints or murmuring, simple acceptance, willing or not!

3. When one faces the loss and accepts the reality, healing will take place in heart. No more shocking, nor more denials, no more depression, no more pleading negotiation, simply accept what it is as the facts of reality. Acceptance brings the wounded and hurt a sense of settlement and closure to what one can not change! Peace, serenity and even new opportunity with a new perspective will start to emerge as we learn to accept the things we can not change. It also gives one the strength and courage to get up and get on with life once again (vv.19-20).

4. This too shall pass (vv.22-23)! Realize that nothing on this earth can last for ever, whether it is the glory of the kingdom or the disgrace of a disaster. As the Apostle Paul powerfully proclaims in II Corinthians 4:18 that what is visible is always temporal and what is invisible is timeless and eternal! A rabbinic story was told about King Solomon in his most triumphant and glorious moment of dedicating the temple with all its grandeur and majesty as never know to humanity. The king asked a well-known artist and theologian to make him an object for him to put on to mark this unparalleled occasion for ever. When the day finally came, King Solomon was formally presented a very fancy ring with these four words engraved on it: "This Too Shall Pass". Seeing the puzzle on the King's face, the wise theologian artist explained: "Your Majesty, these words carved on your ring will forever serve the purpose of reminding you that you will neither be overly exalted when things are going great, not overly discouraged when things go wrong." What great wisdom and what wonderful balance in life. We all need this balance so as to be warned against going to the extremes of the bi-polar disorder! Indeed no matter what happens to you or others, and how you feel about it, life goes on!

5. Life goes on with a renewed perspective gained in His presence in the sanctuary (v.20, see also Psalm 73:17). The famous American poet Robert Frost once philosophically exclaimed: "I can sum up everything

I have ever learned about life in three words: life goes on!" How simple, true and accurate this is! II Samuel 12:20 informs us that once he learned to accept, David began to act, act actively, no longer merely react passively. Not only was he active, King David, a man after God's own heart in spite of his frailties and failures, he became proactive! He got up from the ground, washed himself, put lotions, changed his clothes, and went into the house of the Lord to worship God and ate at his own house. David knew that he was forgiven of the Lord based on his sincere confession and based on the Lord's unfailing compassion.

Like the Prophet Elijah who suffered greatly from discouragements, intimidation, false expectation, and consequently depression in I King 19, David also got up, got over it, got things to eat and got on with life again, as life always goes on, no matter what! Do not dwell on the past; do not look much backward or inward or downward! Look onward, upward and forward in the name of Jesus. The promises of God are not behind us; they are before us! The Kingdom of God is not behind us; it is before us! As Paul the Apostle writes under divine inspiration in Philippians 3:12-14: Not that I have already obtained all this or made perfect, but I press on to take hold of what Jesus took hold for me. One thing I do, forgetting what is behind and straining towards what is ahead. I press on toward the goal to win the prize for which god has called me heavenward in Christ Jesus! What a faithful soldier of the cross and a mighty warrior of the Lord for us to imitate and emulate for ever! Thank you, Lord, for your unconditional and unfailing love. Your mercies, O Lord, never come to an end, for they are new every morning, new every morning! Great is your faithfulness, O Lord! Amen!

I once read some deeply alarming words from a wise but anonymous Jewish rabbi that really spoke right to my heart. I'd like to share with you here as we all can draw some good and valuable life lessons from the glimpses of his observation, warning and solid and sound advice. You will see how accurate and true all this is:

First, I was dying to finish my high school and start college; then I was dying to finish college and start working; I was dying to marry and have children; then I was dying for my children to go old enough so that I could go back to work. But then I was dying to retire, and now I am dying . . . and I suddenly realized that I forgot to live.

To make money, we lose our health, and then to restore our health, we lose our money. We live as if we are never going to die, and we die as if we never lived. Please do not let this happen to you. Appreciate your current situation and enjoy each day with gratitude.

Prayer of Serenity by Reinhold Neibuhr

God, grant me the serenity to accept the things I cannot change,
the courage to change the things I can,
and the wisdom to know the difference.
Living one day at a time, enjoying one moment at a time;
accepting hardship as a pathway to peace;
taking as Jesus did, this sinful world as it is, not as I would have it;
trusting that you will make all things right if I surrender to your will;
so that I may be reasonably happy in this life
and supremely happy with you forever in the next.

Chapter 9
The Triple A Battery
of Passionate Ministry

This chapter is unique and may not fit typically as a section of a book. Nevertheless I decide to include it here to shed some light from our busy life. It is based on an early devotional and a world missions newsletter I wrote to ministry partners. I hope that they will together encourage and bless you with some valuable life lessons for living the victory.

Man of God in a Godless World

In order for us to lead fruitfully with authority, we must learn to live faithfully under His Authority; For to lead like Jesus, we must first live like Jesus—The Principle of Impartation!

In order to present Jesus powerfully & productively, we must first represent Him purposefully and positively!

As a matter of fact, only when we are prophetic, purpose-driven, passionate, positive and pro-active goal setters and go-getters, then can we become powerful, productive and persuasive for the Lord and His Kingdom!!! Amen & Hallelujah!

I encountered the following inspiration from Ted Engstrom's book The Making of A Christian Leader, to share with you today for mutual encouragement, equipping and empowerment in the Lord. The world we live in needs:

Men and women of God
who can NOT be bought;
whose word is their bond;
who put character above wealth;
who possess opinions and a will;
who are larger than their vocations;
who do NOT hesitate to take chances;
who will NOT lose their individuality in a crowd;
who will be as honest in small things as in big things;
who will make no compromise with wrong;
whose ambitions are not confined to their selfish desires;
who will NOT say they do it just "because everyone else does it";
who are true to their friends through good report and evil report, in

adversity as well as in prosperity;
who do NOT believe that shrewdness, cunning, and hardheadedness are the best qualities for winning success;
who are NOT afraid or ashamed to stand for the truth when it is unpopular;
who can say "NO" with emphasis when all the rest of the world says "yes".

In order to really make a difference as a disciplined, determined, dedicated, diligent and dynamic disciple of divine discernment and decision, we must LEARN to Think Differently and then Live Differently (Pro 23:7 . . . As the Mind goes, so the Man follows!) just as Jesus the Lord had to LEARN obedience through what He suffered (Heb 5:8) and just as Paul the Apostle had LEARNED to be content in whatever the circumstances (Phil 4:11)! Life is a process, a life-long learning process with many life lessons for us to discover, develop and deploy.

Don't waste your life for the devil or the world; rather be always willing and ready to risk your life, and even lose your life for Christ and His cause! Then you find the life Jesus promises.

My brothers and sisters of like purpose and passion, of like vision and mission, be correctly informed in your head, be profoundly inspired in your heart, and be actively involved with your hands today by the infallible, inerrant, indestructible and indispensable Word of Life! Have a good and Godly day today and everyday, for what eternal value is there if it is a good day but not a Godly day?!

The Triple A Battery: A Necessity for Victorious Ministry

I hope you like my title here: The Tripe A Battery for Missions Ministries: Authenticity, Anointing, and Authority—the indispensable keys to faithful, forceful, flourishing and fruitful missions for the Kingdom of God!!! Authenticity sets us free from the devil of deception and distraction and destruction; Anointing breaks the yoke of bondage and allows us to serve with enthusiastic passion, power with a Kingdom purpose (Mt 6:33); and Authority enables, empowers and equips us with His approval to successfully carry out His Missional Message with His Miraculous Methods—as the famous Hudson Taylor once said: God's work done God's way will never lack God's supply! I have found this notion to be totally truthful and trustworthy after some 30 yrs of ministries, with almost 25 years now in World Missions Ministries, Hallelujah, PTL, and to God be all the glory!

Esther my wife served low-key with great wisdom and effectiveness for 3 wks in China, leading many to faith in Jesus, making disciples and supporting spiritually and financially many of our persecuted saints there in the house churches! Your support and prayers went with her to dozens of leaders on our churches and Bible schools where they are: Persecuted, Pentecostal, passionate, purposeful, powerful and productive!!! Thank you all for continuous partnership!!! Pray constantly for her as you all know the tense and hostile situation!

As for me, I am always busy for the Lord, and am always happy in the Lord, grateful for the many open doors of opportunities to add values and make a difference wherever He sees fit to place me! I have jus had 4 wks serving the Lord Jesus in the Philippines, Mongolia and Korea... preaching in so many churches of the 3 nations, including a huge Youth Convention with thousands in Amadeo, Cavite Prov, Las Filipinas! I also taught in several Bible colleges, seminary and even at the great Korean Bible Univ where over 50 young Chinese Christian leaders are in strict training to go back and produce disciples after studies! I even ministered as many times before, in a big Mongolian jail among hundreds of prisoners in the heavy snow on April 23 in Ulaan Baatar, Mongolia, and 8 Chinese got saved that same night also in our ethnic Chinese church's evangelistic service in UB Mongolia, PTL!

How grateful I am to the Lord and to you all that He gave me so many opportunities to minister the Word with AAA batteries ---- resulting in several young Filipinas who were delivered from demonic oppression due to sex slavery and other causes (Acts 10:38 -- The Presence of the Father, the Purpose of the Son and the Power of the Spirit —all in one verse -- please check it out!), leading well over 100 souls to faith in Christ, and making disciples among our national leaders and Bible schools! Our God is so good! Not only is He GOOD, Our God is GREAT, GRACIOUS & GLORIOUS!!! Therefore, in response to Him, we must Give, Grow, Glow and GO just as the Lord Jesus did in Matthew 9:35, with the passionate focus, energy and urgency in John 4:34-35 when He declares to us:

> My food is to do the WILL of Him who sent me and to finish His work! Do you not say that in 4 months then comes the harvest? But I declare to you: Lift up your eyes and Look unto the fields, for they are already ripe for the harvesting!

I hope and pray that you enjoyed reading this short praise report to you with our joy and thanksgiving! Please pray for us to richly blessed and mightily used of God as we launch out into the deep to serve Him in 8 days by ministering in different settings in South Africa, and then June, Sept and Nov... Three months out for His harvest in the Far East to win more souls and make better disciples for Christ the King! And of the increase of His the Kingdom, Power and Glory, there shall be no end. Amen, Amen & Amen!

I received a fairly complete summary of our Christian identity (author unknown) from a friend by to share with you. It has blessed me and I like it much. Enjoy the bell below and ring it often to yourself when in doubt or question, and ring it to the ears of our fellow sojourners. This is the very foundation of our identity, based on whose we are and who we are in Him as our intimacy, for we can not really know who we are until and unless we know whose we are (Psalm 100:3, Acts 27:23). Moreover, we can not effectively exercise our divine authority if we do not know our true identity derived and associated with His divinity. Through our daily relational and spiritual intimacy with the Lord, we will know deeply our identity, exercise confidently our God-given authority with His Spiritual liberty (II Cor 3:17) to both win and live the glorious victory!

The Bell
I KNOW WHO I AM
I am God's child (John 1:12)
I am Christ's friend (John 15:15)
I am united with the Lord (1 Cor. 6:17)
I am bought with a price (1 Cor. 6:19-20)
I am a saint (set apart for God). (Eph. 1:1)
I am a personal witness of Christ (Acts 1:8)
I am the salt & light of the earth (Matt. 5:13-14)
I am a member of the body of Christ (1 Cor 12:27)
I am free forever from condemnation (Rom.8: 1-2)
I am a citizen of Heaven. I am significant (Phil.3:20)
I am free from any charge against me (Rom. 8:31-34)
I am a minister of reconciliation for God (2 Cor.5:17-21)
I have access to God through the Holy Spirit (Eph 2:18)
I am seated with Christ in the heavenly realms (Eph. 2:6)
I cannot be separated from the love of God (Rom.8:35-39)
I am established, anointed, sealed by God (2 Cor. 1:21-22)
I am assured all things work together for good (Rom. 8: 28)
I have been chosen and appointed to bear fruit (John 15:16)
I may approach God with freedom and confidence (Eph. 3: 12)
I can do all things through Christ who strengthens me (Phil. 4:13)
I am the branch of the true vine, a channel of His life (John 15: 1-5)
I am God's temple (1 Cor. 3: 16). I am complete in Christ (Col. 2: 10)
I am hidden with Christ in God (Col. 3:3). I have been justified (Rom 5:1)
I am God's co-worker (1 Cor. 3:9; 2 Cor 6:1). I am God's workmanship
(Eph. 2:10)
I am confident that the good works God has begun in me will be perfected
(Phil. 1: 5)
I have been redeemed and forgiven (Col. 1:14). I have been adopted as
God's child (Eph 1:5)
I belong to God !

Keep this bell ringing!!
Working for God on earth does not pay much, but . . .
His Retirement plan is out of this world!!

Chapter 10
The Ten "H" Focuses
in Christian Discipleship

Among the many divine dimensions of dynamic discipleship, there are ten particularly important aspects to be focused on and emphasized in this entire life-long process of information for the head, formation in the heart and transformation of the hand (behavioral and life style challenges). I would like to summarize them up with ten words that all start with the letter "H". They are: head, heart, hand, habit, humility, honesty, holiness, hunger, help and hope. Let me explain them to you one by one.

1. The Head

Proverb 27:3: As a man thinks in his heart, so is he.

II Peter 3:1: Dear friends, this is now my second letter to you. I have written both of them as reminders to stimulate you to wholesome thinking.

Philippians 4:8: Finally, brothers, whatever is true, whatever is noble, whatever is right, whatever is pure, whatever is lovely, whatever is admirable—if anything is excellent or praiseworthy – think about such things.

Your life is what your thoughts make it --- Marcus Aurelius.

The mind is a terrible thing to waste. God has gifted each of us with a smart brain and we are to use it for His glorious purpose on earth while living in this increasing complex world of depression, deception, distraction and destruction. Some people, including many of God's people, would rather die than having to think for themselves. Not only are we to teach and preach, "Let my people go," what we also need to proclaim is, "Let my people think!" And the message of old in Isaiah 1:18 is still loud, clear, fresh, true and highly relevant for us today as an eternal contemporary like the Holy Spirit is, "Come now, let us think together," thus invites the gracious and wise Lord. Let us love the Lord our God with all our minds.

To live the life of victory, one starts with living authentically and genuinely, and truthfully according to the teachings of the Word of God in all the aspects of life, such as faith, family, friends, foods, focus, finance, to mention only a few. Then one needs to think theologically in order to live with abundance, victories and prosperity.

2. The Heart

Proverb 4:23: Above all else, guard your heart, for it is the wellspring of life.

Psalm 37:4: Delight yourself in the Lord, and He will give you the desires of your heart.

As the seat and center of the human personality, the heart, without a question, is capable of all kinds of desires, some are pure, holy and lofty, while others are selfish, wicked, and satanic. In order to properly identify and handle them, one must have a core or a center. For us, it has to be the Word of God and the biblically standards set forth in it. The Bible instructs us on the divine desires, what God really wants from His creatures like us: truth, holiness, righteous, compassion, faith and obedience, among others. In light of the biblical truths and principles, we can then carefully evaluate and seriously examine our own human desires in terms of intents and motives. We must constantly monitor and correct our hearts, channel and adjust our hearts and the desires to the teaching of the Word. Our spiritual alignment to the holiness and righteousness of the Lord is a daily necessity. Moreover, we are obligated to expose, teach, show and warn others with both precepts and examples, with the help of the Holy Spirit and to the very best of our abilities, and as much as possible, as did the pious Ezra set us a good example to follow. "For Ezra had devoted himself to the study and observance of the law of God, and to teaching its decrees and laws in Israel." (Ezra 7:10).

3. The Hand

Isaiah 41:10: So do not fear, for I am with you; do not be dismayed for I am your God. I will strengthen you and help you; I will uphold you with my righteous right hand.

Ecclesiastes 9:10: Whatever your hand finds to do, do it with all your might, for in the grave, where you are going, there is neither working nor planning nor knowledge nor wisdom.

If the head represents reason and the heart represents emotion, the hand then represents action. In the Bible, "the hand of God" has been used to refer to His mighty power, presence, protection and provision as His tangible and visible love for us His creation. The laying on or imposition of hand upon another person symbolizes divine healing and confirmation in the practice of ministries. The lifting of the hands is a common gesture of our adoration and submission to the Almighty God.

The hand here is a symbol of labor and work. It is the observable and measurable behavioral pattern that will drive an influence and make an impact. When one confidently behaves outwardly according to what he or she sincerely believes in the heart and thinks in the mind, it produces wonderful results in and effects on relationship with others. Let us not just become mere hearers and empty talkers of the Word. Rather let us put our hands to our faith with consistent and persistent deeds and works, or as I often say, faith is a verb, and put some feet to your faith. The book of Acts is not a book of talks but one with activities and actions of the Holy Spirit in the apostolic ministries of the early church. We must get busy and become more diligent with our sturdy and strong hands to finish the task assigned to us by the Lord, just as He set the example for us to follow in John 9:4, a divine and perfect example of authority, energy and urgency to go out and get the job done.

4. The Habit

The Greek philosophical guru Aristotle once famously uttered, "You are what you repeatedly do! Excellence therefore, is not an act, but a habit." Without exception, we are all creatures of habits. All of us have formed certain habits over the many years we have lived, be they good or bad, positive or negative, constructive or destructive, or whether you are aware of them or not. The habits we form can and will either make us or break us. Therefore the cumulative success of your life really does depend on your daily consistent and constructive habits. Effective and productive disciples of the Lord deny themselves, carry their cross every single day, and follow Jesus (Lk 9:23).

Here is a good proverb for you to consider on the significance of human "habits". Habits begin as harmless thoughts --- like flimsy cobwebs --- then, with practice, become unbreakable cables to shackle or strengthen our lives (Waitley, p.121). What a powerful statement on our habits, and how true it is in our daily lives!

If it is so in general, it is more so in particular with the teaching of the Word of God. We are to know and obey the Lord faithfully, daily and consistently, not just out of momentary excitement or on emotional highs. In serving the Lord, to be truly spiritual, we must be steady, stable and then we will be strong! We must be intentional and purposeful in our life, starting with me and right now, for today matters and every day it is an intentional choice! "Choose for yourself today whom you will serve, but as for me and my house, we will serve the Lord" (Josh 24:15). This is the day that the Lord has made (Ps 118:24). I will choose to be thankful and joyful in Him and live for Him today, and every day! In this way, the mind, the heart, the attitude and the actions of Jesus will gradually sink into our innermost being and become our own as we turn our eyes to Him and fix all our attention on Him. His passion will be our passion and His Gospel will be our gospel. He is both faithful and powerful, and He will help us to accomplish His kingdom purpose and priority when we are willing and obedient.

5. Humility

Philippians 2:8: He (Jesus being in very nature God) humbled Himself and became obedient to death --- even death on a cross.

Luke 18:14: For everyone who exalts himself will be humbled, and he who humbles himself will be exalted.

Just as pride is extremely perilous to our soul, and is the worst enemy in life and ministries, humility is our best and the greatest friend and asset to victory! Therefore, the Bible clearly and repeatedly instructs us to be humble, because our God opposes the proud and exalts (gives grace to) the humble. God Himself declares loud and clear in Proverbs 8:13, "I hate pride and arrogance." This is so because pride and arrogance, the two sides of the same coin, are an abomination to the Lord (Prov 16:5). Not only is it the first and earliest sin recorded in Isaiah 14 of the prideful Lucifer, pride is core and the essence of all the seven deadly sins (MaHaney, P. 30). Jonathan Edwards named sin as the "worst viper that is in the heart" and "the greatest disturber of the soul's peace and sweet communion with Christ." Pride is the most hidden secret and deceitful of all lusts and it is the most difficult to root out (MaHaney, P. 34).

Pride is the most serious sin in the eyes of God and there is no sin more offensive to Him than pride itself. Pride carries with us many logic-defying and blinding effects which lead and cause total destruction to the proud. At the center of pride is the sinful human desire to contend with God for supremacy and for self glory instead of depending on the Lord or acknowledging God as the Provider, Savior and Sustainer of lives. We in the church today, more than ever before, need more Christian leadership with a humble heart of true servanthood, as exemplified by the Lord Himself in John 13. We must make a conscious effort to fight again the spirit of proud egomania which dresses itself with excessive and glamorous labels, logos, titles, and self-centered and self-serving egos, which add together to nothing more than a bundle of idols that make the humble Lord sick!

The gaze of God's grace is surely upon the humble and the meek and the contrite in heart. In Isaiah 66:2, the Lord Himself proclaims that "This is the one I esteem: he who is humble and contrite in spirit, and trembles at my word." We please God with our faith, with our holiness and also with our sincere humility of heart and life. And since God is decisively drawn to the humble, let us therefore humble ourselves before the Lord and in due time, He will lift us up (James 4:10). As His children and people, let us humble ourselves, (and always stay humble from the heart!) and pray, and seek his face daily and turn from any of our wicked ways. Then and only then will the Lord hear our humble cries, forgive us all of our sins, and revive and restore us again unto Himself for His glory and His Kingdom purpose (II Chron 7:14). This is a wonderful promise if we will first fulfill the premises!

6. Honesty

Honesty is not just the best policy, for Christians it must be our only policy. Honesty is the most basic of humanity. Anything more or less than honesty is of the evil one who is notoriously referred to as the "father of all lies" who actively works in the human heart to try to pollute it with perversions and fill it with deceits (Jer 17:9). What an evil devil we have do daily deal with under the fallen structure of the human soul. But thanks be unto God that greater is He who lives in us than the devil who roams around to and fro to devour the weak and the side-tracked.

An honest person is a sincere person, a truthful person, and consequently a trusted person in both the motive and motion, intent of the heart and action of the hands. Proverb 12:17 declares that a truthful witness gives honest testimony. We must strive to always know the truth, live in the truth and speak the truth in love, and the truth will set us free from all kinds of deceptive devices of the devil and evil people. There are also three dimensions to honesty, just as to love and forgiveness etc. the first dimension is upward with God, to be honest with God who knows all things any ways; second is inward with ourselves, to be honest with the self because we are by human nature selfish and we can all easily be self-deceived (Gal 6:7); and the third is outward to others, to be honest in our dealing with other people.

7. Holiness

Romans 12:1: Therefore, I urge you brothers, in view of God's mercy, to offer your bodies as living sacrifices, holy and pleasing to God — which is your spiritual worship.

II Corinthians 7:1: Since we have these promises, dear friends, let us purify ourselves from everything that contaminates body and spirit, perfecting holiness out of reverence for God.

Hebrews 12:14: Make every effort to live in peace with all men and to be holy; without holiness no one will see the Lord.

Without a doubt, the exhortations of the Scripture prod the believers and followers of the Lord to the pursuit of holiness. The pursuit of holy living should be the normal standard for God's people the saints. We must be holy as the Lord our God He is holy. His Word is called the Holy Bible; His Spirit is the Holy Spirit; His people, namely we, are called by Him as his saints, a holy nation (I Peter 2:9). The early church prayed to God in the holy name of Jesus. We must be holy from the inside out, and not just the outward appearance of "legalistic holiness" of religious ritualism and ceremonialism. Our personal pursuit of holiness must be must be accompanied by the spirit of disciplines for sure, but it must be removed from the works of the law and from mere self-affliction and asceticism. In our life of holiness, we must center our attitudes and activities on the Word and the Spirit of God. We must learn to live by faith in, and with obedience to Jesus Christ whose redemptive crucifixion allows the believers to be crucified to the world and to become alive to the Lord (Gal 2:20, 6:14). A life of holiness is characterized by freedom from sinning, by a denial of the lust of the flesh, of the eye, and the pride of life, and by the cultivation and manifestation of the fruit of the Holy Spirit in one's daily life and relationships.

8. Hunger

Psalm 42:1-2: As the deer pants for streams of water, so my soul pants for you, O God. My soul thirsts for God, for the living God. When can I go and meet with God?

Matthew 5:6: Blessed are those who hunger and thirst for righteousness, for they will be filled.

Human hunger is both a physical phenomenon and reaction from the stomach, and a strong emotional desire from the heart. When you are really hungry with an empty stomach, you are eager and ready to eat about everything to fill up the belly and it takes pretty good; but when you are not hungry, nothing seems to have much taste to it.

Spiritually speaking, it is the same law in operation in the physical. When we are too comfortable and everything is easily obtainable with so much effortless convenience, we become too complacent and lukewarm in our intimacy and walk with the Lord. This was doubtlessly the case of the church in Laodicea in Revelation 3:14-20. Due to the lack and even loss of their first love, these Christians have become self-reliant, self-confident and even arrogant and boastful. The Lord sternly rebuked them for their lukewarmness with the warning that "I am about to spit you out of my mouth." (v.16). As always, the Lord rebukes and disciplines those He loves. This is tough love as love must be tough if it is to be responsible and mature. But along with serious and severe rebukes, the Lord Jesus also offers us sound and solid remedies: to buy gold "refined in the fire." (v. 18). In other words, it is the Lord's desire that the Laodicean Christians restore back their hunger for the Lord and the things of the Lord, not things of the world. He wants them, as He also commands us, to acquire the fire and restore the hunger for more of His Word, more of His Spirit, and live with more faith in Him, more favors from Him and more fruit for Him! In Christ, to be healthy, we must be hungry. Let us hunger and thirst for more of Him, more of His Kingdom and more of His righteousness in our lives and ministries. The more we sincerely hunger after Him, the more the Lord will fill us up with His presence, His purpose, His passion and His power! Amen, Praise the Lord!

9. Help

Psalm 46:1: God is our refuge and strength, a very present help in trouble.

Ecclesiastes 4:9-10: Two are better than one because they have a good return for their work: If one falls down, his friend can help him up. But pity the man who falls and has no one to help him up.

Acts 20:35: In everything I did, I showed you that by this kind of hand work, we must help the weak.

The Christian life must be lived with the help of the Lord and with us helping each other as the family of God and the body of Christ our Lord! No one can handle life alone and live in victory. We must live in constant union and intimate communion with the Lord and with each other because we need the Lord and we also need each other. Indeed the Lord is our very present help in times of our troubles, trials and tribulations! All we need to do is to call on Him calmly and even cry out to Him wholeheartedly in faith, trusting that He will fill us with His wisdom and courage to deal with what we have to deal with. He is always there ready to strengthen and help us out with His righteous and mighty hand (Is 41:10).

With the help we gratefully receive from the Lord, we must be ready and eager to help each other, as is read in the fine example of the tent-making missionary apostle Paul to the Ephesian elders of the church (Acts 20:35). First of all, we must be frank and open to seek and ask for help for our needs. Peter obeyed the Lord and caught such a huge number of fish. He had to humble himself and signaled others from the other boat to "come and help" (Lk 5:7). Then we need to realize that the weak, the needy, the sick and the lonely around us desperately need our help. They need our financial, emotional and relational helps in their difficult situations. There are different levels and kinds of help, and they will all cost us something, time, talents, treasures. Pray to the Lord for His heart of compassion and passion for souls, and my God shall supplies all our need, be it psychological, material, mentally or relational, according to the riches of His glory in Christ Jesus (Phil 4:19), so that we can be the hand of God extended unto our very needy world with His mighty Word.

10. Hope

Romans 15:13: May the God of Hope fill you with all joy and peace as you trust in Him, so that you may overflow with hope by the power of the Holy Spirit.

As long as there is a God, there will always be hope.

Your failures are never fatal or final with God.

Your future shall be as bright as the promises of your God!

The best help we can give to this world is hope.

I more I live, the more I am convinced that life must have meaning, and that life must have hope, for hope deferred makes our heart sick, but when the desire comes, it is a tree of life (Prov 13:12). He who has no hope in life has no life at all. The ones who have stopped hoping have actually stopped living! But praise the Lord that Jesus Christ came to offer us life, new life, abundant life and victorious life, the life that the devil and his demons have tried to steal, kill and destroy (John 10:10).

The Bible is a book of faith, hope and love. If Hebrews chapter 11 is the faith chapter, then Romans chapter15 is the hope chapter. Colossians 1:27 boldly informs and affirms that Christ in us in the hope of glory not only here and now, but more importantly there and then! As disciples of the Lord Jesus, we must be filled with His Word and endued with His Spirit from on high, so that our life of hope will reflect and project to this world of hopelessness. Those who are hopeful are also joyful, and joy is very contagious to those around. The joy of the Lord is our strength to deal with all of life's difficulties.

Chapter 11
All Aboard "the Gospel Ship": The Eight "Ships" of Leadership

Godly leadership entails at least 8 "ships" for us all to get on board. They are followership, fellowship, friendship, discipleship, worship, hardship, stewardship and finally, the equally valid and valuable kingdom partnership for completing the Great Commission together as we already see the Finish Line in these last days. Let us now consider them briefly in their proper priority and spiritual order one by one.

1. Followership

I Corinthians 11:1: Follow my example as I follow the example of Christ.

Following Jesus is unquestionably the single most important aspect of all true and real Christian leadership. The very first words of Jesus (Mk 1:17) and the very last words of Jesus (Jh 21:22) to His number one disciple Peter and in fact to all the others like us as well is loud and clear: "Come follow Me, and I will make you to become fishers of men! You must follow Me." In order to lead others fruitfully, the leader must personally follow the Lord faithfully, not merely by eloquent words and wonderful concepts or precepts, but by authentic daily deeds and concrete life examples (I Cor 11:1). Effective leadership starts with followership and ends with followership. Let this same mind, spirit and heart be in you which is also in Christ Jesus (Phil 2:5). The moment we as leaders have stopped following, we stop fishing. When we have ceased following The Leader our Lord, we have ceased to lead others in the right path, the path of the cross that leads us into His eternal kingdom. When one is distracted from his or her singular focus on daily and personally following Jesus, sooner or later the leader will fall into all kinds of snares of Satan, and will become the devices of the devil, and thus become a disciple of a disgrace to His holy name, as have been tragically evidenced by far too many clergymen and laymen alike. The most common devices of the devil, as have been dealt with in details in previous chapters, have been and will always be money, sex and power. In the words of the Apostle John (I Jh 2:16), they are the lust of the eye, the lust of the flesh, and the vain glory (pride) of life.

2. Fellowship

Proverbs 27:17: As the iron sharpens iron, so one sharpens another.

II Corinthians 13:14: May the grace of the Lord Jesus Christ, the love of God, and the fellowship of the Holy Spirit be with you all.

"Fellowship" means that we are "fellows on the same ship," the same gospel ship with Jesus the Lord as our life Captain. In order to have meaningful fellowship, we must be willing to intentionally spend both quantity and quality time together both in the Lord and with each other. I am convinced that there is no real quality if we have not been willing to have some quantity because the most precious and powerful life lessons are usually not taught, but caught, when the teachers are least expected to formally do a lecture or teaching session. As our mentor and model, the Lord Jesus showed us repeatedly by examples that He made the time and took the time daily to intimately commune in spiritual solitude with the Father way before the dawn of the day. And He did so frequently as His routine and habit. This was the secret of His anointing and authority, power and victory in overcoming all the challenges and difficulties. Not only so, He spent years eating, talking, walking, serving and sleeping with His disciples, both declaring to them clear kingdom principles and demonstrating to them His authority with many effective object lessons. Likewise, we must be like Jesus, live like Jesus first, and then lead like Jesus in Christian leadership.

3. Friendship

John 15:13-15: Greater love has no one than this, than to lay down one's life for his friends. You are My friends if you do what I command you. No longer do I call you servants, for a servant does not know what his master is doing; but I have called you friends, for all things I have learned from the Father I have made know to you.

What a friend we have in Jesus! True friends learn from their Master just as Jesus had learned from the Father. This act of learning requires humility, teachability, sincerity, sensitivity and great dedication. To form a special friendship with the Lord, we must be attentive, eager and quick to learn from Him; to form a great friendship with other people, we must not just intend to teach them something, but first humbly and diligently draw from them by listening to their life stories with the ears of our hearts and with no presumptions.

True friends know the Lord and His Word, and true friends know each other because they spend lots of time sharing life together. To know is to be known. The Good Shepherd our Lord again sets up a great example in John 10:14-15 with four dynamic principles of "knowing" for leadership: the leader is known by the Lord; the leader knows the Lord; the leader knows the followers; the leader is open, authentic and transparent enough to be known by the followers. In other words, his life is an open book, and he has nothing to hide from the Lord or from any others. His heart is righteous and his motive is pure, and his mission is therefore, powerful, for purity is the root of power itself.

True friends love the Lord passionately and love each other sincerely. Love must be sincere, hating what is wicked and evil and loving what is good and right (Rom 12:9). True friends devote to one another in brotherly love and honor each other above themselves. They bear with each other, support each other, pray for each other, forgive each other, encourage and admonish each other in the Lord.

True friends do what the Lord commands. Friendship is not a static statement of a stale relation; it is a dynamic and growing action, action of obedience. Jesus calls us His friends and loves us as His friends. And if we really love Him, we will obey what He teaches in daily lives. We will be richly blessed in the future, not because we have just known the Lord and His truths, but because we are willing and obedient to do them (Jh 13:17). We must go and do His will just as Jesus the Son of God went and did the will of Him who sent Him (Jh 4:34), leaving us a model and example to follow. He brought glory and praise to the Father God by having faithfully finished the work (Jh 17:4) assigned to Him to do on earth even before the foundation of the world.

True friends sacrifice as Jesus our very best friend did on behalf of our iniquities and transgressions. To serve the Lord and others is to sacrifice our own time, talents and treasures as real service will cost us something. Sometimes it costs us very dearly, including that of our own lives. "Greater love has no one than this that one lays down his very own life for his friends." The Apostle Paul urges us to present our bodies as living sacrifices (Rom 12:1) in service to God and for the benefits to others as well, which is only our reasonable act of worship in following the example of the sacrificial and suffering servant Savior.

4. Discipleship

John 8:31: If you abide in My word, you are My disciples indeed.

John 13:34-35: A new commandment I give to you, that you love one another; as I have loved you, that you also love one another. By this all will know that you are My disciples, if you have love one for another.

John 15:8: By this My Father is glorified, that you bear much fruit; so you will be My disciples.

True disciples obey the Word of Christ in relating to people and in discipling and disciplining others. Faith comes by hearing and hearing by the Word of Christ (Rom 10:17). For us to disciple others, we must be first disciplined by the Lord Himself through His Word, His Spirits, and Godly wise mentors. We live a life of discipline and obedience before others first, before we are qualified and fit to effectively disciple them.

True disciples love one another, just as the Lord Jesus loved us. The Bible is a book of love for God the author and finisher is love! If we do not love others who are visible and tangible all around us, how then can we say that we love our Lord who is the invisible Spirit? When we love others with the love of God in our hearts, we become more and more like Christ.

True disciples bear much lasting fruit to glorify the Father. Gifts, spiritual gifts especially the sensational ones such as healings, prophesies, tongues and miracles etc, are plenteous, rampant as a matter of fact, even confusing and deceiving to many of us; but fruit, the authentic spiritual fruit outlined in Galatians 5:22-23, is quite rare these last days. One of the tests in the Spirit that the Lord Jesus provided for us in Matthew 7:16-20 is the test by the fruit, not by words, but by deeds, not by gifts, but by fruit. A bad tree can not bear good fruit and a good tree can not bear bad fruit. "Thus by their fruit, you will recognize them." This refers to our actions, our deeds, the heritage we cultivate and the legacy we leave behind us for all to see and examine.

5. Worship

John 4:24: God is spirit, and His worshipers must worship in spirit and in truth.

Effective leaders must be sincere, passionate and devout worshipers of God. We are to worship God in spirit because God is Spirit, and where the Spirit of the Lord is, there is liberty (II Cor 3:17). We are also to worship our Jehovah God the Lord in truth because Christ Jesus is the way, the truth and the life (Jh 14:6). As disciples we must know the truth and live the truth before we can effectively and authentically speak, present and teach the truth to our own disciples with total spiritual freedom. The truth, the whole truth (the good, the bad, the ugly and the indifferent) and nothing but the truth, Jesus promises us once and for all in John 8:32, will set us free. Indeed lies and deceits are nothing but bondage to the liar and those whom he or she lies to; but the truth, no matter what it is, is liberty and freedom. As leaders, we must invite and involve our followers in the acts of worship, and in all kinds of services unto the Lord as acts of our spiritual worship, for worship is both an active act of life out of an attitude of gratitude from the reverent heart on fire for Who the Lord is and for what He has done for us starting from the rugged cross. We worship the Lord Jesus with all our heart, all our mind, all our soul and all our strength for the Lord God is good and he alone is worthy of our worship!

6. Hardship

II Corinthians 1:8: We do not want you to be uninformed, brothers, about the hardships we suffered in the province of Asia. We were under great pressure, far beyond our ability to endure, so that we despaired even of life.

Christians in many parts of the world such as communist nations and Islamic states go through many hardships in serving their Lord. As a matter of fact, there are more Christians now dying as martyrs for Jesus in this season of church history than in all the other seasons combined. But the Christians in the West, particularly in America, by and large have forgotten the necessity and the costs of bearing the cross of Christ. As Dr. Joseph Stowell (1996), the former president of the Moody Bible Institute, rightly points out that like smorgasbord Christians, we pick and choose al that pleases our taste buds and leave what is less palatable behind. But there is no such a thing as a free lunch, as the old adage truthfully declares. Anything of value and everything of worth in life comes with a price, at times a very high price. While the pleasure and power of following the Lord are real and substantial, the hardship of following Jesus can include insults, betrayals, jails and even martyrdom as Jesus plainly points out at the very outset (Luke 14:25-33, 21:16-17). Following Christ is not like going shopping. According to Stowell (p.197), "In the scheme of followership, Chris is up front about the cost... Our willingness to pay the price of a cross is the pivotal issue of being a fully devoted follower. If I refuse crosses, then I can not be a follower; if I follow, crosses are inevitable."

Leaders must take the lead in sharing the suffering and sacrifices of the Lord, not in gaining prestige and position and possession and more perks. Only then can we encourage others to take the authority and develop the strategy to overcome in the Lord with the experiences we have had in Him and through Him. The message of the great leader Paul in II Cor 1:3-11 is very powerful and relevant for us all today. It came from all the Pauline experiences of suffering for Jesus and bearing his many crosses as fully and proudly displayed in II Corinthians 11. Please take the time to read it carefully. We can learn so many profound life lessons from the passage. Here is just the gist of it for your consideration:

1. Life in this world is full of troubles, pressures, stress, and suffering;

2. In order to explain and encourage others, I have to personally experience it;

3. No one has to suffer alone, as we do have the Father of compassion and God of comforts;

4. There are of necessity, three dimensions of suffering (just like love and forgiveness) mentioned here: the sufferings of Christ, of us and of other people;

5. Christ the Suffering Servant comforts us so we can comfort others with the same comfort that He has comforted us;

6. We learn patience, endurance and obedience through the things God allows us to suffer, just as Jesus did, leaving us an example (Heb 5:8);

7. By relying on God our Divine Deliverer and though our prayers of faith in Him, we shall overcome if we do not give up;

8. We continue to give thanks to our gracious Father and the Lord Jesus who fill our hearts with hope (vv.7, 10). Therefore, we do not lose heart!

7. Stewardship

II Corinthians 9:6: Remember this: Whoever sows sparingly will also reap sparingly, and whoever sows generously will also reap generously.

If we care, we will share, and when we share, we show that we truly care. Luke 6:38 commands us to give unto the Lord and onto the needs of others (be it spiritual, financial, relational, emotional or psychological), and He in turn will give us much more than we could have ever given. In other words, in order to receive bountifully from the Lord and others, we must be willing and eager to give generously and even sacrificially. This is the infallible principle of life: the principle of the harvest --- sowing and reaping. No sowing, no reaping; little sowing little reaping; and more sowing more reaping. "Give, and it shall be given unto you!" What a promise with a premise! Don't just focus on the promise by neglecting or ignoring the premise, for without fulfilling the premise, there will be no delivering of the promise! No conditions, no benedictions!

We are stewards of the graces of God, and we are owners of nothing, absolute nothing! The Lord is the owner of it all, including our very lives (Mt 20:1). We have brought nothing into this world when we were born, and for sure we will be able to take nothing out of this world when we die. Whatever we have is a gift of His grace, and we are to be wise managers of the many blessings of God while He allows us a brief period of time to administer them with human diligence and divine intelligence. As stewards of the Lord, we must enjoy His bounty with gratitude; invest His resources to grow and bless others, and never to be greedy for money. Godliness with contentment is great gain (I Tim 6:6). As stewards we are also responsible in teaching our disciples how to make money, save money and give money wisely by biblical precepts and personal examples. With intentionality and responsibility lived out in front of others, we will enable and equip them with spiritual maturity in stewardship of our temporary time, talents and treasures.

8. Partnership

I Corinthians 9:22-23: I have become all things to all men, that I might be all means save some. Now this I do for the gospel's sake, that I may be partaker of it with you.

No one alone can accomplish the Great Commission. Everyone needs others to help and should enlist partners and recruit fellow workers for the Kingdom work of God (Lk 5:7). The time of the day is getting shorter and the night is quickly coming when no one can work (Jh 9:4). We must discern, decide, discover develop and deploy coworkers and equally valid and valuable partners to finish the tasks still remaining ahead of us. We see this urgency of the kingdom in the life of Jesus (Jh 4:34-35), and in His parable of the workers in the vineyard in Matthew 20:1-17, which is loaded with such spiritual significance. Indeed we are living in the last days and we are the church of the eleventh hours. We must be like Jesus, work diligently ourselves and recruit actively all the other work forces for the Kingdom of God, for when the twelfth hour finally arrives, we will not be able to do anything else.

When we have spent sufficient time with our disciples in our mutual followership of the Lord, in fellowship and friendship with each other, in worship to God, in experiencing and enduring hardships like soldiers of the Cross of Christ, and the principles and practices of responsible stewardship, we as leaders should recognize the maturity and capacity of the workers and authorize them as kingdom partners with vital tasks, as the Lord Jesus did and taught us to do likewise in Luke 10. What we need to warn them is that as kingdom partners, they should not be self-absorbed for personal gains; they should not assume or presume to be right; they should focus on Christ and His Word, and not carnally compare with anyone else; they should not grumble and gripe with complaints which is highly displeasing to the Lord; and they should pervert or distort the grace principle of the kingdom of God by self-righteously judging others as being unworthy. Let us together as mentors and disciples, fix our eyes on Jesus at all times, and let us get up, get over it, get out, get busy, get going, and get the job done, and do it well. Only in this way, will we all finally but certainly hear from the gracious words of the Lord, "Well done, your good and faithful servant! Enter into the joy of your Lord!" Praise the Lord! I can hardly wait to hear the sweet sound of the Spirit and the joyful and proud voice of my Lord soon! Hallelujah to the name of the Lamb!

Chapter 12
From Simon to Peter,
From A Reed to A Rock

And I tell that you are Peter, and on this rock I will build my church, and the gates of Hades will not overcome it. (Matt 16:18).

Jesus' first word to Peter: "Come, follow me, and I will make you fisher of men." (Mark 1:17).

Jesus' last word to Peter: "Follow me… You must follow me." (John 21:19, 22).

Without a doubt, Simon Peter was the most interesting, intriguing, lively and colorful character of all the followers of Jesus in the New Testament. There are many "firsts" and "only one" that are associated with Peter. Let us look us take a quick glance at the list:

He was the first follower of Jesus;

He was the only one who tried to refuse Jesus in the washing of his feet;

He was the only one who rebuked Jesus for talking about His death;

He was the only one among the disciples who walked on water;

He was the first one who boldly confessed Jesus as "the Christ, the Son of the Living God";

He was the first in the inner circle of Jesus to witness His transfiguration;

He was the first and the only original disciple who tried to do God's work man's way – protecting Jesus from harm by using the sword;

He was the only one who denied Jesus three times and was later challenged with the agape love three times by Jesus;

He was the pillar of the church, the first of all the apostles, and obviously the closest to Jesus;

He preached the first sermon on the day of Pentecost, leading thousands to faith in Jesus;

He was reported by history as the only one who eagerly died upside down on the cross for Jesus;

He was, according to Catholicism, the first ever Pope of the universal church of Jesus.

Simon Peter was a faithful man of God, a fruitful man of God and a mighty man of God. Under the pressure of the circumstances, be it the intimidating fear of the Jews or the fierce persecution of the Gentiles, however, he became very weak (not wicked like Judas). He was rebuked by the Lord Jesus for his lack of faith (Matt 14) and by the apostle Paul for his hypocrisy (Gal 2). Yet in spite of his momentary doubts and weaknesses and failures, Peter did faithfully follow Jesus his Lord and Master to the very end. From a simple and sinful shakable Simon (meaning "a reed") the fisherman, to becoming a stable, strong and solid Peter (meaning "a rock") the top apostle, we can learn so many wonderful life lessons in this maturing process of metamorphosis of character, purpose, vision and mission. Based on my many years of fascination with and exploration of the life and faith of Saint Peter, I have come up with ten of the most significant passages in the New Testament to learn various vital life lessons. These passages deserve our full attention and total concentration for they are full of spiritual wisdom, supernatural power, and practical applications.

I. Launch Out into the Deep (Luke 5:1-11)

It is a truthful saying that our final net worth in the kingdom of heaven depends on our current network with each other on earth. In other words, the degree of our ministry network with each other determines and decides the level of kingdom net worth in that the more intensively and extensively we net work with each other of like purpose and passion, of like vision and mission in spreading the Word and speeding the light, the higher will be our net worth as the faster of the return of the King too (Matt 24:14)! We must learn to minimize our minor differences between denominations and maximize our commonalities in goals and resources in fulfilling the Great Commission and finishing the task assigned us. Just as the kingdom of God was at hand with the arrival of King Jesus, so the end in sight shall come with the return of the same King of Kings. The faster and closer all the churches work together to spread the Gospel to all the world, the sooner will be the second coming of the Lord. This is the pure and simple gospel truth we must believe in absolutely and live out resolutely.

Matt 13:47: Once again the kingdom of heaven is like a net that was let down into the lake and caught all kinds of fish."

Mark 1:16-18: As Jesus walked beside the Sea of Galilee, He saw Simon and his brother Andrew, casting a net into the lake, for they were fishermen. "Come, follow me," Jesus said, "and I will make you fishers of men." At once they left their nets and follow Him.

A prayerful and careful study of the Luke 5:1-11 text reveals some powerful, practical principles and life lessons on following Jesus and fishing souls. Let us read it together and then observe the following life lessons:

1. Listen to the Word of God and hide it in your heart (vv.1, 3). The Word of God as incarnated in Christ the Lord, is the non-negotiable and absolute priority , authority and centrality of our life (Acts 17:28), and the Word here is the planted seed that will meet your need. Men shall not live by bread alone, but by every word that literally proceeds from the very mouth of the Lord Jesus Himself, the incarnate Word of God (Matt 4:4).

2. Let Jesus enter into your boat (v.3). Learn to lean on Him and He will lift you to your potential. Miraculous, marvelous and majestic things will happen in your life when Jesus gets into it as the Leader and Lord of life.

3. Launch out into the deep and let down the nets for a catch (v.4). Accept the challenge and obey the command, no complaints, no excuses, just do it! It does not matter whether you understand or not, like it or not, or feel like or not! Since Jesus issued the command, all we need to do is "Just Do It!"(v.5, see John 2:5). Remember that if we do not launch out, we will never get deep. So many lives do not get into the depth that the Lord designed and desires of them because they are not challenged or willing to get out first! First out, and then deep!

4. Learn once and for all that obedience is better than all the sacrifices (I Sam 15;22) and in all things we must obey God before men (Acts 5:29). If you are not finishing, you may not have been following; and if you are faithfully following, you will be bountifully fishing! Now that is a life lesson worthy of our learning! The obedience of Peter and the others brought enormous abundance to their boat and lives which would never be the same! (v.6).

5. Look for help from others (v.7). The wise words of Jethro to Moses the son-in-law are quite appropriate here: Listen to me know and I will give you some advice. May God be with you. The work you are doing, although very significant, is too heavy for you and it will only wear you out. You cannot handle it alone. You need to recruit and enlist people who are God-fearing and capable, systematically train them, carefully delegate the work to them and closely supervise them. (Exodus

18:18-21). Our net worth depends on our network. This is a trustworthy principle for life. Don't be egotistical. Be cooperative and contribute as a team player! The kingdom work is a net work; it is a team work. So train your team and put the team to work, together with you serving as one among them, just like the Lord Jesus (Luke 22:27).

6. Live in abundance, prosperity and victory with the presence and the power of Jesus who makes all the difference in boat of our lives. He will not sink your boat; He will only sanctify your life for His higher purpose! (vv.7-8). A sanctified vessel, pure and holy, tried and true, shall be put in places of effectiveness to bear fruit, more fruit and lasting fruit for the Lord (John 15:16). Jesus confirms and affirms in John 15:8, "This is to my Father's glory, that you bear much fruit, showing yourself to be my disciple."

7. Learn from Peter and the other disciples (Andrew, James and John) in Luke 5:1-11as they manifest so many wonderful and desirable spiritual qualities as current fishermen who would be catching many men for the Lord (v.10). Such qualities made them both faithful followers and fruitful leaders for the years to come. They were: thirst and hunger for God's Word (v.1), heart of availability for Jesus (v.3), the virtue of hard work and team work (vv.5, 7, 10), their willing obedience in spite of questions or doubts of the unknown (vv.5-6), their sincere humility, deep reverence and heartfelt repentance as the holiness of the Lord always reveals our sinfulness (v.8). One final spiritual quality we must learn from them the hard way oftentimes is their self denial, total submission and reckless abandon to follow Him (v.11). Their spiritual successes came from their willing sacrifices. If one is willing to faithfully follow and model after Jesus, she or he will fruitfully lead and model for countless others. Now that is a life lesson that we all need to learn, being discipled to disciple the nations by the grace of God and for the glory of God! Let us look unto Jesus and lean on His Word of promise and power like these early disciples. The strategies they show us here will surely bring us also many victories in the Father's fishing business. Amen!

Hear these challenging words of a dear friend, a man passionate for God with a hot pursuit for His vision and mission to "launch out into the deep":

I am beginning to believe that time after time in one way after another, the Lord issues the same call: Launch out into the deep! Whether for salvation, baptism in the Spirit, a new challenge in spiritual formation or a call to service—the command remains the same . . . The fields are white unto harvest. The power of

God is ours . . . We are soldiers of he mighty King. Catch hold of the hem of His garment, and launch out into the deep! (Rutland, pp.194-195).

II. The Confession from the Heart of Conviction
(Matt 16:13-20)

1. Jesus uses questions and answers as an effective way in disipleship (vv.13,15);

2. In order to have Him realized and actualized, Jesus has to be visualized, vocalized, internalized and personalized in each of our individual lives (v.15);

3. True spiritual revelations come only through the Father in heaven (v. 17); they are not our fantasies or vain imaginations.

4. Kingdom authority (the keys) empowers the believers to overcome all the obstacles of the enemy and live a life of victory by God's grace and for His glory (v.19);

5. Timing is crucial and critical. There is a "kairos" for everything. God's will and God's time always work harmoniously together with each other (v.20). Disciples need to pray for discernment, patience and courage to be who God has created them to be, and to do what the Lord has called them to do.

III. Counting the Cost of Discipleship (Luke 14:25-35)

1. In order to be a dynamic disciple of divine destiny, it is imperative that one recognizes always that Jesus Christ is the absolute priority in all things (vv.25-26).

2. The One who is the absolute priority of both our being and doing demands total loyalty (v.26-27). Be faithful to Jesus and His call on our live even to the point of death, and He will give us the crown of life (Rev. 2:10),

3. Before one decides to follow Jesus seriously, he or she needs to sit down and calculate all the costs involved, carefully and prayerfully (vv.28-32, Lk 21:16-18). There will be major sacrifices and even terrible sufferings involved.

4. He who is not willing to forsake all is not worthy to be His disciple (v.33, see also Luke 5:11). Jesus first gave Himself wholly to His disciples. Consequently He asked them to do likewise: give themselves

away for Him and His cause.

5. Discipleship as part of real Christian leadership is about causing influence, making an impact on the lives of others for the better, for the cause and glory of Jesus (vv.34-35).

IV. The Trials and Triumphs of the Christian Life
(Luke 22:31-34, 54-62)

1. The promises of God never fail. The Lord always performs in His own time that which He personally promises us (vv.34, 56-60);

2. Satan is always out there to tempt and intimidate us – "sift you like wheat" (v.31) with the full intention to weaken us and destroy us, but take heart that the Lord Himself is praying for us that we will not fail the tests. He tests us in order to purify our hearts and strengthen our faith and use us later to strengthen others (v.32);

3. The denying and disowning of Jesus by Peter was not because of evil motives of wickedness, but a heart of temporary and circumstantial fearfulness and weaknesses. God alone knows the heart and He looks only at the intent of the heart (I Sam 16:7);

4. Remorse and repentance is the key to restoration of the heart and revival of the spirit (v.62). The sacrifices of the Lord are a broken spirit, a broken and contrite heart, the Lord will not despise (Ps 51:17). Brokenness is the door to blessedness, for the Lord can not bless us if He does (if we do not allow Him to) break us. No breaking of the self, no blessings from Him. More brokenness, more blessings to come!

5. Effective leadership for others comes from one's faithful followership of Jesus (v. 54). Even with great fear of persecution and even as he did deny the Lord Jesus three times, Peter never did forsake Jesus even once. He always followed His Lord, "at a distance," and eventually upside down on the cross.

V. You Man of Little Faith: The Faith Challenge
(Matt 14:22-33)

1. The secret to Jesus' successes is none other than spiritual solitude: spending quality time apart from the crowds and the disciples, alone with the Father in intimacy and prayers (vv.22-23). This is called the theology of withdrawal which the Lord practiced often and set us an example for personal spiritual retreat, renewal and revival. Without this most vital and spiritual discipline, life and ministry will fall apart sooner or later, sooner

than you think. But with it as the infallible, stable and strong foundation, we will experience much victorious and abundant fruition.

2. The Lord intentionally allows plenty of winds and waves to occur in our lives so as to manifest His glory and teach us lessons on faith, focus, trust and obedience (v.24). Winds and waves, as disturbances and turbulences, are a natural and inevitable part of human life. What's important is not what happens to us or around us, but how we look at it and what we can make out of what happens.

3. While fear of the circumstances makes us doubt, faith in Jesus causes us to be courageous conquerors of all life's storms vv.26-27, 30-31).

4. Faith is the key to all the promises of God v.31). It defeats all fears and doubts; it gives us courage and confidence. Without faith, it is impossible to please God (Heb 11:6), but with him who believes, all things are possible (Mk 9:23).

5. The call of Jesus always remains the same: "Come!" "Come unto me, all you who labor and are heavy laden, and I will give you rest" (Mt 11:28). "Come, follow me, and I will make you to become fishers of men" (Mk 1:17). Come to Jesus today, by faith, and with confidence; Come to Jesus with singular focus on His presence and His promises and His purposes!

VI. Life Lessons on Servant Leadership: Foot Washing
(John 13:1-17)

Jesus the Lord is questionably our Supreme leader. He is our supreme leader because He exemplifies real Servant leadership which always stands readily, willingly and humbly to help us in times of critical needs. The word "SERVE" can be an acronym with special significances as follows:

S — Seek a way to meet a need;

E — Every day go do a good deed;
R — Remember Jesus showed us how;
V — Volunteer your time, talents and treasure now;
E — Exalt the Lord and Eagerly bow!

1. Godly leaders serve others out of a heart of love (v.1);
2. Godly leaders serve others out of humility of the heart (v.4);
3. Godly leaders serve others out of a desire for holiness of life from

the inside out (v.10), for without holiness, no one can see God (Heb 12:14);

4. Godly leaders serve others not just by talking the fine talk, but more importantly, by walking the consistent walk, by setting an authentic example for all to see the Law of the Picture, not in words, but in deeds (vv.4-5);

5. Godly leaders serve others by asking the right and relevant questions and providing the clear answers, challenging Peter and the others to grow in grace (vv.12-14).

6. Godly leaders serve others personally with purity, and collectively with a call and command for unity of the Spirit among all the team members (v.8).

7. Godly leaders serve others by challenging others to put their faith into practice v.17), for action is the very foundation of victory and prosperity.

8. Godly leaders serve others with the promised blessings for lives of obedience (v.17).

VII. Knocked Down, but Not Knocked Out (John 21:1-22)

1. Without the presence and the guidance of the Lord Jesus, the efforts on our own would be in vain, futile, and the boat of our life would remain unfulfilled and empty (v.1-3, see Lk 5:5).

2. Obedience to the Sovereign and Omniscient Lord Jesus brings divine providence (v.v6, see Lk 5:5). Obedience is not a matter of casual chance, but an intentional choice, even if we do not understand the command. Our obedience to Jesus is the key to our life of victory, confidence and abundance as we study the two powerful commands from both the Old Testament prophet (I Sam 15:22) and the New Testament apostle (Acts 5:29).

3. The greatest challenge of life is the challenge to love God with all our heart, all our mind, all our soul and all our strength (vv. 15-17). Peter denied Jesus three times, and hence forth Jesus challenged him three times.

4. To truly lead is to daily feed (vv. 15-17). Christian leadership, as the Lord both declared and demonstrated to Peter and to all of us through Peter, starts with faithfully following Jesus (vv.19, 22), and ends with faithfully feeding the flock.

5. The divine truth about joy in the kingdom of God is summarized

for us in John 21:18. True joy, not momentary emotional high or happiness, comes when we learn obedience to do what we need to do, not selectively doing what we'd like to do. It was through death that Peter obtained the true life, and it was through Peter being crucified upside down on the cross that His Master and Lord was glorified.

VIII. The Promise of the Father as Preached by Peter
   (Acts 2:14-41)

1. The promise of the Father is the gift of the Holy Spirit (vv.4, 38).

2. The baptism of the believer in the Holy Spirit endued him with courage and power (v. 14, Acts 1:8) for holy and victorious living, and effective soul winning (v.41).

3. A Spirit-filled life is one of signs and wonders, dreams and visions, tongues and interpretations in the name and for the glory of Jesus (vv.17-20). It is still the Lord's desire for us all today to be filled with the fullness of His Spirit with all the gifts and fruit, and it is our duty to seek and desire it with all our hearts (v.39).

4. The baptism of the Holy Spirit with outer manifestation and inner transformation in the believers, enables and empowers them with divine authority, extraordinary energy and a strong sense of urgency in the last days to run the race and finish the task assigned to us by the Lord Jesus (vv.17, 41, see John 9:4).

5. The centrality of Pentecost is neither the outpouring of the Holy Spirit, nor the effectiveness of the witnesses. It is Jesus of Nazareth who is the Author and Finisher of our faith (vv.22, 38) for this same Spirit of Pentecost is the Spirit of Jesus the Lord. Jesus said that "I, if I be lifted up, I will draw all men unto Me!" (John 12:32). "You shall be witnesses unto Me" says Jesus in Acts1:8. This was fulfilled with three thousand souls on the day of Pentecost and is being fulfilled today and everyday all over the world.

6. This gift of the Father brings conviction and repentance to the sinners and joyous hope to the saints (vv.25-28), following the clear steps of faith growth as outlined in verse 38 all in the name of Jesus Christ.

7. Once being Spirit filled, Peter was Spirit led and empowered from being a fearful follower of the Lord at a distance to becoming an anointed, bold and authoritative apostle of the Lord. His Pentecostal proclamation was so productive because it was full of spiritual conviction (v.37), personal boldness and unity of the Spirit (v.14).

IX. A Vision from Heaven (Acts 10:1-48)

1. When one spends time in deep spiritual devotion, the Lord Jesus will fill him or her with divine visions and revelation of the Kingdom of heaven (vv.9-11);

2. Many times God purposefully stretches us in order to strengthen us (vv.13-16). He wants us to get out of our own comfort zone of racial background and ethnic relations to receive His kingdom vision: the evangelization of all the nations.

3. The Spirit shows us the same vision one time after another, not for vain repetition, but for urgent and important emphasis to "get up" and "get going" for some immediate actions of obedience (vv.13-16, 19-21). Stop thinking and start acting. Peter received the divine challenge and responded decisively without hesitation.

4. True visions from heaven are always accompanied with spiritual and physical manifestations and confirmations (vv.5, 17, 19).

In order to recognize the will of God and do the work of God, we must listen to the sound of the Spirit (vv.13, 15, 19), which is often a still and small voice in our heart and soul (I King 19), and learn from the Holy Spirit with humble cooperation. We must fully cooperate to allow the Spirit of God to powerfully operate.

5. Our ministries of teaching and preaching the Word must center squarely on the person and work of Jesus of Nazareth. Christ-centered ministry will invariably experience Christ's anointing and authority, guaranteed with the presence of the Father and the presence of the Spirit to fulfill the purpose of the Son (vv.36, 38).

6. The great divine revelation for Peter from this vision is the truth clearly stated and experientially declared in verses 34-35: "God does not show favoritism but accepts men from every nation who fear Him and do what is right." I say "Amen" to that!

7. Without a doubt that this local vision must become a global mission—"telling people the good news of peace through Jesus Christ who is Lord of all." (v.36). In these last days, this vision from heaven, this mission for worldwide evangelization must become our personal passion. This is every true Christian's inescapable obligation because it is the Lord's Great Commission (Mk 16:15)! Then the end shall come (Matt 24:14)!

X. Keep Growing in God's Grace (II Pet 3:17-18, 1:5-11).

Finally, my study of Peter the great Apostle of the Lord leads me to a touching and moving passage of authority, urgency and practicality. It is I Peter 4:7-11, which offers five fantastic ways as to how to "praise god through Jesus Christ in all things". It starts with "all things" and it ends also with "all things". First the passage from Peter, and then the message to us all:

> The end of all things is near. Therefore be clear minded and self-controlled so that you can pray. Above all, love each other deeply, because love covers over a multitude of sins. Offer hospitality to one another without grumbling. Each one should use whatever gift he has received to serve others, faithfully administering God's grace in its various forms. If one speaks, he should do it as one speaking the very words of God. If anyone serves, he should do it with the strength God provides, so that in all things God may be praised through Jesus Christ.

Principle One (v.11): The centrality and the authority of the Word of God. More than anything else, always make absolute sure that you speak the very words of God with authority, power, passion and conviction in our ministries of teaching and preaching. The Word of God centers on and around none other than God in human flesh – Jesus the Lord. Christ-centered preaching and teaching is the absolute key to a victorious and abundant living! (John 1:1-17, Luke 24:27, Acts 4: 12-13, 17:28, Phil 2:9, John 15:26, 16:14).

Principle Two (v.7): No prayer, no power; little prayer, little power; more prayer, more power! A prayerful life is a powerful and purposeful life! A prayerless life, on the other hand, is not only a powerless life, but also a sinful life! Be clear minded and self-disciplined to pray, and pray to know Christ and the Word more intimately, to love Christ and His Kingdom cause more passionately. Pray to be more faithful and fruitful in life, and pray to be more fiery, focused, fervent and fearless in ministries.

Principle Three (v. 8): Since God is love and we follow God, we must love each other with the same love He loved us (John 13:34-35) sincerely and deeply as true disciples of Christ the Lord.

Principle Four (vv.10-11): Serve! Serve the Lord with gladness and serve each other faithfully with the grace and strength that God has provided for us. I am convinced that to really love each other is to sincerely and heartily serve each other. Anyone can be great, I am convinced, if she or he is willing to serve, for true greatness in Christ comes from humble and faithful service with the right attitude!

Principle Five (v.9): Be hospitable to one another without complaints or grumbling! Offer the gift of hospitality to restore and renew and revive others, and do so with the spirit of joyfulness and cheerfulness, for God loves a cheerful giver of warm, loving hospitality!

What a great giant of faith Peter was! How precious and powerful are all these life lessons he has imparted unto us through his constant contacts with Christ! Let us learn and grow in the grace of the Lord Jesus (II Pet 3:18), and in all things, may all the glory and honor and praise and powers go to Jesus, for after all it was not at all about Simon Peter. It was, and it is and it will always be all about Jesus the Christ, the Son of the Living God, our Mentor, Master and marvelous model in all things! Let us grow up to be more and more like Him who still calls us all with a loud voice: "Come and follow". Let us bear the fruit that Peter lists in II Pet 1:5-9: the fruit of faith, goodness, knowledge, self-control, perseverance, godliness, brotherly kindness, and above all these, love! Let all we do be done in love, with the love of God in our hearts (I Cor 16:14). Speaking the truth always, in love always (Eph 4:15), so that we can grow up to fullness of Christ the Lord who is the head of the church! Praise the Lord forever more!

Chapter 13
The Making of A Leader

The indisputable leadership expert Dr. John Maxwell always emphasizes and wholeheartedly believes that "everything rises and falls on leadership"! More than anything else in the organization, it is the leadership of that organization that ultimately determines its successes or failures. The churches, especially the western churches in Europe and America, are losing so much of its traditional influences, and the primary reason for the lack or loss of impact is the serious lack of spiritual, dynamic and particularly visionary leaders, for as Proverbs 29:18 declares that without vision, the people perish. Nothing is more important than godly leadership in the church or para-church organization, and the best source on leadership is the same as it has always been for thousands of years: the Holy Bible. If anyone wants to learn and improve his or her leadership potential, one must go to this greatest book ever written on the subject. After all, who can possibly teach us more and better about effective leadership than God Himself? God Himself is personally inviting us to participate in His work, and partner with Him, learn from Him and lead others fruitfully by following Him faithfully (I Cor 11:1, see also Gen 1:26 the interesting paradigm: "Let us . . . " and "let them . . .")

The Making of a Leader: The Jesus Way

In Mark 1:17, the Lord Jesus personally invites us to "come and follow" Him before we can "go and lead" others. If we will come, He will make us to become, and if we are not willing to first of all, come, then we will not be able to become. Come sit at His feet like Mary in Luke 10, seeking that One Thing, intimate fellowship and close relationship with the Lord. Then we can go in the power of His presence to be fruitful fishers of numerous men.

And as they were eating, Jesus **took** the bread, **blessed** and **broke** it, and **gave** it to them and said, "Take, eat; this is My body." (Mark 14:22).

In this most significant verse quoted above, the Lord Jesus reveals to us four foundational principles and essential steps in the process of Christian spiritual formation and godly leadership making. Let us examine them one by one.

Step I: Taken

This first process "taken" refers to the potential leader's personal realization that he or she is not here incidentally, coincidentally, or accidentally, but providentially, for such a time as this with an urgent and specific purpose (Esther 4:14). It denotes our "special divine chosenness," so to speak. Many are called of the Lord, but few are chosen by the Lord in such a crucial and critical time to make a difference in the world for the glorious expansion of the Kingdom of God. The church did not call or choose us; the religious system or denomination did not call or choose us; rather it is Jesus Christ our Lord who initiated the call to us (Mk 1:17) and chose us for the honor and privilege to be transformed by Him and to transform others for Him. Jesus declares in John's gospel 15:16, "You did not choose Me, but I chose you, and appointed you so that you should go and bear fruit, and that your fruit should remain." What a joy and peace to know that, that in spite of our utter unworthiness, it was the gracious Lord Jesus who called us and chose us to follow and serve Him, to be blessed of Him to be a blessing unto many others. He has indeed chosen us for Himself and has taken us in His hand for His glorious cause! Don't you ever forget this fundamental truth: He who has taken us will take care of us as we trust Him, obey Him and serve Him wholeheartedly!

Step II: Blessed

Not only have we been chosen of the Lord to His Kingdom services, we have been so blessed with multiple blessings beyond any measure! His blessings upon my life and family over the past many years to me personally have become too numerous to even begin counting, and too amazing to even describe. When people greet me with "How are you doing, Bro. Hong?" I often reply with the sincerity and from the profundity of my heart by saying "better than I will ever deserve" and "Blessed! I am too blessed to be depressed!" The Abrahamic promise that God gave in Genesis 12 has been fulfilled many times over in my own personal life and missions ministries. I am filled with an attitude of great gratitude and a heart overflowing with thanksgiving for His multitudes of blessings upon me, my marriage, my family and my God-given missions. He has truly prospered me over the past 30 years following Him according to His three-fold promises of blessings outlined in III John verse 2, that "you will prosper in all things, and in health, even as your soul prospers in the Lord".

I am so grateful to the Lord for His salvation of my soul, for His healing of my body many times, for His touching and renewing of my mind, for His strengthening my feeble and sometimes carnal, human spirit by the purity and the power of His blessed Holy Spirit of truth and wisdom and joy, and for His transformation of my life for His glory and honor. Indeed the Lord Jesus Christ has abundantly blessed me spiritually, academically, financially, relationally, psychologically, physically, missionally, and ministerially. Much greater shall be the blessings to come, for the Lord always saves the best for the last, and I am fully expecting it in the future, for I always remember myself and remind others around me that our future dreams in the Lord shall be as bright as the promises of the Lord, and that our future dreams will be much greater than all our past memories put together! Don't ever allow your past memories to become bigger than your future dreams! How wonderful and marvelous it is to see the blessed promises of God fully fulfilled in my own faith walk with Jesus. Be always mindful of the Word of God when Jesus answered and said, "Assuredly I say to you, there is no one who has left house or brothers or sisters or father or mother or wife or children or lands, for My sake and for the gospel's, who shall not receive a hundredfold now in this time ....with persecutions—and in the age to come, eternal life." (Mark 10:29-30).

Step III: Broken

The Lord Jesus now only has personally called us and specially chosen us for Himself, not only has He bountifully blessed us with the multiplicities of blessings in all areas of life, of necessity, He has to break us, break our own will for His Will, break our own ambition for His Kingdom direction, and break our own stone-hard hearts and carnal mind so that we might have His tender gentle compassionate heart and His tough spiritual mind (Phil 2:5, Lk 10). Just as a horse that needs to be broken so as to be obedient and useful for its owner, so must we also be broken before we can become humble and obedient for the Master's use! Just as there is no glory of the beautiful crown without the agony of the excruciating cross, also there is no abundance of His blessings without His strict and disciplined breakings! If there is no breaking, then the channel of blessing will be blocked until nothing can flow through it. No cross, no crown; likewise, no breaking, no blessing; much brokenness, much blessedness!

I love to sing the songs which invite the Lord and His Holy Spirit and His Holy Scripture to break us. Have your own way, Lord, have your own way, for You are the Potter and I am just the clay. Break me, make me, mold me, fill me and use me! Spirit of the Living God, fall fresh on! One of the most dangerous elements in the service of the Kingdom is the self-willed spirit which is unbroken, for it does not want to follow His Word, His will and His way. The sacrifices of God are a broken spirit, a broken and a contrite heart --- these, O God you will not despise... Purge me with hyssop, and I shall be clean; wash me and I shall be whiter than snow. Make me hear joy and gladness that the bones you have broken may rejoice (Psalm 51:17. 7-8). May the Lord break us like He did the bread in his hands, like He did with His own body (which is us!); may the Lord break all of us with the same conviction and burden that broke His own heart so that we may have a heart like His very own! May the Lord Jesus Christ break you and me today and everyday so that we can understand authority and learn about surrender and submission within the Kingdom of God (Edwards, p.xvii).

Step IV: Given

The last but not the least indispensable life lesson and crucial step in the making of a leader according to the Lord is that we must be "given" out as a living sacrifice, holy, acceptable and totally obedient and pleasing to the Master. Giving is the very nature of God according to John 3:16; it is also the nature of love. For God so loved that He gave. One can give without loving, but to be truly like Jesus, one can not love without giving! He gave up His own life for us while we were still rebellious sinners against Him, and he did so solely because of love (Rom 5:8). God has loved us with an everlasting love and has given us so many excellent and wonderful gifts both spiritually and materially. What can we render unto the Lord, or give back to Him for all His benefits and blessings toward us? The same loving and giving God commands us to love others as ourselves. He also requires that we give so that He will give back more for us to give out (Luke 6:38).

As we are willing to give out and give up the things precious to us such as material possessions, creaturely comforts and contextual convenience, projected images and social status, God will give back to you a hundred fold according to His unfailing promises in Mark 10:30, and what He gives is of eternal and kingdom value and worth! Paul the apostle emphasizes in II Cor 9:6-7 that we are to give cheerfully and generously as we purpose in our heart, and not sparingly or grudgingly. When we sow bountifully, we will also reap bountifully. God loves a cheerful giver. When we love and give cheerfully and bountifully, we will become more and more like the Lord Himself who gave Himself to us completely!

Just as He is the light of the world (John 8:12), we must be also the light of the world for Him (Matthew 5:14, 16). Just as Jesus want around to do all kinds of good works (Acts 10:38) in the presence of God the Father and in the power of the Holy Spirit, we must also let out light of love and life shine so brightly before the world that they will see the good deeds and give glory to God the Father through Jesus Christ the Son. And just as Jesus Christ is the bread of life (John 6:35) and this bread refers to His body and we are His body, so we though many, are one bread, for we all participate of that one bread (I Cor 10:17). We are the bread to be broken, as Jesus was and did, to feed the hungry and starving world with His gospel of hope, peace, joy and love. What an implication and what a costly spiritual life lesson!

Here are a few simple but profound concepts on leadership for us all to consider. To lead is to personally heed; to lead is to show the deed; to lead is to sow the seed; to hoe up the weed; to lead is meet the need; to lead is to feed; to lead is to bleed, and to lead, one must speed! Let us now consider each of these principles concisely and precisely.

1. To lead is first of all, to personally heed

To heed is to take serious notice of something. To heed is to give full and undivided attention to someone or something. Proverbs 15:32 correctly points out that whoever heeds instruction gains understanding. Ecclesiastes 7:5 affirms the truth that "it is better to heed a wise man's rebuke than to listen to the song of fools." The mighty prophet Samuel asked, "Has the Lord as great delight in burnt offerings and sacrifices as in obeying the voice of the Lord? Behold, to obey is better than sacrifice, and to heed than the fat of rams." (I Samuel 15:22). Having not shunned at all from declaring to the Ephesian elders the whole counsel of God, Paul the apostle urges them to "therefore take heed to yourself and to all the flock, among which the Holy Spirit has made you overseers, to shepherd the church of God which He purchased with His own blood." (Acts 20:28). More than anything else, to lead is indeed to heed the Word of God and the still and small sound of the Spirit. Heed before you lead.

2. To lead is to show the deed

A true leader, more than talks the talk, she walks the walk, daily and consistently, for all to observe. He says what he does and does what he says. Practicing what one preaches is the essence of integrity, being the wholistic and being the same inside out for all to see. Just as we are learning by doing, our followers and disciples also learn by observing and involving in what we do, for we are what we repeatedly do, and not what we incessantly say. Action speaks louder to the people than all the words put together. We will be blessed if we do what Jesus the Lord did for us (Jh 13:15, 17), and in so doing, people will see who we are, by influenced by what we do, and thus this earned credibility of people of the Way testifies and glorifies our Lord (Matt 5:16...I Tim 4:15). This is an infallible law of the picture, leading not just by anointed precepts, but by authentic examples.

3. To lead is sow the seed

Psalm 126:5-6 provides yet another great law of leadership: sowing in tears and reaping with joy! He who continually goes forth weeping, bearing seed for sowing, shall doubtless come back with rejoicing, bringing his sheaves with him. Leading is seeding and there is no leading others toward the goal without seeding into them the same purpose and passion. This means that the leader must be constantly recharging and replenishing himself through the Word, the Spirit, mentors and useful resources to help him grow healthy first, and then he is positioned to invest in others by adding values to their lives, be it spiritual, relational, financial or psychological. A leader plays the role of the host to house and bless others with care, counsel, correction and compassion.

4. To lead is to hoe up the weed

In one of his most powerful and applicable parables, the Lord Jesus illustrates this leadership principle with the sower and the seed. ""Still others, like seed sown among thorns, hear the word; but the worries of this life, the deceitfulness of wealth and the desires for other things come in and choke the word, making it unfruitful." (Mk 4:18). The devil for sure does not want us to be faithful to or fruitful for the Lord. He is trying his best to desperately sow weed among the wheat of our life in order to confuse us, debilitate us, and choke the potential of victory and abundant life out of us. But when the enemy attempts to sow, we must be vigilant and vigorous to hoe! To effectively lead is to actively and wisely weed! We must be ever prayerful and careful with our own spiritual intimacy, purity and vitality, and we must watch out for our disciples and followers (the sheep) to first protect them again the evil devil and then to provide for them the healthy and nutritious food to eat and grow!

5. To lead is to meet the need

As it is has well know in businesses, to be successful, a business must have at least three key elements: a quality product or service to sell, a credible publicity to promote, and a real and existing need to meet! John 6:1-14 tells of the miracle of Jesus feeding the five thousand. A miracle teaches a spiritual and eternal life lesson by solving an existing problem and meeting some existing needs. In this case, the need is food, and to meet this need, a miracle was performed. There are obviously many ways of look at this beautiful story, but the one thing that touched me the most is this young lad who is available and willing for the Master's use. He came prepared to give all that he had to Jesus and somehow, Jesus made more than sufficient foods out of the five loaves and two small fish to meet the need of the multitude. Give whatever little you might have, and the Lord will take it, bless it, break it and multiply it to bless many more needy people (v.11). As a result of the Leader Jesus meeting the need, the people were well fed to follow Him and the Lord was glorified as the true Prophet (v.14). This is the value and essence of this and any miracle of the Lord Jesus: to meet a physical and temporal need, and to teach a spiritual and eternal lesson!

6. To lead is to feed

John 21:15-17 repeatedly emphasizes the leader's relationship with the Lord first and then with the people he or she leads. If we love the Lord, we must obey His voice which is to "feed My sheep," for to lead is to feed. Feed their human spirits with His Holy Scripture, and saturate them with the Word, the will, the wisdom and the ways of God so that they will be encouraged, equipped, emboldened and empowered to make wise choices and take decisive actions to walk with and work for the Lord and His glorious cause of the Great Commission. As leaders we are to empower people by adding values to them. To add real values to people, we must make a impact, drive an influence and somehow creates an income as there are mouths to feed and bills to pay in the earthly lives of the followers.

7. To lead is to bleed

Leadership entails a lot of wounds and hurts as a natural and necessary process, without which there would be no quality product.

To bleed means to experience life as Jesus the Wounded Healer did, prophesied by Isaiah 53 and performed by Jesus Himself bleeding on the cross of Calvary. Our Lord was one fully acquainted with sorrow and grief, being slandered, betrayed, rejected (Mk 6:4), sold, beaten, and crucified for our iniquities, yet He sinned not and learned obedience through the things He suffered (Heb 5:8). How much more should we as leaders learn from the precious Lord? As a matter of fact, we have to learn, and learned it the hard way, the way of the cross, as Jesus did and promised us His genuine disciples in Luke 21:16-19. Therefore, be ready to be hurt as you will be, often not necessarily always by the opponents of the faith, but by the exponents of the same faith, whether intentionally or unintentionally. Often times those whom you love and care the most can bitterly disappoint you and deeply hurt you the worst. But the leader must always focus on Jesus and His Word so as not to grow weary or lose heart (Heb 12:2-3).

8. To lead is to speed

Spread the Word with rapidity, and speed the light with velocity. Matthew 24:13-14 admonishes us never to give up, but to be patient and perseverant to endure to the very end in carrying the Gospel to the whole wide world. Then the Jesus will return a second time when all have heard and the end shall come. Not only must we have the Kingdom authority and Spirit power, we need, as Jesus did, develop a strong sense of urgency in speeding the spread of the Gospel of God's grace (Jh 4:35). Like the Lord Jesus Christ, we must also work hard to reach the finish line and get the job done while it is still done, for when night comes, no one can work (Jh 9:4). We as servant leaders must never stay idly by (Matt 20:3, 6) for this does not please to the Lord Who will not prosper us or our ministries. Let us not be the wind watchers and cloud looker of Ecclesiastes 11:4; rather, let us be decisive and diligent disciples to go all out and get the Master's job done in the name of Jesus and by the power of the Holy Spirit! Let us be like the seraphim that Isaiah the prophet saw with six wings, with two covering the face in holy reverence of God, with two covering the feet in humility, and with the other two wings flying with active urgency to speed the heavenly vision to earthly action! Hallelujah Praise the Lord, what a majestic and marvelous vision we need to get hold of in our soul as well!

A final important word must be added about leadership the Jesus way, and that is that leadership at all levels is a long learning process throughout one's entire life time! It is never too late to start and it is never too late to learn, and this takes both a sense of passionate urgency and a spirit of true humility and enduring patience. According to the well-know leadership expert Dr. J. Robert Clinton (pp. 180, 194), effective and productive leaders all have a lifetime dynamic ministry philosophy that evolves continually from the interplay of three major factors: biblical dynamics, personal gifts, and situational dynamics. If they expect to produce and reproduce over a whole lifetime, leaders over necessity must develop this philosophy that simultaneously honors biblical values, embraces the challenges of the times in which they live, and fits their unique gifts and personal development. We need more leaders and we need better leaders. We desperately need more Christ-like leadership to face and overcome the increasing challenges and difficulties in both the church and the society in these last days and end times.

Chapter 14
Leadership Personalized and Simplified

After having spent a lot of quality time in intimacy with the Lord, after being filled and remaining full with the presence and power of the Spirit of the Lord, and after effectively equipping the team with the Holy Scripture and the Holy Spirit by both biblical precepts and personal example, I believe the Christian leader will have five essential steps or stages to follow through in order to lead in vision and victory: make up the mind, calculate the cost, take the risk, assume the responsibility, and pay the price. These must be consistently carried out determinedly and decisively by the grace of the Lord and with the help of many others. Let us now examine these five elements one by one:

I. Make Up the Mind

Ecclesiastes 11:4: Whoever watches the wind will not plant; whoever looks at the clouds will not reap.

Luke 9:62: Jesus replied, "No one who puts his hand to the plow and looks back is fit for service in the kingdom of God.

Luke 21:14-15: But make up your mind not to worry beforehand how you will defend yourself. For I will give you words and wisdom . . . "—Jesus.

James 1:6, 8: When he asks (of God), he must believe and not doubt, because he who doubts is a like a wave of the sea, blown and tossed by the wind. He is a double-minded man, unstable in all he does.

James 4:8: Come near to God and He will come near to you. Wash your hands you sinners, and purify your hearts, you double-minded.

"Making up one's mind" means to be decisive, to be firm, and to be steadfast. The phrase also means to be unwavering, unhesitant, unquestionable, undoubtful, and unmistakable. It means to live one's life with no ambiguity, no remorse and no regrets! For one to be and to do all these, he or she must know the Lord intimately and know His Word and will thoroughly. This person must have faith and obedience, and not fear of any threats or doubt over the promises of the Lord. This is a learning process and growing process in that the more we put our faith to our feet, the more we become steady, steadfast and firm on the Word of God. The more we exercise our faith in Jesus, the more we become faithful in and fruitful to Him.

Once you see an opportunity for ministry and know beyond the shadow of a doubt in you heart that it is His will backed up by His Word, you must decisively seize it and use it fully for His greater glory, for opportunity of a life time can only be seized during the life time of that opportunity. Strike while the iron is hot, and work hard for the Lord while it is still day, for when night comes, no one will be able to work (Jh 4:35, 9:4). Once a harvest is lost, you will have nothing from the filed for the whole year. Once a generation is unreached, we will be held responsible for eternity due to our negligence or indifference. Therefore, be strong, be courageous, be firm and be decisive! Set a worthwhile goal that has eternal values and purposes to it and go all out to passionately pursuit. Don't mind what others say for it does not matter in view of the kingdom and eternity. Remember this: those who do mind usually do not really matter, and those who matter normally do not mind! Go ahead, get out, get busy with the work of the Lord, and by God's grace together with others of like vision and passion, get it done, the sooner the better!

II. Calculate the Costs

Luke 14:28, 31: Suppose one of you wants to build a tower. Will he not first sit down and estimate the cost to see if he has enough money to complete it? . . . Or suppose a king is about to go to war against another king. Will he not first sit down and consider whether he is able with ten thousand men to oppose the one coming against him with twenty thousand?

This is another critical step or stage in Christian leadership: spiritual and strategic planning with careful and prayerful evaluation, calculation and estimation before boldly launching oneself deep into action! Mature Christians must first pray and then plan accordingly by taking a careful look at one's resources, be it physical, mental, relational, financial or spiritual. In the process, one will come across many possible obstacles and challenges (I Cor 16:9), but always remember that you do not determine the difficulties in light of your own personal resources. Always consider the goal of God and utilize fully the faith factor in prayers and planning. Learn to prioritize matters in light of their importance first, and then, only then, their necessity and urgency. Always put the first things first and embrace them with all you personally have, and all you can muster from others.

King David once pointedly said that he would not give God an offering that would not cost him anything, for he understood it clearly and correctly that true love is very costly. It cost Jesus on the cross to show and demonstrate His genuine love for us and for our reconciliation with the Father God! Those you love the deepest also usually cost you the most. Don't be afraid of the cost of disciple in terms of time, energy, money and even your life! Though the cost is high in the kingdom service, the reward of eternal life in glory with the King is worth it all. It is when we are willing to risk and lose our lives for Him and His name, we indeed then will find the true meaning and full fulfillment of life itself.

III. Take the Risk

Matthew 10:39: Whoever finds his life will lose it, and whoever loses his life for my sake will find it.

Luke 21:16-19: You will be betrayed by parents, brothers, relatives and friends, and they will put some of you to death. All men will hate you because of me. But not a hair of your head will perish. By standing firm you will save yourself.

Acts 20:24: However, I consider my life with nothing to me, if only I may finish the race and complete the task the Lord Jesus has given me —the task of testifying to the Gospel of God's grace.

Human life on earth is extremely fragile and temporal, like a mist or a vapor as James 4:14 describes it, "What is your life? You are a mist that appears for a little while and then vanishes." There is no such a thing as absolute safety or security in this world. The enchantment of safety is really just a myth, and the promises of security are but an illusionary mirage. Life is in fact full of risks and loses on a daily basis. The very definition and nature of the word "risk" is the possibility or probability of injuries and or losses, physical and psychological injuries, and losses of face, finance, health, body parts and even one's life. Risks are woven into the very fabric of our finite life on earth. When you take a risk, even a calculated and necessary risk, it is possible that your action may endanger your life and the lives of others involved.

The risk of following Jesus is very real as promised in Luke 21:16. Daring to risk our lives for spreading of the Gospel is right. As Pastor John Piper forcefully points out in his great book *Don't Waste Your Life*, that "playing it safe" may not always be wise or right, and that losing one's life is quite different from wasting it. It is better for us as disciples of the Lord to make up our mind and go ahead to obey Jesus in spite of the high risks involved. It is far better to lose our life for the service in the Kingdom of King Jesus than to waste it in the world and for the devil (pp. 79-89).

II Samuel 10:12, Esther 4:15-16 and Daniel 3:17-18 all provide us with powerful real life examples for the cause and the glory of God! In the first case, when Israel was surrounded by the overwhelming hostile forces, the Godly commander Joab decisively divide the army of Israel into two major camps, with one for His brother's leadership and the other following him to fight. After making preparation and giving words to be of good courage, Joab boldly took the risk of all the others to fight to death, trusting the Lord to do "what seems good to Him." In the second case, Esther, very much similar to General Joab, after preparing all that needed to be do and doing the very best she could do, bravely took the risk, declaring that "If I perish, I perish!" In the final example of the three courageous young men Shadrach, Meshach and Abednego, they proclaimed the real essence of the Godly faith and the risks of faith, no matter what the costs! This is exactly what Paul meant in Philippians 1:21, to live is Christ, and to die is gain. Paul risked his life many a time (Acts 20:22, 21:13) for preaching the gospel of God's grace, not knowing what might happen to him, and not even fearful of dying for Jesus! Jesus died for us all, and let us be willing and bold to live and die for Him. The One is for all, and therefore all should be for the One, for whether we live or we die sooner or later, we belong to Jesus, and nothing can separate us from the love of God in Jesus Christ (Rom 8:39).

A word of cause must be given about the dangers of risking our life but for the wrong reason (Piper, vv. 90-91). It is always and absolutely right to risk our life for Jesus and the glory of the kingdom. But if we are not careful and prayerful enough, we can become too fixated on self denial and self sacrifices that we become unable to enjoy the proper pleasures of life that God has given us. Through taking risks for Jesus ourselves, we might be drawn to self-righteousness, self-exaltation and glorification. We might scorn the lazy and the cowardly and thus feel the superiority of our own spirituality and life. When we decide to risk our lives for His sake, we must do so with "childlike faith in the sovereign rule of God in the world and in His triumphant love" (p.90).

IV. Assume the Responsibility

John 2:5: His mother said to the servants, "Do whatever He tells you."

Luke 37: Jesus told him, "Go and do likewise."

Luke 17: 10: So you also, when you have done everything you were told to do, should say, "We are unworthy servants; we have only done our duty." — Jesus.

Intentionality and responsibility lead to personal victory and spiritual maturity. That indeed is a life lesson I have learned over the many years of active and passionate global missions ministries. Great vision without a strategy and consistent action will not bring about any fruition. I have learn that it is always the right time to do the right thing for the right reason, for this will be pleasing to the righteous God who will powerfully prosper you! Always do your very best with all that you have gotten. No excuses, no complaints, no slothfulness, and no procrastination.

It is our responsibility as the children of God to live with obedience to the Great Commandment of love for God and for our neighbors; It is also our solemn responsibility to finish the Great Commission with a passion for Christ and a compassion for souls for Christ's sake. Together with His personal examples before us, Jesus commanded us to do likewise. We must heed to the motherly advice (as mothers know best) of Mary to the servants in the weeding at Cana in Galilee: Whatever Jesus tells you to do, go ahead and just do it! No doubts, no questions, no fears and no worry. Just Do It! Because of the humility and sensitivity of Mary, and because of the responsible obedience of the servants, the very first miracle in the Lord's ministries took place with amazingly great results in John 2:11, "He thus revealed His glory, and His disciples put their faith in Him." As the greatest leader ever, Jesus always found a way or made a way for the followers to be responsibly involved in the Word of faith and in the work of ministry so as to allow them to grow stronger experientially, for He knew that one of the best ways of effective learning is by actually and actively doing. We must resume our God-given responsibilities of knowing Christ personally and making Christ known globally until all have heard. The best way know Him is to obey His Great Commandments in Mark 12:30-31, and the best way to make Him known is to enthusiastically carry out His Great Commission (Matthew 28:18-20) in the presence and power of the Holy Spirit. Let nothing and nobody distract us from fulfilling your life mission which should be the Great Commission to go into all the nations and preach the Gospel to all people!

V. Pay the Price

John 12:24: I tell you the truth, unless a kernel of wheat falls to the ground and dies, it remains only a single seed. But if it dies, it produces many seeds.

In order to go up in life, one must learn to give up, for there are no serious successes without substantial sacrifices. In order to receive the final prize, the great reward that Lord Jesus has promised us if we will obey Him (Luke 6:31-36), we must be willing to pay the price, including the ultimate price, risking and even losing our lives for the cause of Christ. Just as there is no reaping without sowing, there is no prize without paying the price. Jesus demands all and deserves all from us because He gave us His all on the cross f Calvary. He did so simply because He loved us and still loves us with an everlasting and unfailing Agape love, even while we were still yet hostile sinners living in iniquities and rebellions against Him (Rom 5:8). Jesus did not just declare His love; He demonstrated His love with both His life and His death! If we really love Him, we will gladly obey what He commands us to do: pay the price for His cause, which includes others' rejection of us, hostility and hatred towards us because of Him, and even possible martyrdom for the Gospel's sake (Lk 21:16-17).

Here is a marvelous little poem penned by one of my famous professors of practical theology, Dr. J. F. May. I received this blessed piece from Professor and Pastor May while attending his course entitled "Expository Preaching without Notes" at the Church of God School of Theology in Sept 1985. It has since served as a personal living reminder for my life and ministry all these past 28 years now, and I sincerely pray that it will be an inspirational blessing to you as you read it, ponder upon it and apply the meaning of the text to your own life context:

Don't ask for blessing without giving;
Don't ask for grace without a trial;
Don't ask for peace without a conflict;
Don't ask for faith without a fight.

Don't ask for strength without a struggle;
Don't ask for hope without a goal;
Don't ask for joy without a burden;
Don't ask power without love.

Don't ask for guidance without obedience;
Don't ask for success without trying;
Don't ask for glory without humility;
Don't ask for life without dying.

Chapter 15
Characteristics of Corinthian Carnality
and How to Overcome Them

Reading through the two Pauline epistles to the problematic church at Corinth, one gets the idea that the church was filled with all sorts of issues, be it physical, financial, moral, doctrinal, ethical, legal and spiritual. You had them all just like the church in this day and age. According to careful research, there should have been another epistle that Paul wrote to the Corinthian Christian, for in II Cor 2:4, Paul said that he wrote them out of great distress and anguish of heart and with many tears over their many problems. This lost letter Paul referred to could have been II Corinthians and the II Corinthians we have could have been the III Corinthians. It must have been a very tense, intense and severe epistle of needed warnings and timely admonitions with clear suggestions for discipline and action, further reconciliation and restoration.

Based on only the I and II Corinthians we do have, one knows for sure that these believers of Christ were pretty unspiritual, immature, worldly, carnal and sinful (I Cor 3:1), for they were not focusing their attention on Lordship of Jesus Christ and His divine attributes, but rather on themselves with much selfishness, arrogance, jealousy, backbiting, quarrels and divisions for power, position, possession, pleasure, privilege and prestige, not at all unlike the situation facing us all today even after two thousand years due to the fallen structure of the human soul and the resulting evil gene in the human nature (Jer 2:13). Indeed the human nature has not changed much at all; neither has the powerful Word of God in its relevancy and vitality to convict and correct us when we humble ourselves before Him. There are several characteristics of carnality among the Corinthians (some are explicit and others are implied and applied to them from the five major historical lessons and spiritual warnings of the people of Israel in I Cor 10) that must be exposed, analyzed, and by God's grace, avoided and even crucified:

Characteristics of Carnality

Comforts—Like the churches today, especially in the affluent and materialistic West, the rich Corinthians Christians lived a life of comfort and everything was convenient in the prosperous commercial city. While comfort and convenience are good to a certain degree, and certainly the carnal weak spirit always craves for more of it, it can turn out to be a source of idleness which is the devil's own workshop (Mt 20: 3, 6). Too much of a blessing can become a curse. The Corinthian Christians were idling around, with lives captured by more comforts and conveniences. But God is always more concerned about the cultivation of our character than the expansion of our comfort, as he is more concerned about our holiness than our happiness!

Complacency—Too much comfort causes complacency and complacency kills both conviction and courage. The Bible repeated warns believers to be on guard against this foolish spirit of lukewarm complacency which God punishes and even destroys (Prov 1:32, Amos 6:1, Zeph 1:12). This dangerous attitude of indifference causes the complacent Corinthian Christians to be insensitive and indolent and indulgent only in themselves, with little or no kingdom ambition for the furtherance of the cause of Christ. As it has been correctly identified, that the opposite of love is actually not spirit of hate; rather it is the spirit of indifference which could not care less about anything or anyone other than the self (known as the evil gene in humanity or the egotistical principle). This spirit of indifference is the root cause of spiritual apathy and lethargy which are two of the greatest dangers in life and ministries.

Comparison—There was a strong tendency among the spiritually infant Corinthians toward carnal comparison simply because they did not focus their attention on the finished work of Christ on the cross. Comparison causes jealousy and envy, discontent and ingratitude. It makes one ready to complain! And that the Corinthians did.

Complaints—Carnal comparison always leads to murmuring and grumbling and griping and complaints. This happened to the people of Israel under the prophetic and Godly leadership of Moses. This also took place with the infants at Corinth who complained that Paul was good in letter writings maybe, but was weak in appearance and had no eloquence in his speech. That was why the Apostle Paul, spiritually discerning their sense of his unworthiness to minister to them, had to defend and assert himself in I Corinthians 2:4-5, "My message and my preaching were not with wise and persuasive words, but with a demonstration of the Spirit's power so that your faith may not rest on men's wisdom, but on God's power." They complained because they had their perspective and priority all messed up, not looking unto Jesus who alone was the Author and the Perfecter of their faith. Let us heed to the biblical admonition, "Do everything without complaining or arguing." (Phil 2:14).

Criticism—A further characteristic of the Corinthian carnality is criticism. They criticized the apostle Paul and they criticized each other.

Instead of appreciating and affirming each other as brothers and sisters in the Lord, we humans all have a fallen tendency to be the judge, with a critical spirit for fault finding. Instead of lending a helping hand, we often extend a pointing finger or even worse, a tight fist. Let us be ever careful in our criticism because it can easily lead to condemnation if it does not have its way.

Condemnation—Condemnation brings spiritual, physical and mental oppression while compassion brings liberation. While we must live our life of clarity and conviction, we must be reminded that we are not the judge of the universe. We are not to judge other people's thoughts and motives. We pray for them, and love them and ask God to take care of it. To them own Master they will either stand or fall. John 3:17 declares that God did not send his Son into the world to condemn it, but to save it through people's faith in Him! And therefore, there is no condemnation for those who are in Christ Jesus (Rom 8:1). Let the only righteous Judge do the judging. As for us, we should follow Matt 7:1-2 that instructs is not to judge others or we too will be judged in the same way we judge others. Quite on the contrary, we should always follow the Golden Rule of life that, "In everything, do to others what you would have them do to you." (Matt 7:12). In other words, in all things we should not do to others what we do not want them to do to us. This sums up the Law and the Prophets.

Cynicism—It is a self-centered and self-righteous attitude that believes that all the other people are motivated only to get and gain benefits for themselves. A cynic is a person who makes cuttingly unkind and negative remarks that the whole world has done him wrong. A cynic is a person who also likes to speak ill and evil of other people. He or she does so because of inward bitterness and internal unforgiveness. Cynicism is a terrible, dangerous and spiritual cancer that grows inside one's soul and will eat that person alive from the inside out! It must be cut out and uprooted and destroyed once and for all. Cynicism should have absolutely no place in the body of Christ, and it should never be allowed in Christian kingdom relationship as it chokes vitality and thus destroy any possibility of victory and prosperity. Instead of getting cynical, we as dedicated disciples of Christ must be forgiving of others and supportive of them joyfully as we live out our life with enthusiasm and optimism!

Overcoming Carnality by the Word of Christ

I strongly believe that when we are filled and continue to be refilled by the presence and the power of the Holy Spirit, and when we are focused and refocused today and every day on the unfailing and unshakable promises of God revealed and fulfilled in Christ, then our life hidden in Christ will promising, prophetic, purposeful, passionate, positive, persistent, proactive, powerful, productive, prosperous and persuasive! Let us look at these effective strategies to defeat all forms of Corinthian carnality and to fully live the victory that the Lord has promised us and prepared for us before the foundation of the world.

1. Be Prophetic

Where there is no prophetic revelation or heavenly vision, the people will cast off all restraints and go crazy (Prov 29:18). To be prophetic, we need to go back to the basics—The Holy Bible which is the book of prophecies and promises from the Almighty God, the source of wisdom, knowledge and understanding. To be prophetic is to be biblical and to be prophetic is to focus on the promises of the Word of God! We can not be promising if we do not delve into the promises of the Lord which make us prophetic in spirit and word.

2. Be Purposeful

Out of the prophetic utterances and revelations, one derives purpose for his or her life and mission in life. The Word of God teaches us that we are fearfully and wonderfully made in the very image and likeness of the Creator God, and that we are here for a purpose. That purpose is to please God in every way, and glorify the name of Jesus in all that we say and do as the Holy Spirit and His power enable us to do (John 15:26, 16:14). We are created to be Christ-like, saved to serve the Lord, formed to be His family, planned for His pleasure and we are made for His missions! This indeed is the purpose of my life in a nutshell. How about you?

3. Be Passionate

Once we discover the real meaning and the central purpose of living on earth, we must take action with a heart of passion. Get enthused in the Lord, be excited and exuberant to go all out, and get busy with what the Lord has clearly called you to do. And whatever you say and do, do it all from sincerity and simplicity of the heart, and with all the might and energy of your hands, as unto God and His pleasure, and not unto man, for it is from the Lord you will receive your blessed rewards (Col 3:23). Never be found lacking in zeal, but keep your spiritual fervor and physical strength in serving the Lord with all you have got!

4. Be Positive

A person who is prophetic in spirit, purposeful with life and passionate about his life's missions is definitely positive in his outlook and perspective. She always looks at the brighter sides of things and the better sides of people. She does not allow the small stuff or petty things of people or circumstances of life to distract or derail her from her hot pursuit of her vision and mission. Positive people not only have faith in the higher source and thus is always focused, they also unites, energize, motivate and inspire others around them to bring out their own best in life with the hope and optimistic attitude daily displayed for all to see and sense. A positive person is respectful and appreciative of others. He works well with others as a team and glad to share credits and honors with people because a positive person is also a secure person. This positive spirit enables the individual to reach out to others with kindness and compassion, and to enlist others for worthy causes by words of motivation and personal examples of inspiration.

5. Be Perseverant or persistent

Perseverance or persistence is not a natural inheritance. It is a mindset and it is an attitude which believes and behaves in such a consistent way as to stay at the task, stick to it until the job is done, and done well! Since it is a mindset and an attitude of the heart, perseverance or persistence must be daily cultivated and conscientiously developed. A character trait closely associated with these is patience. A hasty person jumps to conclusions based on a very partial impression without any serious exploration or examination or investigation of the matter, but a patient person gains wisdom and understand steadily. There is indeed no wisdom without patience, just as there is no maturity without assigning and assuming real and serious responsibility. And it order to develop it, one must has faith and possess conviction in the prophetic promises of the faithful Lord. One must have a clear goal to achieve and a strong desire to pursue the goal. He or she must develop a plan or strategy before any activity. Additionally, the persistent should be prepared and be willing to go through strict disciplinary training and pay the precious price before achieving the precious prize! Having role models is also crucial in growing perseverance. The persistent widow of the Bible is a good example!

6. Be Proactive

A person of proactivity is one who actively takes the initiative in life and gladly resumes the responsibility to make wise choices and tough decisions in the midst of hard and even hostile circumstances. A proactive person does not passively react to the environmental conditions with natural instincts or impulses based on mere feelings and emotions, but respond to what's happened confidently based on his or her own carefully internalized values and profoundly personalized principles. According to Dr. Stephen Covey (p.71), "responsibility" is a compound word of "response-ability"—the ability to choose your response. Highly effective people are highly proactive people who recognize that responsibility. They do not blame circumstances, conditions or conditioning for their behavior because their behavior is a product of their own conscious choices, based on solid and sound values, rather than a product of their conditions based on reactive feelings. In the final analysis, it is not what happens to us that hurts or helps us, but rather our response to what happens to us. Proactive people know how to take the initiative and how to respond with wisdom, decision and precision based of principles. Principled living (always doing the right things for the right reasons) invariably leads to a victorious life.

7. Be Powerful

A life of principles is a life full of power for it is not turned and twisted every which way by the winds and waves, or the fads and fashions. When we live prophetically from the Word of God and purposefully for the glory of God, we can not help but be full of enthusiasm and energy to get the job done and do it with excellence.

8. Be Productive

The natural result and reward of a life driven by purpose and filled with passion and power is productivity. This life is an intelligent life, and it is also a diligent life what the Lord is pleased with and richly blesses. This faithful life totally submitted and completely surrendered to the Master's purpose well pleases the Lord. In turn, the Lord will prosper this life of faith with much lasting fruit for all to see and emulate.

9. Be Prosperous

The purpose-driven life is not only a passionate life and a powerful life, it is also a prosperous life, for the Lord gives this person the gift (divine ability) to be successful in whatever she or he touches. The Bible declares that the Lord delights in the prosperity of His servants (Ps 1:3, 35:27, Josh 1:7, III Jh 2). It is the Lord who gives us the power and wisdom to get wealth and prosperity Deut 8:18). He is so please when His own children live, not in the bondage of poverty, be it financial, relational or spiritual, but in the victory and glory of prosperity! The Lord Jesus Christ causes us to succeed and prosper in all things, especially in priority of the soul, so that He can establish His covenant, and use us to confirm His unfailing and infallible covenantal promises to be truthful and trustworthy for all to see, obey and follow. We as the people of God with His wisdom and disciple and diligence, will lend to others but not borrow anything from them; the Lord will make us the head and not the tail; we shall only be above, and not be beneath, if we will prayerfully heed His commandments this day and if we will carefully observe and obey them! (Deut 28:12-13). Amen!

10. Be Persuasive

To be persuasive is to be influential. To be persuasive is to be able to positively and inspirationally impact other people who have contacts with you. Passion, like joy and love, is infectious and contagious in constructive way. Prosperity is a blessing not just to the individual, but to all who are associated with the prosperous person far and wide, as in the biblical example of Joseph of the Old Testament. As a result of his godliness, faithfulness and divine wisdom, Joseph was so blessed beyond measure from the poor pit to the powerful premier that he was able to subsequently bless his family, his tribe and his whole nation, leaving a legacy to the whole world as a savor and sustainer of lives and resources. What a wise steward of God who demonstrated both faithfulness and fruitfulness for us to seriously imitate in the purpose and passion, vision and mission of our own lives and ministries!

Chapter 16
Christ-Centered Counseling as Challenge, Choice and Change: On Cultures, Contexts, Conflicts and Confrontations

For though I am free from all men, I have made myself as a servant to all, that I may win the more . . . I have become all things to all men, that I might be all means save some. I do all this for the sake of the gospel that I may be partaker of its blessings with you. (I Cor 9:19, 22-23).

Preach the Word; be prepared in season and out of season; correct, rebuke and encourage – with great patience and careful instruction. (II Tim 4:2).

"I am the way, the truth and the life" — Jesus Christ in John 14:6.

To be a Christian is to be like Christ; to be truly like Christ, one must center his head, heart, purpose, passion, vision and mission on Christ. Just as our teaching and preaching must be Christ-centered, our life and counseling must also be Christ-centered. It is in Christ Jesus our Lord that we live and move and have our beings (Acts 17:28) victoriously and eternally, for He is the beginning and the end, the first and the last, the Alpha and the Omega, the author and the finisher of our faith! Jesus Christ has to be centrality and the originality and destiny of all we are and all we do. He is much more powerful than the tripe A battery, for He is the Anchor of our soul, the Answer to our desires, the Anecdote of our life, the Antidote to our problems, the Anointing of our missions, and Authority of our ministries.

Over the past 30 years, I have tried incessantly to become a diligent student and even a serious scholar of counseling, especially Christian pastoral counseling (advice rendering which includes teaching, encouraging, exposing, rebuking, correcting, modeling and challenges to action), and Christo-centric cross-cultural counseling. In this chapter, I would like to share with you some of the highlights and insights in this area so as to equip you for the mission and the ministry that the Lord may have called you: Christian counseling across cultures.

In I Corinthians 9:19-27, Paul the cross-cultural Kingdom servant leader named quite a few cultures, the culture of the Jews, the culture of the Gentiles, the culture of the lawless, and the culture of the weak, the poor, and the powerless (vv.19-22). Not only did he name all the people in these various cultures who needed to be reached, gained, won and saved with the gospel of God's grace and glory, Paul also provided several insightful, indispensable and invaluable strategies to accomplish the objective: the salvation or redemption of souls in all cultures. Here is a brief list of his methods that a cross-cultural leader must develop and deploy:

1. Genuine Humility (v.27);
2. Spiritual and cultural Sensitivity and relevancy (vv.20-22);
3. Principled Flexibility (v.22);
4. Adaptability & adjustability (vv.20-22);
5. Connectivity, networking and partnership (v.23);
6. Purposefulness or intentionality (v.19);
7. Unquenchable passion and energy (v.22);
8. Focused urgency (v.24);
9. Confidence and Certainty (v.26);
10. Kingdom Authority (vv.24-26);
11. Direction and determination (v.24);
12. Strict discipline (v.27);
13. Optimistic hope for eternal rewards (v.25).

Paul lived a life of dedication and discipline for he clearly knew that what he was doing was part of his eternal life destiny with incomparable and unparalleled kingdom rewards and glory. He led by the excellence of his example, devoid of any slightest sign of pretense and hypocrisy. He lived a life with a purpose-driven urgency, and in turn he pleaded all of us to follow him as he faithfully followed Jesus (I Cor 11:1). He further urged others to run the Christian race of grace with purpose and passion, focus and force, willing to sacrifice, suffer and surrender to the Master, running to win the incorruptible crown of victory and glory, as we are all predestined to in Christ Jesus even before the foundation of the world.

Human Culture: Definition, Nature and Character

Culture can be generally and inclusively defined as "the ways of life of a given people in a given place at a given time." It refers to arts and artifacts, attitudes and activities, beliefs and behaviors of the said people, race or ethnicity. Cultures all have the same basic nature as follows:

1. Culture, being human in origin, is not perfect just as human beings are not.

2. No culture is neither totally demonic, nor completely divine.

3. Culture by nature is only a neutral tool, vessel or instrument of expression and action.

4. Culture is not the object of God's compassion. Human soul and its redemption are.

5. God is not for or against any particular human cultures; He works in, through, above and beyond them all to accomplish His ultimate salvific purpose. For more scholarly information, read the excellent classic *Christ and Culture* by H. Richard Niebuhr, 1951.

Additionally, all human beings are cultural beings, whether he has been enculturated in his own particular culture, or she has been acculturated in a cultural context which is not originally her own. All human cultures share the following most basic characteristics:

1. Cultures are learned beliefs and behaviors;

2. Cultures are shared within their contexts;

3. Cultures are dynamic and not static. As the well-know saying declares, the only constant in life is change itself, although some cultures change and adapt to change more rapidly than others. There is not s single culture that has not changed at all over the millenniums.

4. Cultures are like a double-edged sword in that they punish and reward thoughts and actions according to their acceptable and desirable cultural norms;

5. Cultures are systemic in that all of cultural elements are either closely connected or loosely linked together somehow. They may not be highly and systematically organized, but they are all related to each other with dynamics and interdependence for some useful purpose.

As human beings from different cultural backgrounds and ethnic people groups, in some ways we are like all others (fallenness, sinfulness, selfishness, aspirations, deep desires to be free and live a better life after the basic human needs for foods, clothes and shelters are met), and this is called human universality. In some ways, due to cultural differences, we are like some others. In other words, we are like those who are more like us to due race, ethnicity, education, economy, religion, geography and political persuasion etc). This is called cultural similarity. And in some ways, we are like no others because we are all unique human beings and none of us are exactly alike in all aspects of life. This is called individual uniqueness which should be respected, encouraged, and cultivated for greater purposes. All of these have to be properly processed and rightly appropriated depending on the context, for even a biblical text would become no more than a pretext and even anti-text without sufficient and correct ramification from and application to the context. Theology in its most basic sense is "faith seeking understanding from within a cultural context." (Augsburger, pp. 140-142). This definition of faith with its three elements also offers three important propositions: (1). Theology relates humans to God who transcends all cultures while being absolutely related to each; (2). Theology is done within a cultural context, and being incarnational, this Christian theology is local and cultural in application and situation, while simultaneously global and universal; and (3). Theology seeks a coherent understanding of relationships between the human and the divine which would allow one to speak glocally with cross-cultural and cultural perspectives. This theology means that all therapy must be "contextually congruent," finding its proper "fit". "To attempt a challenge or change from an alternative context is both vanity and insanity." (Augsburger, p.140). And based on my 30 some years of intra-cultural and inter-cultural ministries of counseling in the Asian, American and Latin American contexts, I know that relationally, human beings, by and large, all want to be accepted, respected, and meaningfully and significantly connected, knowing that they are in some big or small way, making a difference or a contribution. I have not met one human being anywhere who desires to be intentionally neglected, or rejected! No, not one, regardless of her or his particular cultural orientations!

Christ-centered cross-cultural counseling as challenge, choice and change

Generally speaking, counseling can be easily understood metaphorically. A metaphor is a figure of speech widely and effectively used in all cultures, and even frequently in the Bible (Matt 5:13-14, 6:22, 7:13-14, 23:33). It is an implicit comparison between two similar things which are essentially unlike each other, without using the words "as" or "like". A metaphor functions for the counselor as a definition and direction of counseling, as a framework and structure to guide and guard both the client and the counselor in the counseling process. The metaphor that one engages can also affect and determine the results of counseling. Counseling is "hide and see"; counseling is "guest and host"; counseling is "wounds and healing," counseling is "scientific empiricism and experimental research;" and counseling is "challenge, choice and change."

People in life, including believers and followers of the way, are often caught in dilemmas, stuck in predicament and hooked with certain harmful addition and habits. Life on earth is full of crisis, be it attitudinal, physical, accidental, relational, psychological, financial or spiritual. In order to "unhook" and help people from the dangerous trappings and subtle snares, the Christ-centered counselor must be sufficiently prepared in wisdom, knowledge and understanding of God, self and others in contexts, and the necessary qualities and skills to deal with the issues and the struggles of life. He or she should at the outset of the therapeutic relationship, let the counselee know, as Jesus did us in John 16:33, that in this life, we all have and will have all kinds of trials and troubles for a purpose. Let him or him clearly realize that in life of self, sin and Satan, trouble is normal, crisis is inevitable, change is constant, and wise choice is absolutely necessary. This way the counselor will not live in fantasy, illusion or delusion, but live in objective reality with sound and solid spirituality and biblical theology to deal with real problems and people associated with us. Several necessary steps should be taken, such as:

1. The counselor provides a Kingdom perspective and priority of life on earth;

2. The Counselor listens attentively and understands correctly the client's values and views according to his cultural and personal context;

3. The counselor clarifies clearly and reevaluates the counselor rigorously and vigorously, speaking the truth in love;

4. This is done in the context of caring and coaching and mentoring and modeling where one's authentic being is more important at this stage than one's doing;

5. The counselor provides insightful and authoritative alternatives and possibilities to the client to see succinctly a different and better point of view, and to accept willingly the challenge to make the wise choice to effect the desirable changes;

6. The client or the counselor, after being confronted or challenged with the past history, be it views or values or attitudes or activities, is again challenged with biblical teachings and wisdom to assume responsibility which leads to maturity, and to make correct choices which will lead to positive change when acted upon;

7. The counselee is the one who does have the right to choose his attitudes and action, beliefs and behavior; but he also is the one who

must be held responsible to carry out the choice with consistence. Rights and responsibilities must go together with each other.

8. This process of self-determination and personal responsibility is crucial in developing in the counselee a strong sense of ownership of feeling and decisions;

9. Action of the counselee should produce certain clear results;

10. Evaluation by the counselor, and reorientation for the client with renewed direction (based on the previous performances and resulting outcomes) will allow the counselee to feel deeper and reach higher.

Cross-Cultural Conflicts and Confrontation

It has always been the desire of the heart of God that we live in perfect unity, harmony, fresh and frequent fellowship with Himself (John 17) and with each other as brothers and sisters in the family of God, the Body of Christ (Psalm 133). We are expected of the Lord to be loving and caring for each other, praying and helping each other, forgiving and reconciling with each other and fully accepting one another, affirming and appreciating each other, building each other up and bearing each other's burdens, thus fulfilling the law of Christ with the dynamics as the Body of the Lord Christ (I Cor 12). Unity is God-like, and the trinity means "three in one" perfect unity. This unity is achieved not by uniformity, coercion to conformity, but by respecting, accepting and appreciating the differences and diversities within the body of Christ, just as the trinity is marked by diversity of distinct roles and functions.

Duane Elmer (pp.25-33) sharply points out that our ability to respect human and cultural diversities and differences and not let them disrupt harmony is indeed a powerful testimony to the love and power of God. But unfortunately, due to our human fallenness, and due to our typical Western, and especially American orientation to the ways of thoughts and actions, individualism and independence are normally lifted with a high premium way above unity and harmony. Elmer firmly believes that one of the main reasons among others unspecified, why God does not send the much needed revival to us is because of "unresolved interpersonal conflicts." If people in the world see broken relationships, schisms, gossips, and people exploiting one another in the churches, a message then about God's love and power will have little effect. Without any question or debate, it has been identified that "the greatest problem among missionaries is relational breakdowns among themselves, and our greatest need is to help them deal with conflicts by building positive interpersonal skills." (p.33). If it is so even among missionaries who are full-time, specially-called ministers and ambassadors of the Lord Jesus, how much more is it factual among the regular folks of different cultures!

People, being created as unique individuals, do have sincere differences of opinions, which are natural, normal, and even healthy for growth and maturity when viewed wisely and handled properly. Being human, none of us is exactly alike in outer appearances, and inner personality characteristics. As the axiom goes, that if two people think, agree and act exactly alike on everything, then one of them is absolutely unnecessary. None of us will ever have a "perfect" relationship on earth with another person that does not have some sort of friction or even fracture. There are as many causes of human conflicts as the conflicts themselves, such as conflicts of interests and serious misunderstanding, distrusts and mistrusts, along with the infamous seven deadly sins traditionally identified, seen in James 4:1-5, and vividly illustrated in the poem of Mother Teresa at the end of this chapter. Other causes of human conflicts also can include the actual or perceived scarcity of available resources, desire to obtain honors and status, privilege and positions, and the craving to enjoy the pleasure and power that come from controlling others. This however is neither the time nor the place to discuss them. What I would like to do is to bring your attention to Matthew 18:15-17 and James 1:19-20 and other passages such as Philemon o as to draw out some powerful principles and life lessons to educate and improve ourselves in this unpleasant and unavoidable area of human life:

> If your brother sins against you, go and show him his fault, just between the two of you. If he listens to you, you have won your brother over. But if he will not listen, take one or two others along, so that every matter may be established by the testimony of two or three witnesses. If he refuses to listen to them, tell it to the church; and if he refuses to listen even to the church, treat him as you would a pagan or a tax collector.

> My dear brothers, take note of this: Everyone should be quick to listen, slow to speak, and slow to become angry, for man's anger does not bring about the righteous life that God desires.

It is not humanly desirable to cause conflicts, neither is it natural for us to embrace confrontation. Conflicts are very unpleasant and confrontations are not enjoyable, unless you are a morbid trouble maker. In fact, you do not have to look for troubles as troubles will be coming your way looking for you sooner or later in life. So do not trouble troubles until and unless troubles trouble you. Don't fear, deny or hide the conflicts; neither try to avoid them or run from them. If you do, you will be controlled by them! When they do come to us, we must be confident and courageous in resolving them by caringly and lovingly confronting them! Since conflicts among peoples are surely inevitable, we must proceed with careful preparation and prayerful consideration before taking any action. One must always bear in mind that the ideal goal of confrontation is never the destruction of relation, but the restoration of fractured and broken relationships so the body can once again healthily function. Conflict resolution is one word: confrontation. If you are really desire to resolve an existing conflict, you must confront. But how does one confront caringly – carefrontation? Here are some most essential guidelines:

1. Take the initiative to make the contacts;

2. Privacy and confidentiality should be initially maintained;

3. Begin with affirmation of that person;

4. Admit that you do have a problem or struggle, and need understanding and clarification;

5. Let the other person(s) involved respond with focus only on the problem.

6. Establish forgiveness and repentance if needed.

7. Compromise on opinions and preferences, and insistence on principles;

8. Witnesses with sound Christian character and reputation are often needed in the process;

9. Seek help from experienced mentors and study the root cause(s) of the conflicts;

10. Deal with the underlying issues and not the superficial symptoms or manifestations;

11. Handle the conflicts immediately, actively and decisively, as soon as possible, for the longer the passive delay, the worse the situation gets;

12. Always speak the truth in love, not in hatred or revenge;

13. Focus on the problem(s) with principles, and not the person(s) associated with the conflicts;

14. Making the matter public and disassociation with the person should be the last resort.

15. Don't hurry, don't fear, and don't worry for worry is the most

unproductive of all human activities on earth! It solves no problems and yet it causes all kinds of problems!

16. Be slow to speak yourself, be quick to listen to the other, and then you will naturally and supernaturally be slow to be angry;

17. Be patient, be wise, be timely, be gentle, be humble, and most importantly, let everything you do be done in love (I Cor 16:14), for love, true love, never ever fails (I Cor 13:8).

"Any Way"—A Poem of Perspective and Power
Mother Teresa of Calcutta

People are often unreasonable, illogical and self-centered;
Forgive them anyway.
If you are kind, people may accuse you of self, ulterior motives;
Be kind anyway.
If you are successful, you will win some false friends and true enemies;
Succeed anyway.
If you are honest and frank, people may cheat you;
Be honest and frank anyway.
What you spend years building, someone will destroy overnight;
Build anyway.
If you find serenity and happiness, they may be jealous;
Be happy anyway.
The good you do today, people will often forget tomorrow;
Do good anyway.
Give the world the best you have, and it may never be enough;
Give the world the best you've got anyway.
You see, in the final analysis, it is between you and God.
It was never between you and them anyway.

Chapter 17
Faith, Family and Friends
and Other Fabulous Factors

Faith: Upward relationship with God

Mark 9:23: Jesus said to him, "If you can believe, all things are possible to him who believes."

Hebrews 11:1, 3, 6: Now faith is the substance of things hoped for, the evidence of things not seen . . . .By faith we understand that the worlds were framed by the Word of God, so that the things which are seen were not made of things which are visible . . . .But without faith it is impossible to please Him, for he who comes to God must believe that He is, and that He is a rewarder of those who diligently seek Him.

Faith is a gift of God, and as a gift, faith can also be cultivated and strengthened. Developing faith in God is a life-long learning process, even and especially in trusting God as our Protector and Provider for all our needs. Throughout the Bible and in my short time of 30 years of knowing, living for and serving Christ by faith, I have found the Lord to be gracious and good, pure and holy, tested and true, well worthy of our total and complete trust. We serve a faithful God who has and will continue to perfectly perform that which He personally promised in His Word! All humans to some extent are liars, be it white lie, black lie or yellow lie, for all kinds of reasons under all sorts of incredibly pressured circumstances, but God is not a man that He should lie. He is always true to His Word. Because He is true, and He is the Truth, He therefore is trustworthy at all times.

Once we have learned the lesson of trusting Christ deeply through biblical teachings, commands, testimonies of others, and most importantly, through our personal experiences with the Lord, immediately our life will be transformed to be full of His joy and peace. In trusting the Lord more deeply, we will have joy unspeakable and full of His glory; In trusting the Lord more deeply, we will have peace, perfect peace, the peace with God and peace from God, the peace of the Prince (Isa 9:6) which surpasses and transcends all human knowledge and understanding. Not only so, when we learn to trust in the Lord with all our hearts (Prov 3:5-6) and no longer lean and depend on our meager human ingenuities or cleverness, we will be fortified with strength, everlasting strength, and He will direct our ways and straighten out our paths! Praise the Lord for these wonderful, powerful and beautiful promises that I have personally and daily experienced all these years. But the best is yet to come for those who will not lose heart, but will keep on keeping on, trusting Christ for everything more and more deeply!

The Bible admonishes us to cultivate an intimate and personal relationship with our Lord Jesus on a daily basis. This is absolutely essential for a victorious life when we have deep spiritual roots. The great Apostle Paul earnestly prays for us to develop deep roots in Christ so that we can be well "rooted and grounded" in the faith and love of Jesus to bear much more lasting fruit to the glory and praise of God (Eph 3:17). The truth of the matter here is this simple: the root determines the fruit! No root, no fruit; bad root, bad fruit; good root, juicy, healthy, delicious and nutritious fruit! No root, no wing! The deeper the roots, the stronger the trees. And that root for us is none other the faith and trust in Jesus and His Word! When we heed His Word and root ourselves in faith with depth, we prosper victoriously and abundantly in life for His purpose. But if not, we will be like the man Jesus referred to in the parable of the sower. "But since he has no root, he last only a short time. When trouble or persecution comes because of the Word, he quickly falls away." (Matt 13:21). What a realistic and accurate commentary by Jesus the Lord on our contemporary western-style artificial and superficial Christianity with so much emotionality and complacency, and so little enthusiasm and commitment! May the Lord help us to reverse the curse through our sincere repentance which leads to genuine revival!

Family: Inward relationship with each other

I Timothy 3:4-5: He must manage his own family well and see that his children obey him with proper respect. If anyone does not know how to manage his own family, how can he take care of God's church?

I Timothy 5:4, 8: These should learn first of all to put their religion into practice by caring for their own family and so repaying their parents and their grandparents, for this is pleasing to God... If anyone does not provide for his own relatives, and especially for his immediate family, he has denied the faith and is worse than an unbeliever.

Faith in the Lord is the most important factor—this Faith Factor overcomes the fear factor. Second only to our faith in God, is one's inescapable obligation to provide and protect the family. Provision and protection, the double aspects of true love for the family, include material supplies such as foods, drinks, housing, clothing and transportation needs, and physical safety from harms and injuries.

Protection and provision go also beyond the material and the physical. As caring responsible parents, we must watch over the children's spiritual, emotional, mental and relational needs and protect them from unwholesome contexts and companions, for bad company corrupts good character. In order to do so, we must model after Christ and model for them in godliness by living a life of love and light right in front of them so that they can see and believe in our claims and words. The best way to train up a child in the way he should go, as President Abraham Lincoln said it right, is that we go that way ourselves in front of them in the fear and favor of the Lord! Parents should set a fine example for the family in matters of faith, love, hope, finance, relationships, words, deeds, disciplines, diligence and intelligence by spending time with each other as much as possible.

Friends: Outward relationship with others

Proverbs 18:24: A man who has friends must himself be friendly, but there is a friend who sticks closer than a brother.

Proverbs 27:10: Do not forsake your friend and the friend of your father, and do not go to your brother's house when disaster strikes you — better a neighbor nearby than a brother far away.

John 15:14: You are my friends if you do what I command — Jesus.

The immediate extension and expansion of our own biological family is the family of faith, the household of God, the body of Christ! The Bible gives us a deep theology of "each otherness," and "togetherness". We, as brothers and sisters in the Lord, are to commit ourselves to loving each other unconditionally (it does not matter whether you really "like" each other or not by the way) as Jesus the Lord loves us. I Corinthians 16:14 commands that "Let everything you do be done in love," for sincere and genuine love is of God and it therefore pleases God when we love one another, not just in words but also in deeds, bearing and sharing each other's burdens, thus fulfilling the law of the Lord who is love itself. "Therefore, as we have opportunity, let us do good to all, especially to those who are of the household of faith." (Gal 6:10).

Not only are we to do good to bless the family of faith, we are commanded to obey Christ to do good to all people, even do good to them who despitefully use us or hatefully persecute us for the faith. We are to be kind and helpful in endeavoring to be a blessing to the people around us and even far away from us where needs exist. The Christian faith is a tri-dimensional relation (God upward, Self inward, and Others outward) with good deeds and constant actions, and actions speak loud than all the words. As we live out our faith in Christ with love and kindness and generosity, we thus are powerfully testifying and sharing the Gospel of God's grace with others without having to get too preachy or wordy to them. By all means, preach the Word, and only if necessary, use words! The best way to share the Word of God is show the love of God through our authentically transformed lives, and shine the light of the Lord as He is the light of the world (Jh 8:12) who has also made us as His light (Matt 5:14-16) for people to see Him through His children's deeds. As we are friends of the Lord and as we obey His commandments to love others as ourselves, more and more friends will be made and will be led to the fellowship of faith in Jesus Christ, thus advancing the Kingdom of God in the whole world with both our precise faith precepts and our effective faith examples.

Fervor/Fire

Romans 12:11-12: Never be lacking in zeal, but keep your spiritual fervor serving the Lord. Be joyful in hope, patient in affliction, and faithful in prayer.

When one is seriously sold out to Jesus with an intimate love relationship with the Lord, his or her life will surely be on fire for the cause of Christ, for the outward manifestation of an inward transformation is zeal, enthusiasm, excitement, fire and fervor for the Word of faith and the work of ministries! The more we are faithful to God the consuming fire, the more the Lord makes us fervent and hot unto Him and his missions. One thing that makes the Lord Jesus sick is a church that has lost its first love for Him and thus has become neither hot nor cold. They are lukewarm. The key solution to this situation is "Back to the Basics," return back to our first love for Him, not theologies, things, theories, and other cheap thrills. Let us get down on our knees; Get back to the Word, and seek the infilling of the Holy Spirit of fire to inflame our soul with the passion from Christ. I daily pray to the Lord in earnest with all my heart: O Lord, let the fire fall; let the fire burn and let the fire spread. O God, let your fire fall upon me; let your fire burn inside of me; and let you fire spread through me! Amen!

Force

Matthew 11:12: From the days of John the Baptist until now, the kingdom of God has been forcefully advancing, and forceful men lay hold of it.

If we are truly on fire for the Lord and for His Great Commission, God Himself will empower us with His divine force to get up, get out, get along, get ahead, and get the job done well! The kingdom of God does not come by mere observations or empty talks; it comes by force, the force of God which is greater than the force of darkness and evil. When one is faithful, God will make her or him forceful, as Acts 1:8 promises along with the baptism of the Holy Spirit. "You will receive power!" That is a promise for all of us who are willing and obedient to the counsel and commands of the Lord! God will fill us with the Holy Spirit of truth and wisdom, and with the spiritual and human and material resources to finish the assigned task when we are hooked with the Source: Jesus the supplier and supplies, the author and finisher of our faith. He never fails to carry out His promises, and His promises, like Himself, are powerful and are the same yesterday, today and forever!

Favors

Luke 2:52: And Jesus increased in wisdom and stature, and in favor with God and men.

Just as the Lord Jesus, being 100% human, increased in favor, we too will grow in favors with God who will cause people to be favorable towards us. As a matter of fact, everything we have is a favor and blessing from the Lord directly or indirectly. He crowns us with the favors of His love, compassion, forgiveness and abundant provision so that we can be blessed to be a blessing to those around us. He has given me innumerable favors in the past years serving Him wholeheartedly, and these include faith, family and thousands of friends as relational favors as well as generous spiritual and financial favors. I am forever profoundly grateful when I meditate and count on the bountiful blessings of Jesus. It makes me more eager and passionate to serve Him more as a result of the genuine gratitude in my attitude. Thank you Lord Jesus! Praise your Lord Jesus for who You are in my life and for what You have done for me and my family! Hallelujah, Amen!

Freedom

II Corinthians 3:17: Now the Lord is the Spirit, and where the Spirit of the Lord is, there is freedom.

When you operate in the faith of God, you move in freedom,

freedom to choose the right thing to do for the glory of the Lord! There are many kinds of freedoms in the world. For me, the greatest freedom is spiritual and personal when I finally got to know the truth in Christ late October 1983 in Kaifeng, China, and gave my heart and life to Jesus. Because of the truth I encountered in Him, I was set free, liberated once and for all from the degradation of Darwinism, the bondage of atheism and the oppression of communism, without God and without hope, with suicidal and homicidal tendencies. Then the truth set me free, free from sins, from the animalistic instincts and impulses, as I began to live according to the teachings of the Word of God! As I deepened in faith in the Lord and frequently fellowshipped with mentors and coworkers, I started to enjoy the freedom of the Spirit away from the pressures of the world. I learned to use the God-given freedom to wisely choose and make friends and enjoy the relational freedom, free to serve and bless many others as I have been so blessed in so doing. I am just simply too blessed of the Word to ever be depressed by the world! The gift of spiritual freedom along with my peace and joy, the devil will never be able to take it away from me because the devil did not give it to me. All these are blessings of the Lord Jesus who loves and gives!

Finance

III John 2: Beloved, I pray that you will prosper in all things and be in health, just as your soul prospers.

Godly living is living holy, and Godly living is living debt free. A life free from debt is a blessed life devoid of all kinds of subsequent stresses and worries. If you live according to the wisdom of the Word of God, you will enjoy many material blessings as your heart and soul continue to be blessed by favors of the Lord! Financial freedom, free from the worries of lacks and losses, is a blessing from the Prince of Peace. The powerful Word of the Lord in Deuteronomy (8:18, 28:1-2, 13) infallibly promises us that if we are diligent in obeying the voice of the Lord and careful in following all the commandments of the Lord, God will then cause all kinds of blessings to come upon us. As a result of them, we will be made the head and not the tail; we shall be above and not beneath; and we shall lend many and shall not to borrow from anyone. In this substantial and tangible way, we shall remember the Lord our God who gives us the power to get wealth, that He may establish His covenant with us. Of all the blessings referred here, certainly included are the blessings of financial freedom from debts, and material prosperity to enjoy ourselves and invest in others for kingdom purposes, even as our soul prospers first in the Lord (III Jh 2)!

Fruit

John 15:8, 16: This is to my Father's glory that you bear much fruit, showing yourself to be my disciples... You did not choose me, but I chose you to go and bear much fruit—fruit that will last.

Galatians 5:22-23: But the fruit of the Spirit is love, joy, peace, longsuffering, kindness, goodness, faithfulness, gentleness and self-control.

Nowadays, spiritual gifts are plenteous and even rampant at times, but authentic spiritual fruit is rare indeed, even in the household of faith, let alone in the secularized, sensualized, sexualized and satanized world we live it. The Lord Jesus commands us to go and bear much lasting fruit for two main reasons: to glorify God and to show others that we are indeed the disciples of the Lord Jesus. He has chosen us not only to be faithful even to the point of death, but also to be fruitful for His glory for all to see. Without a question, in order to be fruitful for the Lord, we must first be faithful to the Lord in things big and small. On the other hand, if we are truly faithful to the Lord, we will be fruitful as good trees that can not bear bad fruits. When we evaluate others, the Lord teaches us pointedly that we are to recognize and know them by the fruits they bear, and not by the words they utter (Matt 7:20). Indeed one must have the gifts of the Spirit in order to minister forcefully and effectively, but these gifts, no matter how spiritual or powerful, are not the end in and of themselves. They are only the means to the end. The central purpose of the spiritual gifts in Romans 12, I Corinthians 12 and Ephesians 4 is to use them to bear much lasting and abundant spiritual fruit for the glory of the Lord so the Christ Jesus can be exalted and uplifted to draw all people unto Him.

Chapter 18
Working Hard and Working Smart:
On Diligence and Intelligence

Blessed on the balanced, for they shall outlast everyone else.

Blessed is he who does what he loves to do while simultaneously making a good living and enjoying the abundant life. This is called the labor of love. We usually will do a great job if we love our job.

As life must have purpose, life also must have balance. As life must have a focus, life must also have a balance. As a matter of fact, life is a delicate balance, a balance between being and doing, a balance between living in the world and being a citizen of heaven, a balance of intelligence of the head and the diligence of the hand, a balance between working smart and working hard, and a balance among the inspiration, aspiration and lots of perspiration. This balancing act is both wonderful and indispensable in reaching goals and living in victory. A balanced life is a stable life and a stable life is a strong life. A life devoid of balance is a life out of order and control. This kind of life is one which will be short lived with an ending in disappointments, discouragements and disgrace, if not in despair, disaster and devastation.

John 9:4: I must work the works of Him who sent me while it is day; the night is coming when no one can work.

I Corinthians 4:12-13: We work hard with our own hands. When we are cursed, we blessed; when we are persecuted, we endure it; when we are slandered, we answer kindly.

I Corinthians 15:10: I worked harder than all of them.

I Thessalonians 5:12-13: Now we ask you, brothers, to respect those who work hard among you, who are over you in the Lord and who admonish you. Hold them in the highest regard in love because of their work.

II Thessalonians 3:8-10: We worked night and day, laboring and toiling so that we would not be a burden to any of you. We did this, not because we do not have the right to such help, but in order to make ourselves a model for you to follow. For even when we were with you, we gave you this rule: "If a man will not work, he shall not eat."

Isaiah 1:18: "Come now, let us reason together," says the Lord.

Daniel 12:3: Those who are wise will shine like the brightness of the heavens.

Matthew 25:1-2: At that time the kingdom of heaven will be like ten virgins who took their lamps and went out to meet the bridegroom. Five of them were foolish and five were wise.

I Peter 3:15: But in your hearts set apart Christ as Lord. Always be prepared to give an answer to everyone who asks you to give the reason for the hope you have. But do this with gentleness and respect.

The Lord Jesus sets us an excellent example from the beginning of his life. Jesus grew in wisdom (Lk 2:52). This clearly refers to His intellectual development with deep cultural insights and great divine wisdom, the ability to think theologically and reason logically. In addition to being spiritual and smart, the Lord Jesus also worked very hard. He declares to us with urgency and challenge to us all that He came to work the works of Him the Father who sent Him while it is still day, for when night comes (and it is coming quickly as we are the church of the eleventh hour according to Matt 20:6), no one can work! It will be too late to do anything. Let us not be foolish virgins in Matt 25, but let us be wise as the days are indeed increasingly evil.

Work Hard: God Detests Idleness & Loves Diligence
(Matthew 20:1-8)

Proverbs 21:5: The plans of the diligent lead to profit, as surely as haste leads to poverty.

Matthew 20:3, 6: He went out about the third hour and saw others standing idle in the market place . . . And about the eleventh hours he went out and found others standing idle and said to them, "Why have you been standing here idle all day?"

Hebrews 6:11: We want each of you to show the same diligence to the very end in order to make your hope sure.

I Timothy 4:15: Be diligent in these matters; give yourself wholly to them, so that everyone may see your progress.

Everything in the world is purchased by labor. (David Hume, *www. wisdomquotes.com*).

Life grants nothing to us mortals without hard work (Horace, *www. quotationspage.com*)

Work while you have the light. You are responsible for the talent that has been entrusted to you. (Henri-Frederic Amiel, *www.quotationspage. com*)

Work is an extension of personality and achievement. It is one way to measure the human worth and humanity. (Peter Drucker, *www. wisdomequotes.com*)

There are no secrets to success. It is the result of preparation, hard work, and learning from failures. (Colin Powell, *www.wisdomquotes. com*)

Your work is part of your life. The only way to be truly satisfied is to do what you believe is great. The only way to do great work is to love what you do. (Steve Jobs, *www.wisdomquotes.com*)

Pleasure in the job puts perfection in the work. All paid jobs absorb and degrade the brain. (Aristotle, *www.quotaionspage.com*)

Real success is finding your lifework in the work you love. (David McCullough, *www. quotationspage.com*)

When it comes to getting the job done, we need fewer architect and more bricklayers (Colleen Barrett, *www.lifequotes.com*) —more perspiration than inspiration or aspiration. We need more walkers than talkers, more practitioners than preachers.

The things that will destroy us are: politics without principle; pleasure without conscience; wealth without work; knowledge without character, business without morality; science without humanity, and worship without sacrifice. (Mahatma Gandhi, *www.wisdomquotes.com*)

The parable of the workers in the vineyard in Matthew 20:1-16 teaches us 10 profound life principles and provides us with such wonderful and applicable life lessons:

1. Develop the proper perspective of the kingdom and the priority of the King Jesus as it is all about Him and His business (v.1).

2. God is the owner of all things and we must be wise and responsible stewards (v.1).

3. In order to work well together, we must at the outset agree with each other (vv.2, 13).

4. God always does what is right regardless whether we like it or not (vv.4, 7, 13).

5. The Lord detests idleness, comparison and complaints (vv.3, 6, 11).

6. We are to work out our salvation with fear and trembling, not assuming and supposing that we deserve this, that and the other (v.10). Thank God for he didn't give me what I deserve.

7. We must work urgently and diligently as we are the church of the 11th hour, with the 3rd hour in Acts 2 for the Jews, 6th hour in John 4 for

the Samaritans, 9th hour in Acts 10 for the Romans and Italians further away (vv.3, 5-6).

8. We will receive our right reward if we are faithful to the end (vv.7-8).

9. The kingdom of God is not about fairness, but about God's mercies and grace (v.13).

10. Matthew 20:16 is the key principle of the Kingdom of God!

Work Smart: God Detests Foolishness & Loves Intelligence (Matthew 25:1-13)

Jesus the Lord once exclaimed in Matt 9:37 that indeed the harvest is plentiful, but the workers are few. To be totally honest, these days readers are plentiful, but thinkers are few, and far in between. The Bible repeatedly urges us to serve and the Lord the Lord our God with all our mind and intellect as it is a gift from God. Let my people think! We must use our head, our brain to reason before making any serious decision, not just depending on how we "feel" or "feel led". The mind is a terrible thing to waste. One well-known evangelical scholar once sadly commented to me that as much as he admired the Pentecostals for their peak emotion and hot passion, he felt that most Pentecostals would rather die than think! What an indictment this is! Unfortunately, it is not too far from the fact and the reality either!

Intellectual growth should commence at birth and cease only at death. (Einstein, *www.lifequotes.com*)

A man of great spirit honestly and courageously uses his intellect and fulfills the duty to express the results of his thoughts in clear form. (Einstein, *www.quotationspage.com*)

The ability to focus attention on important things is a defining characteristic of intelligence. (Robert Shiller, *www.quotationspage.com*).

To repeat what others have said requires education; to challenge it requires brain (Mary Pettibone Poole, *www.quotationspage.com*)

The more intelligent one becomes the more original and creative he or she will be.

Chapter 19
Thoughts on Gates and Doors

Matthew 7:13-14: Enter through the narrow gates. For wide is the gate and broad is the road that leads to destruction, and many enter through it. But small is the gate and narrow the road that leads to life and only a few find it.

Matthew 7:7: Ask and it will be given to you; seek and you will find; and knock the door will be opened to you.

John 10:1-4: I tell you the truth, the man who does not enter the sheep pen by the gate, but climbs in by some other way, is a thief and a robber. The man who enters by the gate is the shepherd of the sheep. The watchman opens the gate for him, and the sheep listen to his voice. He calls his own sheep by name, and leads them out. When he has brought out his own, he goes on ahead of them, and his sheep follow him because they know his voice.

Acts 14:27: On arriving there, they gathered the church together and reported all that God had done through them, and how He had opened the door of faith to the Gentiles.

II Cor 2:12: The Lord had opened a door for me . . . to preach the Gospel of Christ . . . in Troas.

Revelation: 3:8: I have placed before you an open door that no one can shut.

Revelation 3:19-20: Those whom I love, I rebuke and discipline. So be earnest and repent. Here I am! I stand at the door and knock. If anyone hears my voice and opens the door, I will come in and eat with him. And he with Me.

Gate and door in the Holy Scriptures symbolize authority and legitimacy. From the verses above quoted, it is not difficult to discern the importance and the necessity of gates and doors in life and ministry. For without them, we will fail to have the divine legitimacy and authority as children of God. Without them, we would be considered illegitimate thieves and robbers whose leader is the one who comes to steal, kill and destroy (John 10:1, 10). But with the door and gate opened up to us by God's watchman on the wall, we are correctly identified and legitimately authorized as the children of God Himself and ministers of the Gospel of God's grace! Along with this legitimate authority, come the power and the energy to go out and do the will of God and finish His work with urgency and excellence, just as Jesus the Lord did (John 4:34-35). We will not become shiftless, lazy, aimless, confused or cowardly, we will be purposeful and passionate, confident and courageous to get the job done for His glory and honor and praise!

"Gate and door" in the Word of God also represent newly open access and unprecedented opportunities that may not have been available to us before. Based on my personal life experience and those of many countless others I know, at the end of our lives of poverty and brokenness and vanities, I know the Lord Jesus opens doors for us as He is the Door and the Gate. Jesus is still lovingly urging us to come and follow me... for "I am the way, the truth and the life, and no one comes to the Father except through Me." (Jh 14:6). Indeed this statement is very exclusive that none of us comes to the Father except through this one and only door—Jesus Christ the Lord! Once that person seizes the day without any delay, and enters the door without any hesitation, he or she will find many wonderful opportunities to live the victory with abundance. She or he will have an endless access and limitless power prepared and available for him or her in the promises of the Word of God. That disciple of Jesus will be enabled and empowered and equipped by the Spirit of God to live and serve the Lord triumphantly!

Finally, "gate and door" in the Bible promise victory and prosperity to those who will walk in by faith for His glory. When we walk by faith in God our source and our strength, and not by sight of ever-changing circumstances or shaky human environments, we will never grow weary and we will not lose heart (Hebrews 12:2-3). Instead, we will walk according to the unfailing and unshakable and unstoppable promises of the Lord, in victories and prosperities in all areas of life and ministry, be it health and healing, signs and wonders, finance and freedom, favors with God and with people, even and especially as our soul prospers in the Lord (III John 2). Let us be daily reminded to listen and follow the very utterance of God to one of His most faithful and fruitful servants Joshua (1: 8) and choose to serve the Lord with gladness and fervor, "Do not let this Book of the Law depart from your mouth; meditate on it day and night, so that you may be careful to do everything written in it. **Then** you will be prosperous and successful."

One of the most interesting, intriguing and amazing verse of the Bible in my thoughts on doors and gates is found in one particular and profound verse of both purpose and passion and power, which deserves our careful and prayerful spiritual scrutiny. It is I Corinthians 16:9. Let us read it both in the NIV and in the NKJV. "Because a great door for effective work has opened to me, **and** there are many who oppose me."

"For a great and effective door has opened to me, **and** there are many adversaries."

What a life lesson revealed through this simple yet deep verse above cited: There are no opportunities without oppositions! There are no victories without adversaries! There is no prize without paying the price! Ultimately it is the principle of the cross and the crown at work: if we are not willing to bear the cross, the cross of pains, indignity and agony, we will not be able to wear the crown, the crown of gains, glory and victory. No trials, no triumphs. No sacrifices, no successes. That is exactly the life lesson that the apostle Paul, as did his own Lord and Master Jesus Christ, is trying to teach us.

Just as the roses are so beautiful to see and fragrant to smell, but has a lot of thorns behind it, so life is full of opportunities, but it is also full of oppositions. As a matter of fact, we should not shun away from oppositions because in them are tremendous opportunities for us to cultivate patience, responsibility, growth, wisdom and maturity. Don't you be easily disappointed when you have to face opposition of the enemy, for human disappointment often is a divine appointment if one will choose never to give up! One should not easily call it a quit to life's adversity either because your worst and most difficult adversity could prove to be your best and most valuable university! I recently read a forwarded message on the word "adversity" as an acronym by Dr. Charles Stanley, which is quite revealing and truthful along the same train of thoughts. It really hits the nail on the head, so to speak. According to Pastor Stanley, "ADVERSITY" literally can mean:

A— Accept the events of your life as necessary and indispensable parts of how God is equipping you in life;

D— Decide and determine to follow the Jesus ways of reacting and responding to the trials and tribulations;

V— Veer neither to the right nor to the left from the path of obedience;

E — Expect fully the Holy Spirit to help you grow and mature through your difficult adversities;

R— Remember always how the Lord has helped you in the past;

S— Set your face like a flint (Isa 50:7) to endure hardship like a soldier of the cross, without wavering or complaints;

I— Invest additional time in your relationship with the Lord;

T— Trust the Lord with all your heart, especially when you do not understand;

Y—Yield to the Lord and yearn to be made ready for the return of our Savior!

The great door that Paul referred to represents open accesses for effective ministries, as is also mentioned by the Apostle John in Rev 3:8 above quoted. From the single verse of I Corinthians 16:9 about this "great door," we can draw at least four major spiritual and vital life lessons in dealing with and winning over our own hardships and difficulties:

1. This great door is forwarded to us as A Divine Opportunity. Time and timings are indeed everything! We must learn to seize the day decisively, for opportunity of a life time can be grasped only during the life time of that opportunity! Time and tide wait for no man, as the proverb goes. We are absolutely living at the end times, the last days, and we are the church of the eleventh hour (Matt 20:1-8). Just like our Lord the owner of the vineyard, we must work while it is day for when night comes, no one will be able to work!

2. This great door is framed as A Devilish Opposition. As has been stressed before, there are no opportunities without some sorts of oppositions. As a matter of fact, where there are more opportunities, there is also more opposition. This is as in the natural as it is in the supernatural. Sometimes those that oppose us are more than we can humanly bear. That's way when we must get down on our knees and go to the Lord with humility, prayer and trust. He will make a way where there seems to be no way. The devil is evil without a doubt and we are not ignorant or negligent of his schemes of lies, and deceits, confusion and intimidation. Even though he is not the Almighty, yet he is actually pretty powerful. But greater is He, and much more powerful is He who lives in us and gives us the opportunities than he who tries to stir up opposition against us! But if God is for us, who can stand against us!

A good illustration to demonstrate this principle at work is the profound passage of II Cor 12:1-10 where Paul received special and unspeakable revelation from the third heaven. But Satan our adversary the devil is not pleased. He tried to do everything within his power to destroy the apostle and thus wipe out the divine revelations he had supernaturally received. But Jesus is more powerful and faithful to perform that which He promised to Paul. As a result, what the devil and the opponents of Paul meant for evil, God purposed it for good (Gen 50:20) so that Paul was kept from ever becoming conceited or arrogant due to the surpassingly great revelations, and Paul learned to live by and depend on the grace of God which is sufficient for all circumstances and superior to all others, be it people, things, events or situations. As long as we stay pure and humble, and as long as we remain faithful and obedient to God and His command, no devil or demons or human opponents will ever be able to defeat us! We are triumphant and always victorious in Jesus because of what Ha has already done for us on the cross of Calvary!

3. This great door is to be faced with A Dedicated Obedience. In order to be victorious, we must be courageous to face and engage the enemy with the full armor of God in us (Eph 6). We will defeat the devil and destroy the demonic influences, not by our own clever ingenuities or strength, but by the blood of the Lamb and by the words of our own testimonies, not being afraid of dying for Jesus the Lamb ourselves. We will never be defeated by the devil if we are devoted and dedicated to God! Moreover, we will always have His divine guidance and supernatural abundance when we follow and serve the Lord gladly with our total obedience! That is a promise and a guarantee that will never fall or fail!

4. This great door is favored to The Devoted Overcomer. I loved and still love the famed Negro spiritual of the American civil rights era, which I learned from a senior student to sing passionately as my first song in English to encourage myself. That was even before I ever heard of the Bible or the name of the Lord Jesus while studying as a sophomore English major in Kaifeng, Henan Province, P. R. China 1982. How time has flown! "We shall overcome; we shall overcome! O deep in my heart, I do believe, we shall overcome some day!" Our gracious and great, precious and powerful Master, Mentor and Model Lord Jesus Christ prophetically informs us in John 16:33, "In this world, you will have trouble. But take heart! I have overcome the world." He who has overcome the world and the devil will help us overcome. And that He did help with the early church in Rev. 12:11, that they overcame the devil by the blood of the Lamb of God and by the words of their own testimonies, not even being afraid themselves to give us their lives and die a martyr's death for Jesus the Martyr who dies for us all. The Lord will help us in like manner if we follow Him faithfully all the way to the end, no comprise and no cowardice, but with all confidence and courage from Him and for His cause.

In like manner, we who are born again, have faith in this Jesus and faithfully follow Him shall certainly and absolutely be victorious also like Him for He has given us the divine authority to overcome the self, the sin and Satan of this world. "For everyone born of God overcomes the world. This is the victory that has overcome the world, even our faith." (I John 5:4). Without faith it is impossible to please God. Greater is He who has given us faith and who lives in us than he who lives in and is of the world. Let us serve the Lord with both diligence and intelligence and endure to the very end. Then we shall not only be saved; we shall have the victor's crown for all to see! You and I can do all things through Christ who strengthens us (Phil 4:13); and we are indeed more than conquerors through Christ who loves us with an ever-lasting love, and nothing, and nobody can ever separate us from this love of God which is in Christ Jesus our precious and powerful Lord (Rom 8:37-39)! What an unfailing promise of God to us all, His devoted overcomers!

Chapter 20
A Chinese Missions Summary
for the Lord's Glory

Greetings to each and every one of you with our profound gratitude to God and to you for your devoted partnership with us in China missions over the past 12 years (May 27, 1998—Jan 10, 2010) in the most precious and peerlessly powerful name of our Lord and Master Jesus Christ! I thank my God every time I remember you and pray with exceedingly great joy to our Lord for His richest blessings to be bestowed upon you that you will be filled with the knowledge of His Word, His Will, His Wisdom, His Way on your walk to faithfully and fruitfully finish His work, being confident of this, that He who began the good work in you and me WILL carry it onto completion until the day of Christ Jesus our Lord to the glory and praise of God (Phil 1:3-10)!!!

I believe that by now (Jan 15, 2010), most of you have heard of the terrible ordeal of persecution I have encountered and endured in my beloved homeland China and the wonderful honor I have undeservedly received from the Lord as a prisoner of the Gospel. They arrested me in the midst of teaching the Word at 6 am on Nov 14th 2009 when we were suddenly besieged and raided by the police on one of our dynamic house church leadership meetings. Only after many hours of endless interrogation and intimidation all day long, they officially let go of me with surveillance for the next 12 days. Then again they arrested me because of faith in and missions for Jesus, and forcefully expelled me from Beijing only after the cold-cell detention, harsh interrogation, and dreadful intimidation for a whole night and day on Jan 9-10, 2010. Even though they declared expulsion to me with the official notice of "Not welcome to return to China" for the next 5 years, yet I thank God for this special privilege to be counted worthy and chosen of the Lord to suffer the CROSS of CHRIST for His righteousness and for His name's sake. Just as I Peter 4:14 declares and promises us, that if we are insulted for His name, we are indeed blessed because the Spirit of glory and of God rests on us!!!

The devil indeed is a dumb devil, and whatever evil he intends to harm me with, God intends it for good to accomplish His supreme purpose, namely, the salvation of many more Chinese souls (Gen 50:20). For I am NOT ASHAMED of His Gospel because it is the power of God unto salvation (Rom 1:16)! And here is my motto for all these past twelve (12) years in China missions (knowing in my spirit that this would happen to me sooner or later) and will always be for me future in Him, that "For me, to live is Christ and to die is gain!" (Phil 1:21) which will be engraved on my tombstone some day as a testimony: our story, His glory, always!

The number "TWELVE (12)" seems to have special spiritual significance and ministerial ramification in the Word of God. Joshua picked up 12 stones to commemorate the faithfulness of God to Israel. There were 12 gates and 12 foundations in the original wall of Jerusalem. There were 12 tribes of Israel; Jesus was 12 when he totally amazed the teachers of law in God's temple with His understanding and answers (Lk 2: 41-47) ; then Jesus "reached" 12 disciples to "teach them and dispatch them" for the ministries; Mark 5 tells us that the woman who was divinely healed of the issue of blood by Jesus had suffered 12 long years under the care of many doctors; and that Jairus' daughter was raised from the dead by the Lord of Resurrection at the age of 12 (V.42). The number TWELVE (12) obviously denotes healing and health from suffering and affliction. It also signifies a brand-new beginning of life, completion and resurrection!!! It is the divine number for HOPE! Romans 15:4 powerfully proclaims to us the central purpose of the Bible in that all that was written in the past was written to teach us, "so that through the endurance and the encouragement of the Scriptures we might have hope! Christ in you today, is the hope of glory (Col 1:27). My prayer for you and me today and everyday is this: May the God of Hope fill you with all joy and peace as trust in Him so that you will overflow with HOPE by the power of the Holy Spirit (Rom 15:13)!

Over the past 12 years, my wife Dr. Esther Yang and I have been faithful in carrying out the Great Commissions (Matt 28:18-20) with the Great Commandment (Mark 12:30-31) in our hearts. As a result of exercising our faith in His promises and willingness to pay the price to win souls for Jesus, the Lord has seen it fit to favor us with fire, force and much lasting fruit (John 15)! Only by His grace and for His glory, we have been able to help establish and support well over 20 Bible schools which have trained and graduated more than 3,000 ministers, preachers, pastors and even missionaries of the Gospel. These preachers are completely sold out for the cause of Christ and totally on fire from the Spirit serving whole-heartedly all over China and even beyond China's borders (serving in Buddhist countries like Thailand, Muslim nations west of China as part of the Back to Jerusalem Movement, and even with 6 workers serving in the most oppressive secluded evil kingdom of North

Korea with its long official name: The People's Democratic Republic of Korea)!!! These modern-day Chinese apostles operate their lives and ministries according to these core values:

1. The Word of God as the only foundation;
2. Christ the Lord as the only centrality and authority;
3. The Holy Spirit as the only guide;
4. The cross of suffering and sacrifice as the only path to Christ;
5. Agape love as the only motivation for evangelization of the world and edification of the body.

They work with passion and purpose, humility and unity with a team approach to ministries, to spread the Gospel, establish churches and sending out missionaries to the unreached people groups. Team spirit, team approach and team work are foundational fountains for our missions, for we believe that while we are good working on our own, we are better working together. One famous African proverb I like much says it all and says it well about life and ministries, "If you want to travel fast, travel alone; but if you want to travel far, it's better that we travel together!" What a life lesson with such wisdom!

Our strategy after much fervent prayers has been simple but central: reach the lost; teach the saved; and dispatch the called (reach, teach, and dispatch)! In turn, these young gospel foot soldiers, being fully equipped to live and die for the Master, have reached hundreds of thousands themselves, set up countless house churches, and even started their own Bible schools to make more disciples among the younger generation in China. The Gospel seed has been effectively sown in fertile soil all over China. As we traveled far and wide among the beloved and hungry people of China all over the provinces, we have had the privilege and honor everywhere, of leading and baptizing literally thousands in 50-gallon grain jars, rivers, bathtubs and swimming pools for Jesus! We now have dedicated disciples all over China to continue the work of God even though I will not be physically allowed to be with them. Hong Yang might be banned and barred from China for a while, but the Holy Spirit can NEVER be blocked from saving the precious 900 millions more Chinese who are yet to have a Bible and to hear the Gospel! Our work in the Lord is not in vain. To God be all the glory and honor, for He alone is worthy! He alone is good all the time!

The revival in China has been the most explosive and spectacular over the past 30 some years in the midst of horrific persecution such as sudden arrests, brutal torture, detention, forced-labor concentration camp, life imprisonment and even martyrdom. Tens of thousands of Chinese saints have suffered and sacrificed their very lives for the advancement of the Kingdom of God in China and beyond. Yes, the disciples of the Lord in China are the kernel of wheat unafraid and willing and in some cases, even eager, to fall to the ground and die so as to produce many seeds (John 12:24). We as a fellowship have grown tremendously from only a few timid preachers in 1998 to now over 3000 bold and productive full-gospel ministers in 2010. From only a few families, the Full Gospel Church of God has now approximately half a million members and many more affiliates mostly in central, NW and NE provinces of the country!

The church of the Lord Jesus is daily persecuted, but she is alive and well, fully Pentecostal, passionate, productive and powerful!!! Christianity in China has miraculously grown from less than one million in 1949 with the communist takeover to well over one hundred million strong! The rapid growth of the underground house churches in China has become an irresistible trend in the nation, and it will surely become the leading missions force in China and beyond China for the evangelization of the world, especially the Muslim world west of China as the Back To Jerusalem Movement advances by force in the name of Jesus! The precious and powerful promise of the Lord is being realized even as I write this summary and report to you, that "Upon this rock, I will build my church, and the gates of hell shall not prevail against it!" (Matt 16:18).

I have often wondered in my mind and pondered in my heart as to why the persecuted underground churches in China, without much financial or missionary support, and not even enough Bibles and training materials, can grow so fast in such a short period of time under 60-yrs of cruel and severe atheistic communist oppression and suppression. Based on my personal participation and keen observation over the past 12 years living and serving among them, I have found the following list as an inclusive summary of the major reasons for their growth and expansion:

1. They love the Word of God. The ministers and Bible students do nothing else but memorize the Word in their heart (even entire books like John and Romans) and even copy out the Bible by hand! They have no interest in liberal theologians!

2. They are fervent in praying day and night, always weeping loudly before the Lord, even repenting and confessing their "sin of lack of zeal," asking the Lord to forgive them of their "lukewarmness"! If we are not praying, we are merely playing; and if we are playing, we are straying!

I have seen more than once Acts 4:31 being realized among the simple, earthy, and innocent followers of Christ!

3. They are zealous in evangelism, passionately winning the lost at all cost! Many signs and wonders follow them who believe in miracles such as healing, exorcism, and even in some cases, the resurrection from the dead. Many illiterate old ladies I know are now miraculously reading the Bible fluently, and one of them is none other than my step mother!

4. They emphasize the absolute sovereignty and the unique Lordship of Jesus Christ and refuse to compromise their faith in any way, willingly paying the heavy and high price of persecution for their faith and work in the Lord!

5. They live not by sight, but by faith and faith alone. Under the circumstances, they are stripped of all the non-essentials of external religion and they embrace the intimacy of Godly relation! Their close fellowship further enhances relations with God and with each other for accountability and discipleship.

6. They are not a fixed temple with a maintenance mentality of religious bureaucracy, but are quite flexible like tabernacle, dynamic, flexible and effective in following the prompting of the Holy Spirit!

7. They are filled with the fullness of the Holy Spirit of boldness (Acts 4:31, 28:31)and spiritual gifts, full of passion and conviction, and not with apathy and lethargy as we see the western churches in comfortable complacency!

8. The governmental persecution, as they tell me many times, is an approval of God over their ministries and is a sure blessing of the Lord in disguise. Never-ending oppression and opposition from the enemy only helps to unite the Body of Christ as the family of God in sharing and caring for each other with vision and missions! There are no hypocrites or spectators or idle analysts, as everyone is expected to serve and lead!

I do pray and Hope that these spiritual life lessons I have learned from the living martyrs of China can enrich, empower, challenge and inspire all of us, spurring us onto more Godliness and Christlikeness in our character and conducts for Him! May we continue, together in faith, to pray and support the Full Gospel house churches in China. May the gracious and great Lord continue to abundantly bless and mightily use each of us, for to me, nothing, absolutely nothing is more fulfilling or pleasing to God than being blessed and used of God to be a blessing to others, especially the persecuted church of the Lord in China and beyond!

Thank you and God bless you for being such dear and special friends with us. Your faithful and sacrificial generosity to the China harvest, has made, and will continue to make a tremendous difference and a powerful impact on millions of souls yet to be reached and discipled for Jesus! Until He comes, we must go! A true Christian is a giving Christian, a growing Christian, a glowing Christian, and by faith, a going Christian!

"Therefore, Go and Do Likewise"!—Jesus (Luke 10:37). And "Now that you know all these things, you will be blessed if you will Do them"—Jesus (John 13:17). Obedience always brings personal confidence, divine guidance, and great abundance, always! Amen!

THE SIMPLICITY OF THE GOSPEL—MORE LESSONS FROM CHINA

Adapted from an internet article by Pastor Billy Humphrey of IHOP
May 13th, 2012

China is home to the largest revival the world has ever seen. Conservative estimates say that 30,000 people are coming to the Lord Jesus daily. That's approximately 1 million salvations per month. These are not simply crusade evangelism stats of people who filled out a commitment card, there are no crusades or mass evangelism efforts in China. Rather, these are actual conversions of people who are added to the church. Truly the Word of the Lord is running swiftly and being glorified!

As one western leader said to me, "Without one Billy Graham or Benny Hinn, only brothers and sisters in the Lord, the church in China is doubling every 1o years. If God can do this in China, the largest communist country in the world, He can do it anywhere." To that I say, AMEN!

The idea that there are no mass evangelism efforts, yet millions are coming to the Lord every year boggled my Western mind. How are they doing it? I don't know that I got the full picture, but what I did learn was actually very simple and very provoking. The Chinese embrace a few simple truths that make a lot of difference. These ideas probably won't seem revolutionary or new to you, they weren't new to me. The power of them is that the believers actually walk them out. It made me realize that there is much I believe, but I don't actually live. I'm asking God to help me to live out the corresponding actions to my faith.

1) Every person is a full time minister. The Chinese church has

incredible leaders and the people hold each leader in high esteem. However, in China because of the restrictions on public assemblies, a leader of a network of a million believers can only meet with 50 -100 believers at any one time. Because of this, no one assumes that the work of the ministry is to left to the leader only. Each believer fully embraces his or her own calling to minister the gospel, lay hands on the sick, cast out demons and do the works of ministry. When you have 150,000,000 believers fully committed to sharing their faith, praying for the sick and doing the works of the ministry, the expansion of the gospel is viral. Col 1:5-6 explains that the nature of the gospel is to bear fruit wherever it is proclaimed. This is what's happening in China. As the church has embraced her mission to declare the gospel of Jesus, the gospel has born incredible fruit and souls are being saved.

2) A simple gospel is a powerful gospel. The Chinese believe that the longer it takes for a new believer to share their faith the less likely they will be to ever share their faith. They encourage all new believers to immediately begin to share the gospel with others. The results have been incredible. Scores of new believers have been won to Jesus by saints who are brand new in the Lord. For me, I realized that I was dealing with unbelief that the simple gospel was still powerful enough to convict and convert the sinner. I had to repent of my unbelief. Romans 1:16 is still true today, "The gospel IS THE POWER OF GOD UNTO SALVATION…" I think we have complicated it in the West. We have so many tools to use, I wonder if we have based our belief in the effectiveness of the gospel upon the effectiveness of the tools we use to share it. Without huge light shows, sound systems, videos, worship teams, dramas, television shows, radio broadcasts, etc… the simple gospel of Jesus Christ has exploded in China. Perhaps we need a renewed faith in the POWER of a simple Gospel.

3) Sharing your faith is an incredible privilege. Often times ministers have to cajole believers in the West to share their faith; even threaten them with the shame of "blood on their hands" if they don't reach the lost for Jesus. In China, believers don't have to be persuaded to embrace the mission of the gospel. They are so grateful for the love and salvation that Jesus has brought them that they feel privileged to share their faith. They are compelled by the love of Christ that has delivered them from the bondage of communist atheism. It's simple gratitude that compels them and therefore sharing the gospel is an incredible honor. Though sharing their faith could result in their own imprisonment, they don't count their lives as dear to themselves and gladly tell others of the joy, freedom and

forgiveness they've found in Jesus. I was convicted when I realized my own dullness and lack of gratitude for my own salvation.

4) You cannot sacrifice too much for the Gospel of Jesus Christ. Everyday in China or any closed country for that matter, believers face an array of challenges that believers in free countries never experience. Every worship meeting, church gathering, time of study or prayer is a risk to their freedom, and in some cases, their lives. Even so, with joyful hearts, they willingly risk their freedom to love and serve Jesus. They don't feel like it is a sacrifice at all. They have no sense of entitlement. They are happy to give their lives fully to Jesus regardless of the risk or cost. They are a living example of how Jesus called us, His disciples, to live.

Mark 8:35 "For whoever desires to save his life will lose it, but whoever loses His life for My sake and the gospel's will save it."

Somehow I actually missed the phrase "and the gospel's." We kind of get the idea that we are to give our lives for Jesus...but losing our lives for the sake of the gospel? In the West it almost sounds reckless to call people to lose their lives for the sake of the gospel. Yet losing your life for Christ and the Gospel was Jesus' main call to discipleship. It is normative Christianity and is commonplace in China and other closed nations. Somehow we've lost this abandonment in our safe, sanitized version of Christianity. Yet, for the Chinese, the call to give it all is a liberating adventure. They know what Paul meant when He said, "For me to live is Christ and to die is gain."

My heart has been freshly pricked with the vision of sharing the gospel with the lost on a regular basis as a normal part of my life. Not leaving the preaching of the gospel to only what happens when I minister publicly, but sharing one on one with people that the Lord brings across my path. My heart has been renewed in the simple truths that the gospel is the power of God unto salvation and Jesus wants the lost just as much as He wants me. He longs for them with deep affections. I want to offer Him whatever I can to see to it that they come to know Him. I pray that the church in America would once again burn with a passion to share the simple gospel and win for the Lamb the reward of His sufferings.

Upon coming back from ministering with the persecuted but passionate and powerful underground house church leaders of China for five days, the Reverend J. Lee Grady (March, 2001) reported that his normal western world of Christianity was "rocked". "I had encountered New Testament-style faith for the first time... I began wondering if what we call Christianity here bears much resemblance to the real thing."

154

Based on his keen and accurate observation, recollection and reflection, Mr. Grady concludes that the leadership of the house church movements is gripped with a sense of urgency to send missions teams from China to closed Muslim nations; their childlike simplicity of faith and sincere humility in life reveal and expose his own trust in technology, materialism and pride. Their infectious passion to fulfill the Great Commissions forces him to see his self-centeredness.

I've had enough of our abnormal, Americanized brand of Christianity. It is as impotent as it is lethal. After spending time with my brothers and sisters in China, I've realized that some of what I see in the church makes God sick . . . How desperately we need the Holy Spirit—our Refiner... we need a return to simple humility. What they have is genuine. We've settled for a cheap imitation (Grady, p.6).

O Lord, please help us to restore our first love for you by going back to the basics! Help us to repent of our sins of terrible lukewarmness, complete complacency, the spirit of lust and pride and greed, and a heart of apathy, and a body of lethargy! Please wake us up, shake us up for your glory! Humble us and break us, fill us and use us for your purpose, I pray! Amen!

Chapter 21
Growing in Grace:
A Personal Process

It is by grace you have been saved (Eph 2:5).

We are justified freely by His grace (Rom 3:24).

But by the grace of God I am what I am, and His grace to me was not without effect. No, I worked harder than all of them, yet not I, but the grace of God that was with me (I Cor 15:10).

However, I consider my life worthy nothing to me, if only I may finish the race and complete the task of testifying to the gospel of God's grace (Acts 20:24).

My grace is sufficient for you (II Cor 12:9). Grow in the grace of our Lord Jesus (II Pet 3:18).

Let us then approach the throne of grace with confidence, so that we may receive mercy and find grace to help us in our time of need (Heb 4:16).

The grace of the Lord Jesus be with God's people, Amen! (Rev 22:21, the last verse of the Bible).

Acts 1:4-8: And being assembled together with them, He commanded them not to depart from Jerusalem, but to wait for the Promise of the Father, "which," He said, "you have heard from Me; For John truly baptized with water, but you shall be baptized with the Holy Spirit not many days from now." Therefore, when they had come together, they asked Him, saying, "Lord, will you at this time restore the kingdom to Israel?" And He said to them, "It is not for you to know times or seasons which the Father has put in His own authority. But you shall receive power when the Holy Spirit has come upon you; and you shall be witnesses to Me in Jerusalem, and in all Judea and Samaria, and to the end of the earth."

In order to grow healthily and mightily in grace, it is imperative that we as disciples and followers of Jesus go through some necessary processes, for without the necessary process, there will not be the quality product fit and ready for any use. The law of the process insists that discipleship and leadership "develops daily, and not in a day" as was evidenced even in the Lord Jesus in Luke 2:52 and Heb 5:8 (Maxwell, p.1336). This is also a life lesson both in the physical and in the spiritual realms. Let us now look at the eight Pentecostal "P's" which all come from one verse, the Pentecostal verse of Acts 1:8.

1. The Perspective of the Kingdom

In this long passage above cited, one can see that there are two kingdoms implied just as there are two worlds in God's creation: physical kingdom of Israel, and the spiritual King of God which Christ said is not of this world. Both of these kingdoms, as the two worlds, the spiritual world and the physical world, are very real and we feel their impact and effect in all aspects of our lives. Everyone sooner or later has to come to terms with them and find ways to deal with them. It does not matter whether or not one believes it or not, for the truth of the matter is that no one can escape from them.

What was in the minds and hearts of the disciples of Christ in Acts 1:6 was a Davidian type of the Israeli national kingdom. It was a kingdom ruled with a powerful King David, an earthly, physical, and thus temporary kingdom—the kingdom of Israel which in general was full of political powers, economic prosperity, military might, victory and glory, lives of leisure, pleasure, comfort and complacency. In particular, it was the Davidian kingdom of national sovereignty and authority with no foreign forces controlling and bullying them, especially the cruel Roman Empire.

But the Kingdom of God as revealed in the Lord Jesus Christ is quite different from that of the disciples. As it is well known to us all, Jesus spoke more intensively and extensively about the kingdom of heaven and the kingdom of God interchangeably than anything else in heaven, on earth or under the earth. Not only did His intimate disciples asked Him about this matter shortly after His victorious resurrection and right before His glorious ascension, the Pharisees like all the others, also kept asking Jesus about the coming kingdom of God. Jesus replied in their case in Luke 17:20-21, "The kingdom of God does not come visibly, nor will people say, 'Here it is,' or 'there it is,' because the kingdom of God is within you." His kingdom is spiritual and eternal and thus it is unshakeable by the forces of evil in this world. His kingdom comes to us by faith and trust and obedience to His commandments, and not by sight, sword, or forces of political, military, and financial might. His kingdom is all about people made in His very own image and about the priceless human souls to be saved by His grace for it is not His will that anyone should perish, but all come to the saving grace of Christ and thus enter into the kingdom of God. Therefore the most important thing that the

Lord desires us to know is the truthful principles and eternal perspectives of His Kingdom.

2. The Priority of the King: Jesus Christ

Once we have the right and correct perspective of the kingdom of God, we will naturally and automatically see and have the priority of the King Jesus, for Jesus Christ the Lord is the only King in the kingdom of God! This is made amply succinct in Acts 1:8 when we are told by Jesus that everything we are, we say, and we do, and everywhere we go should be all about "Me" – Jesus. The Lord Jesus pointed out on the road to Emmaus to the foolish disciples who were slow of heart to believe in all that the prophets have spoken, declaring that all the Scriptures were concerning Him, about Him and for Him (Lk 24:27), and that it is in Jesus that we live and move and have our beings abundantly and victoriously (Acts 17:28). The whole and single purpose of the Holy Scriptures with all the signs and wonders is summed up in the words of Jesus, "I, if I be lifted up, I will draw all people unto Me" (Jh 12:32), and in the Gospel of John 20:30-31, "And truly Jesus did many other signs in the presence of His disciples, which are not written in this book, but these are written that you may believe that Jesus is the Christ, the Son of God, and that believing you may have life in His name."

God the Holy Father exalts Jesus Christ to the highest place and gave Jesus a name that is above all names. At the name of Jesus, and nobody and nothing else, every knee shall bow and every tongue shall confess Jesus Christ is Lord to the glory of God the Father. In the same way, God the Holy Spirit came down among us to testify, verify and glorify the same truth that Jesus Christ is Lord! He is the way, the truth and the abundant and eternal life! And Christ Jesus in you is the hope of glory (Col 1:27). This was made so clear to me through Hebrews 12:2 when I was arrested and interrogated day and night for preaching and teaching the name of Jesus in China Nov 209 and then again Jan 2010. This powerful life verse ever since has genuinely become my source, my strength, my song, my sustenance and sufficiency, my salvation and satisfaction: Fix your eyes on Jesus, the Author and the Finisher of your faith! And if we are willing and obedient to do this command, our premise and our duty, then we will have the guaranteed promise in the next verse (v.3) that you will not grow weary and you will not lose heart! Hallelujah, Praise the Lord Jesus. He is so faithful and so powerful and so beautiful, all the time!

3. The Promises That Can Not Fail

In Acts 1:8, we are given two promises by the Lord Jesus. "You shall receive ..." and "You shall be ..." To live a promising life of victory, we must get hold of and hold on tightly the infallible and unfailing promises of God! As people of faith, we do not live by the projections of the world or the protections of the "systems" of men, we live securely and move confidently by the promises of the Almighty God! When you learn to live by faith, you learn to live with all His promises outlined for you in His Word which also permeates and saturates your heart and mind. Your future, according to His promises, shall be as bright and brilliant as the promises of God Himself. And as long as there is a God, there is always a future full of hope because Christ the Lord in you by faith is the hope of His glory. Never allow your past memories to ever become bigger than your future dreams from the kingdom of God and for the kingdom of God.

Therefore, my dearly beloved body of Christ, as Romans 5:1-5 instructs us, we shall rejoice in the glory of this hope of God through our Lord Christ who is the hope of glory (Col 1:27). Again I shout, "Rejoice!" for the joy of the Lord is our strength. But not only so, because of this most blessed hope we have, we also rejoice in our sufferings and persecution, knowing that tribulation produces in us the quality of perseverance and the nobility of the Christ-like character of joy unspeakable full of glory and of peace from the Prince of peace which surpasses all human knowledge and understanding. And this hope out of the promises of God does not disappoint us because the love of God has been poured out into our hearts by the Holy Spirit that Jesus has given us!

4. The Power of the Holy Spirit

John 15:26: When the Counselor comes . . . the Spirit of truth . . . He will testify about Me.

John 16:14: He (the Holy Spirit) will bring glory to Me by taking from what is mine and making it known to you.

Acts 10:38: How God anointed Jesus of Nazareth with the Holy Spirit and power, and how He went around doing good and healing all who were under the power of the devil, because God was with Him.

I Corinthians 2:4: And my speech and preaching were not with persuasive words of human wisdom, but in demonstration of the Spirit and of power.

Romans 5:5: And hope does not disappoint us, because God has poured out His love into our hearts by the Holy Spirit, whom He has given us.

It is imperative for all the children of God to be filled with the Holy Spirit (Eph 5:18), the Spirit of holiness, the Spirit of wisdom, the Spirit of truth and the Spirit of unlimited power to serve the Lord and defeat and subjugate the devil for God's glory! One can not serve victoriously in His kingdom work without being endued with power from on high. N order to live a powerful life for Jesus as an effective witness, you need to be Spirit-filled and Spirit-led at all times. Then you will be able to walk boldly in the Spirit, live victoriously in the Spirit, and you will not gratify the desires of the sinful nature of the human flesh (Gal 5:16).

5. The Purpose of the Spiritual Power

Power, no matter what kind it is, always has a purpose, whether it is carnal or spiritual, for there is no power or the desire for power without specific purpose(s). Carnal power does everything it can to carry out the desires of the sinful nature such as egotistical pride and possession, pleasures, privileges and position to control and manipulate others to one's own advantage. Spiritual power however, works in conflicts against the secular power. "You shall receive power when the Holy Spirit has come upon you and you shall be witnesses to Me," thus says the Lord as the clear purpose of this mighty spiritual power in Acts 1:8. This power that comes from the Holy Spirit is first of all holy in nature. It is pure in motive and intention. The power of the Spirit is given to the church with the three-fold purposes for the exaltation of the Savior Jesus Christ, for the edification of the saints the Body of Christ, and for the evangelization of the sinners of the world wherever they may be found. But the most important among them is to make us effective and productive as witnesses of Christ to win souls for Jesus, the more the merrier, until all have heard that Jesus saves and Jesus Christ is the Lord, the Son of the Living God!

6. The Presence of God

Acts 10:38: How God anointed Jesus of Nazareth with the Holy Spirit and power, and how He went around doing good and healing all who were under the power of the devil, because God was with Him.

Hebrews 13:5: Keep your life free from the love of money and be content with what you have because God has said, "Never will I leave you; never will I forsake you."

Those who are filled with the promises of God, the power and purpose of the Holy Spirit, are the ones who also live and walk with a keen awareness and a strong sense of the presence of the Lord Jesus in their lives. The Bible assures and guarantees us in many passages the ever living presence and very present help of the Lord through His Word, His Spirit and His saints in times of our troubles and tribulations (Ps 23, Ps 46:1-2, Matt 28:20). The presence of the Lord makes us strong, confident and glad, for Psalm 16:11 declares, "In Your presence is the fullness of joy," and this unspeakably glorious joy of the Spirit in our hearts is our strength to defeat and subjugate the devil and live and enjoy His victory (Neh 8:10). In His presence, hearts are mended and encouraged; in His presence troubles vanish and disappear; in His presence, Satan will have to flee; and in His presence we have the victory and prosperity! This authoritative and anointed covering satisfies our soul, and sustains us to the finish! The presence of the Lord in our lives makes all the difference in the world! It makes us more than conquerors through Him who both always loves us (Rom 8:37) and continues to strengthen us (Phil 4:13). Let us go all out in Jerusalem, in all Judea, in Samaria and even unto the very end of the world to spread His Word and Speed His Light, just as the early church did (Acts 1:8).

7. The Planned Process

Every fine product must go through some strict and even fiery process in manufacturing; and every successful person must have gone through the painful process of hard work with many sacrifices. If you take out the necessary process, you will surely not have the desired quality product, just as gold has to go through the fire in order to become more pure. As a matter of fact, there would be no famous heroes of the Hebrews to encourage us such as Shadrach, Meshach, and Abednego were it not for the burning fiery furnace in Daniel 3. There are no genuine triumphs without some serious trials, and there is no favor or fruit without some purifying fire.

In order to go strong and go global, one must start where he or she is, faithful and flourish and local. If we are not faithful and fruitful locally, we will never be able to be faithful and fruitful globally, for one can not give outwardly to others what he does not already possess inwardly himself. We can not reproduce globally what and who we are not locally. In this aspect, the change of location really changes nothing! One can not transplant who he is not. Even though where we go and what we preach and teach for the Lord are important to a certain extent strategically, what is much more important and essential is whose we are and who we really are in terms of the integrity of the heart and the character of uprightness. In our growing in grace, we must go through the required process according to the plan which has been proven reliable and successful regardless of regions or locations. Be local in roots and go global with wings. Be a dynamic disciple of glocal vision and missions!

8. The Price We Must Pay (Acts 8:1)

There is no grand prize without some heavy and high price. He who is willing to pay the price will also receive the prize. When we are willing, obedient and faithful to bear the cross, we will be able to wear the crown, the crown of victory, life, and glory (I Cor 9:24-25). This is made amply clear in the Pauline theology of ministries in almost all His epistles. While the process of carrying out the Commission is a lot fun and joyful, it can also be troublesome, difficult and at times painful as we experiences losses of face, money, properties, body parts and even our very lives. Jesus prophesied in Luke 21:16-17, "You will be betrayed by even parents, brothers, relatives and friends. They will put some of you to death. All men will hate you because of Me," and the Lord Himself fulfilled that very prophecy with His own death on the cross on our behalf. But look at this divine paradox in the next verse, "But not a hair of your head will perish." (v.18). How do you reconcile the tension here between the bodily death and the non-perishable hair on the head? I believe Jesus is talking in relation to the eternal kingdom perspective and not from the temporary earthly existence. I have found the answer in Romans 8:38-39 that whether in death or in life, nothing can separate us from the love of God that is in Christ Jesus.

Therefore, to live on earth is to witness Christ with fruitful labor for all to see in the world, and to die is heavenly gain for the Kingdom of Christ which is much better by far (Phil 1:21-23). Whether we live or die, or how long the Lord allows us to live for Him on earth, it really does not matter that much any more when you have personalized and internalized the perspective from King Jesus. Whether we live or die, we always belong to Jesus, and the end of this life is but the beginning of the eternal life with Jesus in the glory and majesty of His presence for ever! Indeed death on earth has been swallowed up in Christ's resurrection victory. Thanks be unto God that He has given us this victory through the redemptive work finished on the cross by our Lord Jesus Christ (I Cor 15:54, 57). With this victory in our heart full of His hope and glory

(Col 1:27, Rom 5:2), let us be willing and ready, like Jesus our Lord, to reach the lost at any cost. Reach the lost no matter what the cost! Winning souls and making disciples for Jesus and for the furtherance of His kingdom on earth, nothing is more important and urgent than these!

Chapter 22
On Faith, Hope and Love: Become An
Eagle Christian with Big Dreams

And now these three remain: faith, hope and love. But the greatest of these is love (I Cor 13:13).

I always thank God for all of you, mentioning you in our prayers. We continually remember before our God and Father, your work produced by faith, your labor prompted by love, and your endurance inspired by hope in our Lord Jesus Christ (I Thes 1:2-3).

Faith is the root and foundation in the past event; hope is the wing and the horizon for the glorious future in anticipation; and love is life's present passion in action! There is no doubt in faith; there is no despair in hope; and there is no fear in love for the perfect Agape love of God drives out and cast away all fears!

Thoughts on Faith

Now faith is the substance of things hoped for, the evidence of things not seen... By faith we understand that the worlds were framed by the Word of God, so that the things which are seen were not made of things which are visible... But without faith, it is impossible to please Him, for he who comes to God must believe that He is, and that he is a rewarder of those who diligently seek Him (Heb 11: 1, 3, 6).

When Jesus saw their faith, He said ... (Mark 2:5).

As soon as Jesus heard the word that was spoken, He said to the ruler of the synagogue, "Do not be afraid, only believe." (Mark 5:36).

The righteous will live by faith (Rom 1:17).

We live by faith, not by sight... So we make it our goal to please Him, whether we are at home in the body or away from it (II Cor 5:7, 9).

For everyone born of God overcomes the world. This is the victory that has overcome the world, even our faith (I John 5:4).

Undoubtedly, the entire Bible is a holy book on faith, faith in God and in Jesus Christ as the Son of God, and with this faith in Jesus name firmly grounded and deeply rooted, we will not perish but have everlasting life (John 3:16, 20:31). The famous faith chapter is the Bible is Hebrews 11. There is no other life factor more important, essential, critical and crucial to me than the faith factor in the Bible, for without faith it is impossible to please god. Hebrews 11:6 tells us that our faith in God pleases Him and I am convinced and confident that our God prospers the faithful in Him. Faith pleases the Lord and the Lord prospers the faithful. It is that simple. III John verse 2 assures us that if we live by and in faith in Jesus Christ as Lord and Master of our life, we will prosper in all things, and will remain in good health, and most importantly, our soul will continue to prosper in the Lord!

In the whole Bible, we encounter only two places where Jesus our Lord Himself, the Creator and the Sustainer and the Master of the universe, was shocked or surprised. Both these incidents had to do the faith factor: plenty of faith or the lack of it. In Luke 7:1-10, Jesus marveled at or was surprised by the Roman centurion's faith, sensitivity, humility and perfect understanding of authority, power and submissions, and thus miraculously healed his servants! Jesus exclaimed to the crowd following him: "I have not found such great faith, not even in Israel!" (v. 9). On the other hand in Mark 6:1-6, Jesus encountered in His own hometown among His very own people the Jews, such stiff-necked and heart-hardened people who would not believe in His Word. As a result of their lack of faith, the Bible tells us that the Lord could not do many mighty works but a few small miracles. "He was amazed at their lack of belief." (v.6). What a sad consequence this is, and what a powerful life lesson to learn!

One of the most interesting, intriguing and inspiring verses of the entire Bible to me is Mark 2:5. It says that when Jesus the Lord "saw their faith," the faith of the four men who carried their paralytic friend, He was moved with compassion. As a result of His great compassion for the suffering and the needy, a miracle of healing and provision took place. I have asked the Lord in prayers as to how to see faith, and how He saw their faith. The Spirit of the Lord led me to the following five conclusions:

1. Jesus saw their faith through their authentic compassion for their disabled and helpless friend. We worship and serve a Lord who is full of mercies and compassion. When the compassionate Lord sees us who are merciful and compassionate to our fellow human beings, He will be moved and touched with more compassion to perform miracles, meet the needs and teach us some valuable spiritual truths and powerful life lessons.

2. Jesus saw their faith through their dogged determination. Where there is a will, there is a way. We may have to give in once a while in terms of minor compromises such as gives and takes, especially in

friendship and marriage relations; we will all one day have to give out, leaving this earth, but we must never ever give up on our faith in and promises of God. Then and only then, will the Lord take notice of our divine determination as His disciplined disciple and empower us to receive favors of god and man and achieve the victories He has won and prepared to give us!

3. Jesus saw their faith through their unfailing vision. I am convinced that what guided the activities of the four month was none other than the vision they saw in Jesus healing their faith! This is just like the woman with the issue of blood for twelve years in Mark 5:25-34. She saw by faith in her mind's eye that Jesus was able and willing to heal her, for she said to herself, "If only I may touch His clothes, I shall be made well"! What faith and what vision that brought her wholistic healing of peace and joy and power and prosperity! As a result of their vision in the healing of Jesus, no crowds could stop them, no doors or windows of the house could present them with a problem. Not even the roof could become a hindrance to the healing of Jesus! They had a dream and possessed a heavenly vision!

4. Jesus saw their faith through their harmonious cooperation to get the job done—bring their friend right in front of Jesus. In order for the Lord to miraculously operate in our lives, we must be willing, obedient, ready and even eager to cooperate, for there is no divine operation without human cooperation. Without God, we can not; and without us, God will not! Not only are we to be humble and sensitive to cooperate with God, His Word, His Will and His ways, we must learn to humble ourselves and cooperate with people of like faith and purpose and passion to finish His work, as did these four men!

5. Jesus saw their faith through their unified action. We are who we are, not by what we say, nor just by what we believe, but by what we do. As someone has declared it so correctly that the biggest gap or the greatest distance is between thoughts and action. So many people have great ideas and fantastic intentions, but they do not do anything about it. Therefore, intentions remain just that, mere intentions. No action, no fruition! What does it profit a man if he says that he has faith but has no works, no deeds and no actions? Can such a faith save him? NO! Faith is a verb, and faith demands action from the faithful. For faith with action is dead! (James 2:17). Jesus challenged the disciples to do unto each other as He had done for them and if they would do so by following His example, Jesus promised to bless them (John 13:15, 17). Let us go and do likewise (Luke 10:37). Let us put our hands to the movements of our

hearts; let us put our feet to our faith, and let us put our money where our mouth is, for talk is weak and totally cheap, but walk is loud and wonderful!

Thought on Hope

If Hebrews chapter 11 is the faith chapter, then Romans chapter15 is the hope chapter. Let us look at the source of our hope, the security of our hope, strength of our hope and the sign of our hope briefly.

1. The source of our hope: the Holy Scripture. Everything that was written in the past was written to teach us, so that through the endurance and the encouragement of the Scriptures, we might have hope (Rom 15:4). The Holy Bible, the Word of God is not able to save us and fill us with the blessed hope in Jesus Christ and in the life to come, it also sustains us with plenty of encouragements; it enables us to endure to the very end without growing weary or ever lose heart! And he or she who endures to the end shall be saved and victorious!

2. The security of our Hope: the Lord Christ Jesus. In the last days, God has chosen to make known to the Gentiles, the glorious riches of this mystery, which is "Christ in you, the hope of glory." (Col 1:27). Christ is our source and sustenance and salvation and all the Scriptures from Genesis to Revelations point to none other than Jesus Himself (Luke 24:27). Our security is not found in our political or financial or educational or even religious systems. Our security is found only in Christ Jesus our Lord! And upon Christ Jesus this solid rock I stand, all other ground is but sinking sand!

3. The strength and Seal of our hope: the presence of the Holy Spirit. If we trust in the Lord Jesus, the Bible promises us that the God of hope will so fill us all that we will overflow with hope by the power of the Holy Spirit (Rom 15:13). Furthermore, we can rejoice in the hope of His glory and this hope does not disappoint us, for God has poured out His love into our hearts by the Holy Spirit, Whom he has given us (Rom 5:3, 5). Just as hope deferred makes the heart sick, so a heart full of hope rejoices and is made glad by the Holy Spirit! A hopeful life is a powerful life, and to live in victory is top live in the hope of the Son of God our Lord Jesus Christ who Himself is declared to be "the hope of glory" in all of us who believe in Him, who follow and serve Him (Col 1:27).

4. The sign and signal of our hope: "all joy and peace" as you trust in Jesus. Romans 15:13 guarantees us that if we keep our trust in Jesus the Lord and are filled by the Holy Spirit, which is not a random suggestion

but a strong command (Eph 5:18), we will have the life manifestation and daily demonstration and natural spiritual extension of joy and peace in spite of all the distresses and hardships of our temporary hostile circumstances. Peace and joy are the clearest signs and signals of a Spirit-filled, Spirit-empowered and Spirit-led Christian life. It is a life with joy unspeakable and full of glory; and it is a life of peace from the prince of Peace, a peace with God and a peace from God. And peace of God which transcends all understanding, will guard your hearts and your minds in Christ Jesus (Phil 4:7).

Thoughts on Love

God is love (I John 4:16). Love must be sincere (Rom 12:9).

For God so loved the world that He gave His only begotten son that whosoever believes in Him, shall not perish, but have everlasting life (John 3:16).

Greater love has no one than this that one lays down his life for his friend (John 15:13).

If you love me, you will obey what I command (John 14:15).

God demonstrated His own love for us in this: while we were still sinners, Christ died for us (Rom 5:8).

We love because He first loved us (I John 4:19).

Speaking the truth in love (Eph 4:15). Do everything in love (I Cor 16:14).

The greatest question ever asked three times in a roll by the Lord Jesus is the love question (John 21: 15-17). The greatest challenge ever issued by the Lord is the love challenge, and the great force in the world is the power of love, for God is love and nothing and nobody is greater than God! True love, like genuine faith, is not merely declaration with words and ideas, but demonstration in deeds and action! From the love life of Jesus especially culminating on the cross for our iniquities and the powerful illustration with the parable of the Good Samaritan in Luke 10, we understand the extravagance of the amazing divine love which attracts us and draws us unto the Lord God (Jer 31:3) and motivates us to work unselfishly for Him (II Cor 5:14). The love of God is timeless and eternal; the love of God is unconditional; the love of God is sacrificial; the love of God is covenantal; and the love of God is secure and reliable. True love notices; true love initiates; true love transcends; true love risks; true love costs; true love remembers; true love returns; and true love richly reimburses!

Jesus the Lord instructs us that the most important commandment is "love the Lord your God with all your heart and with all your soul and with all your mind and with all your strength. The second is this: Love your neighbor as yourself. There is no commandment greater than these." (Mark 13:30-31). Both the Golden Rule (Matt 7:12) and the Royal Law (James 2:8) are further explanation and illustration of the Great Commandments in daily life situations. Ephesians 4:15 commands us to always speak the truth in love. This is a delicate balance and it means that we must not love anything that does not have truth in it; and that we must not trust anything that does not have love in it. Truth and love, God is both! What a good God and what a great Lord we serve!

The Bible is God's love letter to a lost and rebellious humanity desperately in need of faith, hope and love from Him. If Hebrews 11 is the faith chapter, and if Romans 15 is the hope chapter, then without the shadow of a doubt, I Corinthians 13, as is known to all, is certainly the love chapter of the Holy Bible! Love is "the most excellent way," Paul declares (I Cor 13:1). When we are kind and patient, humble and unselfish, forgiving, protecting and providing, we are most like God as these are love in action and God is this love! Thus love is God is action. When we are bitter, unforgiving, insincere, rude, proud, disobedient and selfish, we are far from God and from the love of God. We would be more like the devil himself. The famous Chinese philosopher, the founder of Daoism of the Yin and Yang, Master Lao-Tzu, eloquently and exactly, accurately and authoritatively points out that "while being deeply loved by someone give you strength, and deeply loving someone gives you courage!" Love really is the most majestic, miraculous, and marvelous thing in the whole wide world! Without love in life, we would gain nothing; and in spite of all our knowledge and science, tongues and prophecies, and even super faith, we are nothing if we have no love (I Cor 13:1-3). A life without love is not love at all.

Souring High on Eagle's Wings: On Becoming An Eagle Christian

But those who (wait on) hope in the Lord will renew their strength. They will soar on wings like eagles; they will run and not grow weary, they will walk and not be faint (Isaiah 40:31).

Like an eagle that stirs up its nest and hovers over its young, spreads its wings to catch them and carries them on its pinions, the Lord alone led him; no foreign god was with him (Deut 32:11-12)

He satisfies my desires with good things, so that my youth is renewed like the eagle's (Psalm 103:5).

Do not think like a chicken, and do not act like a chicken. God has created you to be a mighty eagle to accomplish great things with extraordinary excellence for such a time as this. Start thinking like the eagle, and acting like the eagle, and you will be an Eagle Christian fit and ready for the Master's deployment!

How does one become a mighty and majestic eagle Christian in this world full of little chickens of mediocrity? Here are several spiritual suggestions for success (Yang, 1998, pp. 21-24):

First of all, one must learn to wait on, trust and hope in the Lord as the source and strength and sustenance and sufficiency in this entire process, for apart from Him, we can do nothing and we will be nothing on our own.

Secondly, we must learn to renew our strength daily like the eagles. Not only must we know the source of our strength which is the Savior, we also must learn to appropriately gain new strength continually. Without the necessary and crucial process of renewal, the eagle would not have the product of majesty, beauty and longevity for 80-120 years, for in order to achieve the right and desirable product, one must go through some vigorous and disciplined process! If one takes out the necessary and painful process intentionally or unintentionally, one will not be able to obtain the quality and proud product. This life law is very appropriate and applicable to all of us.

Third, we must be active and proactive to learn to discern our own spiritual condition and carefully examine our own situation like the eagles. Eagles do not eat dead stale meats, and they are active and not stagnant in life style. They periodically check out every feature on their bodies and often sharpen their talons again the rough and sharp edges of the stone mountains. They are discernible and brutally honest with any problems.

Fourth, we must purge out any defection and sin in us and among us as the eagles frequently do. They plug out the old and broken feathers, expose their bare nakedness and ugliness. They are unafraid of their vulnerabilities. The Word of God teaches us that he who covers up his sin shall not prosper, but he who exposes and renounces sin will find mercy, protection, provision and prosperity (Prov 28:13).

Fifth, we must wash ourselves, clean and bathe ourselves in the Son. The eagles go to the nearby lake or pound to wash thorough the wounds and clean the blood. They find a solitary and safe place of sunshine to bathe under the sun and receive healing.

Sixth, we must be faithful in protection of and provision for our mates and families and the Body of Christ. The eagles in the painful process of renewing their strength, depend on their faithful mates to protect them from harm, and provide them with foods and covering.

Seventh and finally, we must learn to be patient in the renewal process. Without patience, there can be no wisdom (Prov 19:11), and without responsibility, there can be no maturity. The Hebrew word "Kauvaw" in Isaiah 40:31, translated into "wait upon," "trust or hope in," literally means "to tie oneself to something or someone with a big and strong chain that can't be broken". It implies firmness, steadfastness, steadiness and patience. No wonder David proclaims in Psalm 40:1-3, "I waited patiently for the Lord, and He turned to me and heard my cry. He lifted me out of the slimy pit, out of the mud and mire; He set my feet on a rock and gave me a firm place to stand. He put a new song in my mouth, a hymn of praise to my God. Many will see and fear and put their trust in the Lord!

Here Comes the Dreamer: Driven by the Dream (Gen 37:19)

Remember this life lesson I have learned and am about to declare unto you now: Don't look backward to the past. Look upward and forward to the future the Lord has prepared for you, for your future dreams are much bigger, better and brighter than all your past memories put together, and that your future shall be as bright as the promises of your God! You can be confident of this one because He who has promised you is faithful and able to perform the promises. The key to your victory and prosperity is your personal spiritual intimacy – abide, reside and remain in Him (John 15;5). You are His resident, and the Lord Jesus is our President! Therefore do not try to make Him or treat Him as a regular resident!

Throughout human history, great endeavors have been carried out by men and women who possess extraordinary capacities to think deep, aim and dream high, who passionately desire to feel deeper and reach higher! Without a doubt whatsoever, people of vision can accomplish and realize unusual ambitions in various fields of research and investigations. Great vision leads to great expectation and great expectation causes great perspiration. And this is especially true and particularly crucial when it comes to the work of ministries and in the final fulfillment of the

Lord's Great Commissions outlined in Matthew 28:18-20. Therefore also attempt great things for God, and always expect great things from God!

In relation to the power of dreams, the famous British philosopher George Bernard Shaw once said: "Some men see things, and say, 'why'? But I dream of things that never were and I say, 'why not'?! One of the most well-know speeches in the American experimental history of democracy in the quest for human rights, liberty, justice and equality which has literally inspired billions of dreamers and visionaries the world over, is the "Dream Speech" of the Rev. Dr. Martin Luther King Jr. "I have a Dream that one day ..." Inspired by the Word of God and based on his dream, King further and forcefully asserted that:

When evil men plot, good men must plan;
When evil men burn and bomb, good men must build and bind;
When evil men shout ugly words of hatred,
good men must commit themselves to the glories of love;
When evil men would seek to perpetuate an unjust status quo,
good men seek to bring into being a real order of justice!

Because of his complete concentration and devout dedication to this divinely inspired dream of what the United States of America can, should and must be, America since then has never been the same to this very day and will never be the same. This is the power of one man's dream or vision that ultimately transformed the entire nation for good, and for the good of the whole human race under any form of oppression anywhere and everywhere. It has served and still serves as an indispensable inspiration to many millions who are still living under the atheistic authoritarian totalitarianism and the dictator's boots of brutal persecution.

Divinely inspired dreams and visions from heaven are so much bigger, brighter and better than all of us put together. They help to inspire our deep desire to acquire the heavenly fire; they help to unite us together as one in mission and commission with conviction, clarity, confidence and courage; they ignite the passion and the compassion within us and move us to bold action for the realization of the common divine destination. Dr. M.L. King the preacher and the prophet of God once proclaimed from the sincerity and the profundity of his soul that, if a man does not have a faith strong enough and a cause worthy enough to die for, he simply is not fit to live! What a statement of courage! What a commitment to a cause!

Dreamers are so essential and fundamental to the righteous and divine cause that we as God's people would be severely handicapped and even totally incapacitated without them. So much so that another noted African American poet Langston Hughes once penned:

Hold fast to your dream and do not let it die;
For when dreams die,
it's like a broken-winged bird that can never fly!

"In the last days, I will pour out My Spirit upon all people. Your sons and daughters will prophesy, your old men will dream dreams, your young men will see visions. Even on my servants, both men and women, I will pour out My Spirit in those days." (Joel 2:28-29). This mighty prophecy was fulfilled in Acts 2:17-18) and still is being fulfilled all over the world to this very day as the Giver of this prophecy, our Lord Jesus Christ, is the same yesterday, today and forever (Heb 13:8). He is still high and lifted on the throne just as Isaiah saw, and He is more than willing and more than able to perfectly perform that which He has personally promised us His children!

Dreams are not just something that occasionally and randomly occurs at night in our sleep; neither are they something that your head conjures up when the conscious or the subconscious has been taken over by the devil with his sinful and evil desires of temptation and distraction. Divine dreams are driven by the Holy Spirit of the Lord Himself to the holy servants of God. These are fundamentally different from the Freudian dreams and interpretations because they are God-given and God-driven visions from heaven for a Godly purpose and toward a Godly destination! They are inspirations and aspirations from a higher call for a higher goal. Nothing can prevent the Kingdom dreamers and Godly visionaries from bringing their dreams to fruition, for greater is He who inspired the dreams within us than he who is of the world (I John 4:4).

However, this does not mean at all that the path to our divine dreams will always be silky smooth and storm-free (I Cor 16:9). On the contrary, the devil will do his very best through the people and circumstances around you to try to block and hinder you from realizing the dreams. He has done so and will continue to do so with such tactics of intimidation, confusion, hardships, starvation, persecution and even assassination. He will cause envy, bitterness, unforgiveness, anger and hatred against us, but being driven by the dream from above, the dreamer is unafraid of the devil and is keenly aware of the devil's devices. Moreover, working together with the people of like purpose, passion and power, the dreamer

174

submits himself or herself completely to God and resists the devil boldly with the full armor of God, and the devil will have to flee (James 4:7). And anyone who is born of God can and will overcome the world and this is the victory that has overcome the world, even by faith (I John 5:4).

When we constantly feed our human spirit with His Holy Scriptures, the promises of God which are the sources of our heavenly dreams, will come alive, afresh, anew and ablaze in our hearts and lives and missions for God! Our ministerial life must be dream driven, purpose and passion packed, and not merely program and project oriented. When we are Spirit filled and Spirit led, there will be nobody and nothing that can stop us for God is with us, and if God be for us, who then can be against us or defeat us! (Rom 8:31). You and I can do all things through Him who strengthens us (Phil 4:13) for Christ Jesus is our source and our limitless resources for the victorious living! And we shall become more than conquerors through Christ who loves us, and nothing, absolutely nothing in heaven, on earth or under the earth, can ever separate us from this love of God found in Christ our Lord (Rom 8:37-39)! Praise the Lord for ever more!

Our dreams often determine the direction of our lives. The Bible tells us in Proverbs 29:18 that where this is no vision, the people will perish. A life driven by a dream from God Himself is the best prevention against our tendency for mediocrity, against the human status quo for just barely being the average, and against organizational bureaucracy and religiosity. A dream-driven life with its passion packed divine purpose is the most effective measure against a mind of ignorance and arrogance, the spirit of indifference, a heart of insensitivity, and a life style of indolence and indulgence in only oneself (Ez 16:49-50). Our dreams also determine the quality of our daily and spiritual lives. Proverb 23:7 says that as a man thinks in his heart, so is he." A dream-driven life is a life of divine discernments, divine decisions, divine directions, determination, discipline and definite divine developments.

Let us take a brief look at the most famous dreamer of God in the Bible (Gen 37-50) and learn some wonderful and useful life lessons from Joseph. Because of the unusual dreams that Joseph had, it caused his parents to be quite uneasy with him and his brothers to be full of envious anger towards him to the point of danger of murder. In Gen 37: 19-20, the brothers exclaimed facetiously and derogatorily upon seeing Joseph coming, "Here come the dreamer! ... Come now and let us kill him."

The story of Joseph is a very remarkable one, from rags to riches, from the pit of the poor and weak Israel to the premier of the rich and powerful Egypt. There are many colorful accounts of Joseph in the

15 some chapters of Genesis and what all happened to him. What is important to us here to learn is not just what happened to him with all the details, but rather what life lessons we can draw and learn from what happened, for life is only 10% of what you make it, but 90% of how you take it. If you can take it with the right attitude, you will make it to the high altitude! And when you can not change your circumstances, hold fast to your God-given dreams and adjust your attitude towards your circumstances. The right kind of attitude will give you fortitude, latitude and altitude and fill your heart with gratitude in spite of the outward situation. Life is best lived and enjoyed from within, and not from without, better to live life from the inside out, and not the outside in.

So then what can we learn from the incredible life of Joseph the Dreamer? At least 4 life lessons:

1. Joseph always dares to dream (Gen 37:1-11);

2. Joseph holds on to his God-given dream firmly in spite of the oppositions;

3. Joseph actively, positively and optimistically and enthusiastically pursues the dream;

4. Joseph patiently and confidently waits and expects the fulfillment of the dream according to God's perfect timing (Gen 50:20).

What does all this mean to us fellow divine dreamers and Kingdom workers today? I believe Hebrews 12:1-3 gives us the implication and ramification for our current action and future direction in the pursuit of our dreams and visions:

Therefore, since we are surrounded by such a great cloud of witnesses, let us throw off everything that hinders and the sin that so easily entangles, and let us run with perseverance the race marked out for us. let us fix our eyes on Jesus, the Author and Finisher of our faith, who for the joy set before Him, endured the cross, scorning its shame, and sat down at the right hand of the throne of God. Consider Him who endured such opposition from sinful men, so that you will not grow weary and lose heart.

Chapter 23
The Ministry of the Word in the Power of the Spirit: How I Prepare My Soul for Teaching and Preaching

The Spirit of the Lord is on me, because He has anointed me to preach
the good news to the poor. He has sent me to proclaim freedom for
the prisoners and recovery of sight to the blind, to release the
oppressed,
to proclaim the year of the Lord's favor (Is 61:1-2 & Luke 4:18-19);

When Jesus had finished saying these things, the crowds were
amazed
at His teaching, because He taught as one who had authority, and not
as their teachers of the law (Mt 7:28-29)

Now the Lord is the Spirit, and where the Spirit of the Lord is,
there is liberty (II Corinthians 3:17).

Introduction:

Indeed, Christ Jesus is our light, our life, our first love, our true
liberty, our supreme leader, most important of all, our Lord of Lords!
Laity and ministers alike must be always about the Father's business
in the three dimensions: the exaltation of the Savior, the edification of
the saints, and the evangelization of the sinner. The supreme task for us
all, of necessity, must be that of showing His life, sharing His love, and
shining His light all over the world until all have heard! Jesus commands
us, saying, "let your lights so shine before men that they may see your
good deeds and praise your Father in heaven (Mt 5:16).

One of the most dynamic and forceful, powerful and productive
ways of shining His light as Jesus is the light, is through anointed Christ-
centered teaching and passionate Pentecostal preaching of the whole
Word of God rightly divided. And this takes a lot of careful and prayerful
preparation on the part of the teacher and the preacher of the Word, as
we will be judged more strictly according to James 3:1. Like working
out our own salvation, we must also approach the Word of God, whether
teaching or preaching, with fear and trembling, for it is God who works
in us both to will and to act according to His good purpose (Phil 2:12-
13).

Someone asked me before about the difference between teaching and preaching of God's Word. After thinking for a few moments, I replied and still believe that to me personally, there is not much of any essential or fundamental difference except that perhaps preaching for us Pentecostals is louder and faster and more emotional in appeal following the spontaneous strategy of the Spirit whereas teaching is more paced and rational. The message is essentially the same although the methods are a little different; the purpose is the same although the plans are diverse. The Apostle Paul of Old wisely teaches us that we are to become all things to all men that by all means we may save some (I Cor 9:22)—a Biblical strategy of principled flexibility, adaptivity, cultural sensitivity, and relevancy.

The following brief list represents some of my key personal convictions in regards to teaching & preaching preparation. It is by no means inclusive and conclusive of all the wonderful hermeneutical and homiletic principles taught in the seminaries I was gratefully honored to be part of, from Cleveland (TN) to Ashland (OH). I pray and hope that what I am about to share will be an enlightenment, an encouragement, and a blessing to my fellow teachers, preachers, and missionaries as we labor together in love in the Lord's vineyard. The list contains following eight (8) vital focuses on preparing the soul (in Greek "Su-Kay" meaning the mind, the heart, and the human will) for the effective ministry of the powerful Word of God: The Word as the foundation; Christ as the center; the Spirit as the indispensable guide coupled with fervent prayer as the weapon of the warfare, love for the Lord and for souls as the motivation, passion and conviction straight from the heart, simplicity and clarity in communication, the concern for cultural context, and for God's sake, don't take the "self," ourselves, too seriously (in other words, get the "self" out of the way, no logo, no label, no title, no idol, no EGO which means "Edging God Out"). Let us discuss each of them concisely and precisely.

1. The Word of God: Study to show ourselves approved of God

Without any doubt whatsoever, the teacher and preacher must spend much of his/her time studying the Word of God, for all Scripture is Theo-nostros (God-breathed), and it is useful and profitable for teaching, rebuking, correcting, training in righteousness, and equipping the saint for every good work (II Tim 3:16-17). In order to teach and preach the Word, we must diligently study and apply the Word ourselves first. As one can not give what he or she does not have, so one can not teach or preach the Word unless he or she has it in both the heart and head! As it was the Master's custom (Lk 4:16) of reading and reciting the Word, so it must be our cultivated habit also as servants of the Master to delve deep into the Bread of life and be well-fed by it! This habitual practice will broaden and strengthen our hearts, enlighten and sharpen our heads, and hasten our hands for His proper use (the heart, head, hand and habit of the preacher/teacher).

No one can know His will apart from His Word, for His Word does not just contain His will, His Word is His will, just as the Bible does not just contain the Word of God, it is the Word of God. No one can have wisdom from God apart from the Word of God. No one can do His work well if he or she is not saturated and sustained by the power and promises of His Word. No one can have a consistent walk with God if the Word of God is ignored or neglected in the "busyness" of the ministries (BUSY— an acronym for Being Under Satan's Yoke!). We will never become people of the Way until we truly become people of the Word! It takes a lot of discipline and discernment on our part to examine the Word daily like the good old Noble Bereans (Acts 17:11). Applying ourselves to His Word by first believing in and then living out the Word before attempting to teach and preach others is not some kind of a spiritual luxury; rather it is my personal practical necessity! And I am more convicted than ever before that we have no business standing up on our feet to speak (teaching & preaching) for God if we do not first of all spend time on our knees before the Lord. What we really need in this day and age is much more "kneeology," and less theology! Let us hide the Word of God in our hearts (through systematic memorization of Scriptures) so that we will not sin against God in both inner motive and outer motion, in both attitude and activities.

2. Christ the Lord as the only absolute center

John Chapter 1 talks in details about the Word... In the beginning was the Word, and the Word was with God and the Word was God... And the Word was made flesh and lived among us... full of life and light, full of grace and truth which can come only through Jesus Christ our Lord, who is both the Son of God and God the Son (John 1:17). Jesus Christ is the eternal Word; He is the living Word, the creative Word, the sacrificial and sacramental Word, the authoritative Word, the inerrant Word, the infallible Word, the unchangeable Word, the unshakeable Word, the unstoppable Word, the incarnate Word, the gracious Word and the glorious Word (John 1:1-14)! The Old Testament is Jesus concealed; the New Testament is Jesus revealed, and the church of the living God is Jesus fulfilled. It's all about Jesus (Lk 24:27)! It is in Jesus Christ we live and move and have our beings (Acts 17:28). Everything in the Bible points ultimately to Jesus, and the preacher and the teacher must be centrally and singularly focused on Jesus and help the audience lift their eyes and "look unto Jesus, who is the Author and Finisher of our faith" (Heb 12:2) and who is also the First and Last, the Beginning and the End, the Alpha and Omega of our lives and ministries. Only in this way, will we not grow weary or lose heart (Heb 12:3, II Cor 4:16-18).

3. Persistent prayers and the anointing of the Holy Spirit

The Bible tells us that after the believers had prayed, the place where they were meeting was shaken. And they were all filled with the Holy Spirit and they began to speak the Word of God boldly (Acts 4:31). What a powerful connection between the power of prayers and the work of the Holy Spirit! It is unquestionably true that where there is not prayer, there is neither the presence nor the power of God! A prayerless life is a fruitless life; a prayerless life is a powerless life; a prayerless life is a faithless life. And in the final analysis, a prayerless life is a disobedient life, and a disobedient life is a sinful life, for anyone who knows the good he ought to do and yet knowingly does not do it, to him, this is sin to him (James 4:17).

One can succinctly see from the first three Biblical quotations at the very beginning of this chapter (Lk 4) the clear dependence of our Lord Jesus upon the anointing and power of the Holy Spirit in His own teaching and preaching ministries. As a matter of fact, the Holy Spirit was present and powerful at work from the very beginning of His conception, throughout His entire earthly life and till the very end of His ascension. If the person and the work of the Holy Spirit were so indispensable even in the life and ministry of Jesus the Lord then, how much more do we need the Holy Spirit to guide us and provide for us in our teaching and preaching right now!

As we pray incessantly and persistently to the Lord according to His will, the Spirit of the Lord will be moved to touch our hearts and move our soul with what He wants us to teach and preach. The Spirit of the Lord reveals the deep and secret things of God to our soul, and enables us to speak it out directly with conviction, compassion, force and authority. Through fervent prayers, the Holy Spirit empowers us with divine wisdom and understanding about the needs of the audience so that we can boldly and directly speak to them, not in words taught by human cleverness, but in words taught by the Spirit with Godly conviction, expressing spiritual truths in spiritual words (I Cor 2:13) . Search me, O God, and know my heart; test me and know my anxious thoughts. See if there is any offensive way in me, and lead me in the way everlasting (Ps 139:23-24). With the conviction and direction of the Holy Spirit's purity and power through our earnest, consistent and persistent prayers, we will not end up doing God's work man's way, or doing the right thing for the wrong reason, which are two common devices of the devil.

4. Love for the Lord and love for souls as the motivation

Before we minister the Word, whether in teaching or preaching, we must double check our motive and examine our motivational structure and system. Do we really love the Lord with all our heart, all our mind, all our soul, and all our strength? If not, it would be impossible to love others as we do ourselves (Mk 12:30-31). The greatest challenge ever issued for all of us is the love challenge, and the greatest question ever asked is the love question (John 21).The Lord has bestowed a new command to each and every one of us, and it is the love command: "As I have loved you, so you must love one another. By this all men will know that you are my disciples if you love one another" (John 13:34-35). Our love must be sincere (Rom 12:9), and we must speak the truth in love in order to grow up to be more and more like Him who is our head (Eph 4:15). Speaking the truth in love means that we must not trust anything that does not have love in it, and neither should we love anything that does not have truth in it!

What was the motive behind Paul's evangelistic outreach, and what motivated all the other apostles to go on their missions even at the very cost of their own lives? Their love for the Lord as manifested in their love for human souls! "For Christ's love compels us …" (II Cor 5:14). I Corinthians 13 warns us that even if we do have all the spiritual gifts and powers to move mountains and surrender our bodies to the flame for the poor, and yet we have no love, we would be gaining nothing and we would be nothing! The entire Bible is likened unto God's love letter to the whole wide world. In order to effectively and efficiently present God's love, we must faithfully and incarnationally represent the love of God in our own lives and ministries. God does not merely want us to have a lovely relation with Him, not does He desire just a loving relation from us. What He wants with us is a love relation, an obsessive love relationship and a possessive love relationship!

5. Passion and conviction straight from the heart

Above all things, we must guard our heart, for it will affect everything we do (Prov 4:23). At the heart of every matter is the heart matter, and heart of every issue is the heart issue. If the heart is not right, everything we do will eventually turn out to be right in spite of trials, errors and failures. God is not looking for mighty hands of abilities, but rather humble and broken hearts of availabilities. After the prophet Samuel had made seven serious mistakes based on human wisdom in selecting and anointing a king for Israel, the Lord spoke to him loud and clear (I Sam 16:7): "The Lord does not look at things man looks at. Man looks at the outward appearance, but the Lord looks at the heart." Preparation for teaching and preaching of the Word should start from an examination of the heart. True ministries take place when the minister speaks heart to heart with the people, not head to head alone. More than just convincing our heads, the Lord wants us ministers to use the power of His Word and the presence of His Spirit to convict our hearts, move our hearts and inspire our hearts to action. Effective preaching and teaching come from the heart, the sincere heart, the grateful heart, the forgiving heart, the gentle and humble heart, the broken and contrite heart, the heart filled with His vision and mission, filled with His purpose, power, and passion.

One thing I have really learned over the years of ministries is that I can not give what I do not have. In fact, no one can whether materially or spiritually! I was deeply offended in the spirit by a high-level official in the church when he taught that "sometimes, you just have to fake to make it!" I am more convinced than ever before that the Lord Jesus hates, among other things, hypocrisy (the art of acting out a performance or a show in a theatrical setting). He constantly rebuked the hypocrites in His sermon on the mount and with the eight woes in Matt 23. It is the yeast of the Pharisees who served the Lord with their lips but their hearts are far away from Him. We must be sincere, authentic, transparent, genuine, and brutally real in our presentation of His Word straight from the heart and from the inside out. My cup overflows and out of the abundance of the heart, the mouth speaks. The Lord was not pleased with the fig leaves of Adam and Eve then, neither is He happy with a bunch of plastic preachers and phony bolognas! Ministries of the Word are not some kind of silly game for a profession, it is a life or death matter and it requires nothing less than fiery passion and absolute personal conviction. Do not even try to excite others with the thing that we are not even excited about. Do not even think about bring conviction to others when we ourselves are not even under the conviction. Don't even try to inspire the fire to others when you have not acquired the fire yourself. Otherwise it would be all just a wishy-washy waste of your and God's time, and we'd make total fools of ourselves! Remember that one can not give what he or she does not have.

6. Simplicity and clarity of communication

Communication is a very essential part of successful teaching and preaching of the Word. Jesus Christ is the Master Communicator as we see in John 4. He is not only sincere (heart condition), but also simple (true communication—KISS: Kiss It Simple, Stupid!) in His counseling and teaching ministry to the alienated and isolated, empty and hungry Samaritan woman at Jacob's well. To communicate is to arouse curiosity; to communicate is to motivate; to communicate is to understand the audience; to communicate is to clearly see the needs of the audience and to boldly and relevantly speak to them; to communicate is to powerfully present challenges; to communicate is to wisely admonish choices; and to communicate is to cause fundamental and transformative changes in attitudes and activities, belief and behavior, conviction and conducts, as was clearly evidenced in the life of this sinful Samaritan at the noon day of the sixth hour when she did not expect anyone to be around the well.

The Lord is able employ the simple to illustrate the profound, the temporal to point to the eternal, the cultural to the universal, and the earthly to the heavenly. His communication is full of clarity and conviction. His style of communication is simple and yet deep, therefore, simply deep. From being perceived as a hostile Jewish man (v.9), to being a prophet of God (v. 19), to being the Christ (v.29), Jesus eventually was being recognized, revered, welcomed and worshipped as "the Savior of the world!" (John 4:42). What a strong and straight-forward communicator our Lord is! This Samaritan woman herself , as a result of the Jesus influence and impact, became one of His most faithful followers and one of His most productive communicators as many of the Samaritans of that town believed in Jesus "because of the woman's testimony" (v. 39). What a transformational communicator our Lord Jesus is! Praise the Lord! Let us wholeheartedly listen to Jesus, lean on Jesus, live like Jesus, and learn from Him so that we can really lead like Jesus!

7. The concern for the cultural context: sensitivity and relevancy

As all of us can see around us, we live in an increasing multi-cultural and pluralistic society. Our world has quickly become a global village with diverse cultures and all sorts of belief systems. In order to prepare our soul well for ministry in this new era, we must not only be well-informed about the Biblical texts, but also be well-versed and experienced in the human cultural contexts, for the text becomes a pretext when we are not keenly aware of its complex cultural context.

We are all creatures of cultures. Human cultures, no matter whose it is, are neither totally divine nor entirely demonic. They all contain elements which the Lord can help us recognize and use for His purpose, which is the redemption of souls, and not the restoration of cultures. While the culture and its values are constantly changing, the Word of God is forever the same. We must be able to discern, distinguish and discriminate between what is cultural and what is spiritual. We need to also find culturally sensitive means and culturally relevant methods to effectively communicate Christ cross-culturally.

The Lord is neither for nor against any particular human culture; rather He is above and beyond all cultures and simultaneously and actively works in and through all cultures to bring about His plan and purpose of salvation. Remember that the Great Commission is not some kind of great Americanization, but Great Evangelization. We must learn to package ourselves wisely and sensitively in this increasingly hostile world in order to be faithful and fruitful. This takes a lot of soul-searching, prayers, humility and an adjustable strategy. Indeed different folks need different strokes. It is not some kind of underwear sales appeal for "one size fits all". To treat everybody indiscriminately can be itself discrimination. Cultural differences are not necessarily deviances. They need to be taken into serious consideration. Human cultures, as long as they do not violate any clear Scriptural principles, need to be respected and honored and even utilized for our work of ministries. In order to really get ahead with our teaching and preaching ministries, we must learn the art and science of how to get along, for no one can really get ahead until everyone can manage to get along!

8. Don't take the "self" too seriously: let go and let God!

The last but not the least item I personally emphasize in preparing my soul for preaching and teaching is not to allow myself get in the way of God. In fact, I try to forget about myself and concentrate on Him and move along with the guidance of the Holy Spirit in my message. In this regard, Jesus says to all of us: "My food is to do the Will of Him who sent me and to finish His Work (John 4:34). The main thing is to keep the main thing the main thing, and the main thing is Jesus, Jesus and Jesus, and not any of us!

Luke 9:23 commands us to deny ourselves. The world stresses self help. Self image, self confidence, self realization/actualization, self esteem, and self fulfillment. But our Lord emphasizes self-denial, self sacrifice, and even self-death! Remember the acronym EGO— Edging God Out! How to avoid it? Don't take the "self" too seriously. Don't worry about the number of people in attendance, and do not be preoccupied with the number of dollars you want to get out of them! Don't fear about the results. Leave it all to the Lord with all your concerns and cares for He cares for you. You just move forward together in faith with the Holy Spirit after much prayers and study of the Scriptures, approaching the throne of His grace with boldness and confidence, and with absolutely zero logo, zero label, zero title and zero ego! This indeed is the kind of heart God will revive, bless and use!

Conclusion:

Command and teach these things. Do not let anyone look down on you because you are young, but set an example for the believers in speech, in life, in love, in faith and in purity (I Tim 4:11-12). Preach the Word; be prepared in season and out of season; correct, rebuke and encourage—with great patience and careful instruction (II Tim 4:2). Watch your life and doctrine closely. Persevere in them, because if you do, you will save both yourself and your hearers (I Tim 4:16). And if we satisfy His conditions on our part and obey His command, we will hear from Him, saying to us: "Well done, good and faithful servant! You have been faithful in a few things; I will put you in charge of many things. Come and share your Master's happiness!"

Chapter 24
The Pauline Passion In Ministry:
An Acts-20 Summary

Without a doubt whatsoever, the most influential and impactful leader of the early church of Christ Jesus our Lord was none other than Paul, the greatest visionary and missionary apostle. From his brutal persecution of the church, through his dramatic and miraculous conversion, his numerous hardships in the endeavors to spread and expand the Christian faith from both inside and the outside (II Cor 11), and to the very end of his life under house arrest and eventual martyrdom, the dynamic Christ-centered and Kingdom-oriented life of the apostle Paul profoundly touched and moved everyone in contacts with him. If anyone wants to have a life well lived with purpose and passion, Paul would serve as one of the best examples in both words and deeds. This is how the entire book Acts of the Apostles ends (Acts 28:30-31) with Paul under house arrest in Rome waiting for his trial which caused him to lose his life for His savior, Lord and Master Jesus: "For two whole years, Paul stayed there in his own rented house and welcomed all who came to see him. Boldly and without hindrance, he preached the kingdom of God and taught about the Lord Jesus Christ."

Without a question, Paul was the most influential leader then, and we continue to feel his tremendous influence now. But the question we need to ask is, "How did this happen?" and "What can we learn from Paul to make our Christian life and ministries more effective and efficient, more faithful and fruitful for the glorious Kingdom of God?" Paul was extremely effective both as a follower of Jesus and a leader for the Body of Christ because the model of his leadership was Jesus Christ; the motive of his ministry was love; the methods of his ministry were biblical and practical; the motivation of his ministry was passion for the Lord and compassion for souls; the foundation of his ministry was the Holy Scriptures; the guidance of his ministry was the Holy Spirit; the authority of his ministry came from a life of total surrender and reckless abandon; the lubricant for his ministry was the relations in three dimensions; the mark of his ministry was joyful service, the measure of his ministry was suffering and sacrifice; the secret weapon of his mission was prayers; the purpose of his ministry was the exaltation of the savior, edification of the saints and the evangelization of the sinner; and finally the product of Paul's ministry was disciples!

According to Dr. John Maxwell in his *Maxwell Leadership Bible* (p. 1388):

> Paul did not become an influential leader because of his eloquence or because he possessed some special talent withheld from everyone else. Paul gained influence because, regardless of his circumstances—whether he sat in shackles during another interrogation, whether he lay in another cold prison cell, or whether he roamed free to do his work—he stayed committed to the One Thing: preaching the name of Jesus . . . through all of this, Paul never failed to vigorously and courageously defend and preach the gospel of Jesus Christ . . . Wise leaders today will do well to follow Paul's example by purposefully taking the Word of God both to the body of Christ and to the unbelieving world.

Of all the convicting epistles of and moving recording about Paul the apostle in Acts, nothing touches me more personally and profoundly than Acts chapter 20, where Paul bid his very last farewell to his disciples, the Ephesian elders (vv. 17-38). I was moved to tears more than once when I read it all the way till the end, the last three verses (vv. 36-38), "When he had said this, he knelt down with all of them and prayed. They all wept as they embraced him and kissed him. What grieved them the most was his statement that they would never see his face again…"

Let us take a serious spiritual look at this purpose, passion and power packed passage in Acts 20:17-38, and let us examine and explore intelligently and diligently so as to draw out ten principal principles and life lessons to assist ourselves to become better servants of the Lord Jesus just like the Apostle Paul was. For the apostle Paul himself inspired and challenged us to "follow my example, as I follow the example of Christ." (I Cor 11:1). "Whatever you have learned or received or heard from me, or seen in me—put it into practice. And the God of peace will be with you." (Phil 4:9).

1. Living a life of transparency and authenticity. He practiced the life lesson of not merely talking the talk, but literally walking the walk (v. 18). Indeed transparency produces trust which is essential and fundamental to any real relationship; and authenticity release the spiritual anointing and brings to you the Kingdom authority to win battles and live in physical, financial, relational, psychological and spiritual victory!

2. Serving the Lord with diligence and humility. He sowed in tears

with many tests of persecution first, and then he could expect to reap and harvest with great joy (v. 19). God hates not only arrogance, but also laziness for it is useless for the Kingdom of heaven. God always blesses humility of heart and diligence of our lives! Psalm 126:5-6 assures us that "those who sow in tears will reap in joy. He who continually goes forth weeping, bearing seed for sowing, shall doubtless come again with rejoicing, bringing his sheaves with him." No sowing, no harvesting; No pains, no gains, No process, no product; No bearing the cross, no wearing the crown! Ultimately, there is no promise without premise! This is a life lesson that can be applied in any area with anyone no matter what place!

3. Teaching and preaching with decisiveness of the mind and integrity of the heart. Paul was the same inside out and the same in public as he was in private, proclaiming the whole counsel of God and the full Gospel of Christ with total determination and without any slight hesitation whatsoever (vv. 20 & 27). He was direct to the points always and did not have any time or intention to beat around the bush.

4. The centrality of Paul's preaching: repentance of sin and faith in the Lord Jesus (v. 21). True repentance includes two realizations: our sinfulness and God's holiness (Isaiah 6); it also involves two necessary turns: turn away from sin and turn toward God! John the Baptist and Jesus the savior both vehemently and uncompromisingly preached repentance, for the Kingdom of God is at hand! "And repentance and forgiveness of sins shall be preached in His name to all nations, beginning at Jerusalem." (Luke 24:47).

5. Faith is a verb, and faith in God is action, without necessarily knowing all the details of the trials and troubles (v. 22-23). What Paul said and did here reminds us of what was said of Abraham the father of faith, "By faith Abraham, when called to go to a place he would later receive as his inheritance, obeyed and went, even though he did not know where he was going." (Heb 11:8). When we know beyond the shadow of a doubt that we are going with God, God is with us, and that He will never leave us or forsake us (Heb 13:5), this blessed assurance of who we are going with makes the questions of when and where and how unimportant. For we know that if god is with us and for us, who then can be against us!

6. Here lies the very key to a life of victory—Acts 20:24: self-denial, self-sacrifice, self-death with steadfastness! "I consider my life worth nothing to me, if only I may finish the race and complete the task the Lord Jesus has given me—the task of testifying to the gospel

of God's grace." What devotion and dedication! What conviction
and consecration! How worthy of our imitation and emulation is this
marvelous and miraculous life of singular focus and unwavering
purpose! Hallelujah and Praise the Lamb! Let us all humble ourselves
before God and learn from Paul, just as Paul followed Jesus (I Cor 11:1)
and just as Jesus bids us to "take my yoke upon you and learn from
me, for I am gentle and humble in heart, and you will find rest for your
souls." (Matt 11:29).

In Acts 20:24, the Apostle Paul clearly implies that the Christian life
is a race toward God who manifested Himself through His only son Jesus
Christ and is a race toward the Kingdom of God. It is a race of God's
grace, a race that demands discipline and diligence, a race that requires
stamina and urgency, working out our salvation with both fear and
trembling (Phil 2:12). AS he eloquently writes in I Corinthians 9:24-27:

> Do you not know that in a race all the runners run, but only one
> gets the prize? Run in such as a way as to get the prize. Everyone
> who competes in the games goes into strict training. They do it
> to get a crown that will not last; but we do it to get a crown that
> will last forever. Therefore I do not run like a man beating the
> air. No, I beat my body and make it my slave so that after I have
> preached to others, I myself will not be disqualified for the prize.

The purposeful and passionate Paul always preached what he
practiced, and practiced what he always preached. No hypocrisy
whatsoever! In fact, the Bible records that Paul even rebuked and
opposed Peter to his face in front of all the others for his hypocrisy
because Peter was afraid of the Jews who insisted on circumcision (Gal
2:11-13). At the end of his life and right before his departure to the
eternal life with the Lord, Paul concluded that, "I have fought the good
fight, I have finished the race, I have kept the faith." (II Tim 4:7). Praise
the Lord for this spiritual grace race to meet Jesus in the heavenly place!
Amen! Let us run to win the battle; let us run to finish the assigned
task, and let us run steadily and swiftly to complete the Lord's great
Commission—Until All Have Heard the Gospel of the Grace of God!

7. The good and true shepherd of the Lord always does two most
essential and indispensable things for the sheep: to provide (vv.20 & 27)
and to protect (vv. 29-31). Paul as a great pastor of the Lord's church
provided the elders at Ephesus with the solid and healthy life-giving
Bread, the Word of God. He also protected the sheep by pointers to and
warnings against the "savage wolves" that would rise and distort the truth

to draw people unto themselves. He warned each of them night and day with tears about the coming seducers and deceivers so that these leaders would be on their guards at all times! The Lord also warns us to be watchful and prayerful so that we will not fall into temptation or satanic traps by being prayerlessly and carelessly lazy, dreamy and sleepy. Jesus the Lord points out a hard truth that indeed the spirit is willing, but the body is weak (Mark 14:38).

8. Leaders must firmly fix their own oxygen masks before attempting to assist any others (v. 28). First of all, keep watch over yourselves, your life and doctrines closely, carefully and prayerfully in such areas of speech, love, faithfulness and purity in motive and motion. Be a good example to others. One lesson we can learn here in life is that one can not give what he or she does not have. Then watch over the flock, the church of God which the Lord bought with His own precious blood! Here is this vital verse, Paul teaches us another major life lesson: the Law of the picture – people do what people see, for talk is cheap (Matt 5:16).

9. Paul lifts up the absolute authority and complete centrality of the Word of God (v. 32). Only by God's grace and the power of God's Word, can we be edified, sanctified and assured of the blessed eternal inheritance waiting for us as we endure to the end! God's Word is saving Word and he who endures to the end shall be saved (Matt 24:23). God's Word is sanctifying Word. Jesus prayed to God the Father to "sanctify them with you truth, for your Word is truth" (John 17:17). In the Christian life, nothing is more important and indispensable than the infallible and indestructible Word of God's grace. As a matter of fact, the Word of God, as the sword of the Spirit, is quick and powerful, sharper than any double-edged sword (Heb 4:12). It is unshakeable, unmovable, unstoppable and unchangeable! It is the foundation and perpetuation of our victory in Jesus Christ!

10. Finally, Paul by biblical precepts and personal example warns against covetousness and greedy, encourages hard work and challenges Christians everywhere to give in order to get rid of greed and get the gospel of God spread all over the world (vv. 33-35). Just like he instructed believers in several other places, Paul urges us to keep our lives free from the love of money, for the love of money is the root of all kinds of evil with many deadly consequences (I Tim 6). Instead of trying to get and garner more for ourselves to spend on our own pleasure and prestige, we must work hard to make money so that we can become self-supporting first, work hard to save money as good stewards of God, and work hard to give away money for the glorious cause of His

eternal Kingdom, with joy and generosity! Since God so loved the world that he gave His only begotten Son Jesus to redeem us, we then should follow Jesus' command to us, "Give, and it shall be given to you. A good measure, pressed down, shaken together and running over, will be poured into your lap. For with the same measure you use, it will be measured to you." (Luke 6:38). "It is more blessed to give than to receive" (Acts 20:35).

Paul the apostle was unquestionably a unique and effective leader of the Christian faith of all times. In order to be a spiritual and Godly leader of the Pauline kind, we must learn from his purpose, passion and optimism! His call was clearly from the Lord (Acts 9), and his purpose was the advancement of God's Kingdom! Paul had a strong passion for ministries and a deep abiding optimism because of the blessed assurance of his ultimate destination as Christ in Him was the hope of glory. (Col 1:27). What a passion-packed passage from the purpose-driven, power-filled Paul (Acts 20:17-38)! Amen! Hallelujah!

Chapter 25
Go Tell It on the Mountain:
The Big G's of God and Man

As one studies the Word in depth, she or he will inevitably discover many of the great divine attributes or characteristics of God. In addition, our beautiful, wonderful, merciful, faithful and powerful Lord Jesus also expects us to respond to Him with certain obligations or duties. In this last chapter, I will selectively share a few of the divine attributes and our own human responsibilities as the children of God.

I. **The Attributes of God: The Lord God He is Good, Great, Gracious, and Glorious!**

1. **The Goodness of God**

Without any doubt whatsoever, we do have and we do serve a good God. This indeed should be the first thing we must be keenly aware of when we come to the thoughts and the presence of our God. Psalm 100:5 declares to us that the Lord our God He is good; His mercies are new every morning and are everlasting, and His truth endures throughout all generations! And surely and certainly His goodness and His love will follow me all the days of my life, and I will dwell in the house of the Lord forever (Ps 23:6)! Thank the Lord and praise the Lord for all His goodness toward us!

The devil comes to steal, kill and destroy, but our good Lord, the Good Shepherd Jesus (John 10:14-15) has come so that we may have life, the abundantly blessed life here and now on earth, and also the blessed eternal life with Him and all the saints there and then in our heavenly home! He created the earth and the whole universe to bless us with fresh air, beautiful sunshine, clear water and ample supplies of resources for all our needs. He loved us so much that He gave His one and only Son to die on the cross for our iniquities and transgression while we were still sinners not knowing what we were doing! The perfect love of God has cast out all our fear which has to do with torment. There is no fear in His love (I Jh 4:18). This God who loves us so much with such great depth, width, length and heights is really a good God. As soon as we truly believe that He is a good God, positive faith and extraordinary successes will all come to us. When we have faith, deep abiding faith in His unchanging goodness, we will prosper because this good God desires for His children to prosper in all things, in good health and especially in our special spiritual relationship of intimacy with Himself (III Jh 2). Let this good Lord be magnified in all areas and all the aspects of your life. He takes pleasure (delights) in the prosperity of His servants and children (Ps 35:27). There is absolutely zero doubt about any of these promises from our Good Shepherd of Psalm 23 and John 10.

2. The Greatness of God

The Lord our God is not only good; He is great, and greatly to be praised; He is to be feared above all gods (Ps 96:4). The Lord our great God is indeed great in promise, great in purpose and great in power! While we always thank the Lord for His goodness to us, we must also praise Him and reverence Him for His mighty greatness! Because of His greatness, we are protected from the evil one, simply because greater is He who lives in us than he who is of the world (I Jh 4:4). Because of His greatness, let us never become lukewarm or mediocre, but strive always to be great in faithfully following Jesus and faithfully serving Him with joy and gladness in His kingdom! Anyone can be great in the sight of the great God if he or she is willing and humble and obedient to serve, for the greatness of the kingdom is found in the faithful service with the right attitude of humility and obedience. This great God expects greatness from all of us by our faithful and humble service for Him, just as the Lord came to serve us as a humble divine servant (Mt 20:20-28,). Thus Jesus sets us an example and sends us an eternal message about kingdom greatness, challenging us to serve as lowly servants (Jh 13:15-17) instead of being obsessed with images and status, positions, privileges and prestige. In so doing, we will be greatly blessed of Him in His Kingdom as He promises us in no uncertain terms. Perhaps few of us can do great things in this life, but all of us can do small things with great love, with the love of God in our heart! Let all we do be done in love and humility.

3. The Grace of God

Nehemiah 9:17: But you are a forgiving God, gracious and compassionate, slow to anger and abounding in love. Therefore You did not desert them.

II Corinthians 13:14: The grace of the Lord Jesus Christ, and the love of God, and the communion of the Holy Spirit be with you all. Amen.

The will of God will not take you to where the grace of God can not keep you! That is the truth we all can trust. We are saved by His grace, sanctified by His grace, freely justified by His grace through our faith in Jesus, Spirit-baptized by His grace and we shall be glorified with Him by His grace! As the Word of God incarnated and the only-begotten of the Father, Jesus the Lord is always full of grace and truth (Jh 1:14, 17). We are who we are only by the amazing and effectual grace of God and His grace toward us is not in vain, as Paul declares in I Cor 15:10. The grace of God is our undeserved unmerited favors He so kindly and bountifully bestows on us. In our sin and rebellion against God, we should have been deserted or even destroyed, but He gives us grace—unmerited favors we certainly do not deserve, as Nehemiah 9 describes in details. Moreover, the grace of God is also the power of God active and operative in our lives to overcome the self, sin, and satanic attacks of all sorts. It assures us the victory through our faith in the Lord if we do not give up or lose heart. We shall overcome, by His grace and for His glory! Amen!

4. The Glory of God

The God we have and we serve is not only good, great, and gracious, He is also glorious! James 2:1 declares our identity as brothers and believers "in our glorious Lord Jesus Christ." The coming day of the Lord is said to be "great and glorious" in Acts 2:20. We are to praise His glorious name for ever (Ps 72:19). The deeds of our God are not only mighty and majestic, but also glorious indeed (Ps 111:3). His presence is glorious (Is 3:8). This glorious God will supply all our need according to the glorious riches in Christ Jesus our Lord (Phil 4:19). When the Spirit of the Lord comes upon us, we are always filled with joy unspeakable and full of His glory (I Pet 1:8). This joy of the Lord which is our strength (Neh 8:10), will propel and compel us to go all out to preach "the glorious gospel of the blessed God" (I Tim 1:11). Praise the Lord for the Gospel of God's grace and the Gospel of God's glory that we should daily experience and diligently share with all the others! In times of opposition and persecution, we must stand firm for the Lord no matter what the cost. Rejoice that

195

you have the privilege to participate in the sufferings of Christ so that you may be overjoyed by His glory to be revealed to you when the Spirit of Glory and of God rests on you (I Pet 4:13-14). I have personally experienced the truth of this promise when being arrested and locked up in China for preaching the Gospel of Christ and teaching the Word of God. What a joy I had! Hallelujah to the Lamb!

II. The Responsibilities of the Disciples: Let us Grow, Glow, Give and Go!

If we fail to plan, we will plan to fail. We either organize or agonize; either evangelize or fossilize; if we do not grow and go, we will dry and die!

1. Let Us Grow

We are commanded by the apostle to grow in the grace and knowledge of our Lord and Savior Jesus Christ (II Pet 3:18). Just as Jesus our Lord grew in wisdom and stature, and in favor with God and men (Lk 2:52), we must also become active in our daily healthy growth in the Lord! In order to grow healthy as faithful followers of Jesus, we must delve deep into the studies and meditation of the Word of God the standard and the source of our authority and power for the victorious Christian life. We must spend time privately in solitude and prayers as Jesus did, cultivating our inner intimacy, relation, character and passion like Jesus the Lord!

In addition, we must put our faith in action before we can see some healthy and spiritual growth. Let us not forsake the regular assembling of ourselves together in Jesus name, to worship and praise the King of Kings and the Lord of Lords. Let us be active in church work, kingdom service and social activities for righteousness and justice for all. Let us serve the needy, the poor and the powerless with a cup of cold water in the name of Jesus. We grow and learn the deep things of God and man when we get informed, inspired and involved to serve, applying and practicing His Word in this dark, lost, sinful, desperate and dying world.

2. Let Us Glow

If we are following, we will be fishing (Mk 1:17, Lk 5:1-11). Likewise, if we are really growing as we are supposed to, then we will certainly be glowing. One can never show you the one if he or she does not even know the way. Just as you can not show what you do not know, we can not glow if we do not grow; and when we grow, we do glow with the glorious love, life and light of the Lord! "You are the light of the world. A city on a hill can not be hidden... In the same way, let you light shine before men, that they may see your good deeds, and praise your Father in heaven." (Matt 5:14, 16). This little light of mine, I am going to let it shine, let it shine and let it shine! Don't hide your light! We are to shine like starts in the universe as we hold out the Word of life in this crooked and depraved generation (Phil 2:15-16). There are basically to ways to shine you're the light: be a mirror of reflection, and be a candle that gives lights. It is much wiser and better to light a candle in the midst of darkness than just to curse the darkness! Share His life, show His love and by all means, shine His light, with real concrete actions of compassion, and with words if necessary! Now that we know these principles and truths, we will be blessed abundantly and rewarded generously if we will go all out and do them as the Lord Jesus did (Matt 9:35).

3. Let Us Give

For our good, great, gracious and glorious God so loved us that He gave, we who are so richly blessed and highly favored should do just the same as He has shown us and for all that He has done for us (Jh 13:15). We are commanded to "give" and the Lord will give back to us, much more than we can ever give (Lk 6:38), not only in the life to come, but even in this very present age (Mk 10:29-31) as we give ourselves for the sake of Christ and the Gospel. We do not give in order to just get more; rather we give because He gave us first, and we give because we love God and love people! We love Him because He first loved us. Let us not only closely guard our hearts against the devil, particularly the devil of greed; let us also give our hearts completely and unreservedly to the Lord and His call and His cause of the Great Commission! Let us willingly and eagerly and enthusiastically give all our heart, all our mind, all our soul, all our strength, all ourselves to the Master and to His kingdom service; and then we will encounter the fulfillment and the fullness of the life that really matters eternally!

4. Let Us Go

"Go and do likewise," Jesus commanded the law expert in Luke

10:37, and He still calling us all to "go into all the world and to preach the gospel to all creation." Go and Do as Jesus went and did (Mt 9:35)! We can not do if we do not go. A turtle is going nowhere however if it is not willing to stick its head out. Have you heard His call yet? When are you ever going to return His call? And how do you intend to respond to Jesus calling? Nothing will happen if we do not "go and do likewise," if we do not obey the example set forth for us by Jesus! Action, decisive and consistent action, is the foundation for your victory, success and prosperity in life as your soul continues to prosper in the Lord!

The key to victory is obedience, and the Peter Principle is the power of obedience in life and missions (Acts 5:29, see also I Sam 15:22). Obedience will fill your inside with confidence. Your obedience will bring down His great abundance and His divine and supernatural guidance. If the Lord Jesus, being the Son of God and Son of man, had to humble himself and learn to be obedient in the natural to the command of the heavenly Father (Phil 2:8, Heb 5:8), how much more should we His followers and disciples humble ourselves and obey His Great Commissions?! This takes great courage and courage is the first of all human virtues, for there is no virtue without courage. Be strong and very courageous because our Lord through His Holy Spirit will definitely go with us and go before us. Going without praying is very foolish, but praying earnestly without going courageously is very hypocritical. The last time I checked, it seemed and still seems to me that the Lord is not very fond of either hypocrisy or the hypocrites! Therefore, let us boldly and bravely behave in accordance with our beliefs; Let us align our lives and our activities with the Great Commission in the right attitude and spirit of the Great Commandment. Let us move with pure motives; Let us practice what we preach. In the holy name of Jesus and with the power of the Holy Spirit, let us go with His goal and go for the gold—the crown of life with righteousness and glory! By His grace and for His glory, we must go before He comes!

A Summary of Fifty Fifty:
50 Life Lessons in 50 Years of Life
Effective Strategies for Living the Victories

Now at the age of fifty years, I start to wonder and ponder afresh and anew at life itself in general, and at my personal life in particular, with plenty of reflections and reexaminations. My soul echoes the sentiment and the sound as that of the influential Rabbi Harold Kushner (1986, p.155, p.162)), one of my all-time favorite authors:

Now at 50, I am not ready to die, and I hope to live many more years, but I am not afraid of dying because I feel satisfied with what I have done with my life, not wasted it, but lived with integrity, done my best, and had an impact on people who will outlast me . . . The question is not "What's life have in store for me?" but "What am I doing with my life?" . . . There is no way to prevent dying, but the cure for the fear of death is to make sure you have lived!

How then, shall we live, and live in victories as the good and gracious, precious and powerful Lord Jesus Christ has promised us in the Word of God? Here is a list of summaries with my personal top fifty life lessons at my fifty years of age. I simply call it fifty fifty (50/50). Please permit me to share them with you below, with my sincere and strong desires that they will encourage and empower your life with successes and victories as well. As the wise and famous Elie Wiesel once said, "Not to transmit an experience is to betray it" (www.Jewish-wisdom.com). Now I will transmit some vital lessons to you from my life experiences:

1. Back to the Basic: The Word, the Word and the Word (John 1:1) with the two centers of the Decalogue of the OT (Exodus 20) and the Sermon on the Mount (Matt 5-7) of the NT.

2. Back to the Basic: Walk in the Spirit (Ephesians 5:18, Galatians 5:16, Acts 1:8, 10:38)

3. The Great Commandment (Mark 12:30): to know Christ personally! The Great Commission (Mark 16:15): to make Christ Known globally!

4. Always follow the Golden Rule (Matthew 7:12). This is the law of reciprocity.

Always fulfill the Royal Law (James 2:8).

5. Trust deep, aim high, work hard, love much, live well and die laughing

6. Practice the Peter Principle: Obedience is better than all the sacrifices (I Sam 15:22, Acts 5:29). Obedience and diligence work well together to bring confidence and abundance! This takes resilience and discipline. A disciple without discipline is a disgrace and a disaster!

7. A balanced life is a beautiful life; A broken life is a blessed life (Mark 14:22)

8. Live a life that matters, by intentional choice, and not by random chance.

9. It is always the right time and the right place to do the right thing for the right reason, not for the potential rewards or the applauses of others, but simply because it is the right thing to do.

10. Always keep the faith with enthusiasm, for that faith you keep will always keep you in abundant prosperity and glorious victory (Heb 11:1, 6, I John 5:4, III John verse 2)!

11. Do not fear and do not worry (Mark 5:36, Acts 27:24, Ezekiel 2:6, Matthew 6:25-33, Philippians 4:6-7, I Peter 5:7). Trust and obey for there is no other way!

12. Remember to first submit to God and then resist the devil (James 4:7). Remember and make sure to always "fix your own mask before assisting others": first heed, and then lead (Acts 20:28, I Timothy 4:16).

13. Remember that humility of heart is your best friend in life and ministries, and pride is your worst enemy and would be your worst nightmare if you don't humble yourself (I Peter 5:5-6).

14. Remember that today matters (Joshua 24:15, Psalm 118:24, Heb 11:1). Yesterday is already history, tomorrow is still a mystery, and today is a gift. That's why we call it "the present".

15. The Laws of Life, Love and Light (John 10:10, 14:6, 3:16, 13:34-35, 8:12, Matt 5:14, 16): The more we give, the more we will receive. Share His life; show His love; shine His light!

16. The Law of the Source and the resources: You can not give what you do not have!

17. The Law of the harvest: Sowing in tears and reaping with joy (Psalm 126:5-6).

18. The Law of the Picture: People do what people see. Nothing is more powerful in influencing people than setting an excellent example before them (John 13:15, I Cor 11:1, Matt 5:16, I Tim 4:12, I Peter 5:3).

19. The Law of the Solid Ground: Trust is the foundation of all relationship and leadership. Being trusted is a greater compliment than being loved. Trust and travel go together.

20. The Law of Sacrifice: Learn to get along to get ahead; to give up in order to go up. No pains, no gains; no sacrifices, no successes; no excesses, no successes; to succeed is to exceed what's expected (Matt 5:40-41); in order to wear the crown in the future, one must bear the cross in the present (Rev 2:10)!

21. Remember the very first ingredient of relationship and leadership: integrity, without which there would be zero positive impact and constructive influence (Job 2: 3, 9-10).

22. Always remember and be constantly reminded: Who called you and Whom you work for and will give an account to (Colossians 3:23-24, Acts 27:23).

23. Remember to value people above things because the most important things in life are not things at all! They are faith, family and friends—upward with God, inward with self and outward with others. And people do not care how much we know until they know how much we care! And if we care, we will share; only when we share, we show that we really care!

24. Hold unto the things of this world loosely and lightly, but hold unto God and the Word of Life very tightly (Gen 32:22-30).

25. Life is burdensome at times, so travel light; shed light; keep things tight; do things right and treat people right; be careful to pick the fight and be prepared to fight the good fight; and don't ever become trite!

26. The first lesson on leadership is followership, for one must follow the Leader, the Lord faithfully before he or she can lead effectively and fruitfully (Mark 1:17, Luke 5:11, John 21:19,22, I Cor 11:1).

27. The first task of an effective leader is to develop and define core values; then concentrate on your core values which lead to vision, vigor, valor and victory. Don't sweat the small stuff (Matt 6:25-31).

28. Focus your attention on faith, have faith in God, and always try to look on the brighter side of all peoples and all things.

29. Closely watch your attitude which determines your altitude; Make wise choices based on the wisdom of God: choose to bless and not curse, to be better and not bitter, to be grateful and not grumpy, to rejoice over what's left and not regret about what's lost, to be regenerative and not stagnant, to be active, positive and not passive and negative, to be optimistic, hopeful rather than pessimistic and hopeless (Deuteronomy

32-33)! Human disappointments can be divine appointments; your worst adversity is most likely your best university!

30. Stop perfuming that skunk; start dealing with the real root causes (I Sam 16:7, Prov 4:23, Isaiah 29:13, Matt 23:25-28); causes and cures always go together.

31. The root always determines the fruit (Luke 6:43-45): heart of availability before hand of ability (Luke 10:38-42). Motive of the heart is more important than motion of the hand.

32. Always genuinely and purposefully bless and touch a heart first before you ever ask for a hand. This is the law of connection: deposit first before you can withdraw!

33. Character Counts the most: Character before charisma, and charisma without character causes catastrophe! Sound and solid character is one's empowering center and core from which all life's energies flow! If I take care of my character, my reputation will take care of itself.

34. Ritualistic religion without intimate relation is pure spiritual prostitution (Matt 7:21-23).

35. Don't be oblivious to the obvious: Priority, purpose and purity before power, passion and productivity (Matthew 6:33). Put the first thing first; Keep the main thing the main thing!

36. A Principled life is a powerful and prosperous life. Nothing can bring you lasting peace and prosperity but the triumph of principles. Live your life by the principles of the Word and not by the pleasures of the world. Always follow unchanging principles of God and not the unreliable persons of charisma! You will never be disillusioned if you refuse to live in any illusion.

37. Meditate on the life analogy of the compass and the clock: direction and action.

38. Meditate on Aesop's fable of the Goose and the Golden Egg: Don't be impatient and never get greedy! Take care of your asset and you will be taken care of!

39. Be thrifty and frugal: If you will take care of your pennies, your dollars will take care of themselves. If your income is smaller than your outgo, then your upkeep will be your downfall! Be a savior and sustainer of life and life's resources in order to be a blessing to many others.

40. Be aware of the devilish dagger (I John 2:16): the luster and lure of money (possessions), sex (pleasures), and powers (the root of pride).

41. Be aware of "the tyranny of the urgent," for what is urgent is not

always what is important; and what is important is always urgent! Carry out the will of God with divine authority, divine energy and a strong sense of urgency (Matt 20:1-16, John 4:34-35, 9:4).

42. Be aware of "the deceit of the visible," for Satan and his workers (even in the church now) do masquerade themselves as angels and apostles of light (II Cor 11:13-15) to try to deceive, distract and destroy many, as they have already.

43. Be aware of "the danger of the gradual," for we can be "cooked" without even knowing it due to our craving for creaturely comforts, and thus complacence, lukewarmness like "the frog in the kettle," and like King Solomon.

44. Have something bigger, brighter and better than yourself to believe in: God and His promises.

Have someone to love and to be loved by: Families and friends Have something meaningful and significant to do here and now: work as a call. Have some common sense, for nothing is more uncommon than common sense! Have somewhere exciting and eternal to look forward to there and then: home in heaven with the Lord Jesus Christ. What a glorious day that will be!!!

45. Face your past with gratitude, your present with purpose, your future with confidence.

46. There is no wisdom without patience: Just as the distance of the journey reveals the strength of the horse, so only the duration of the times tests the condition of one's heart!

47. Intentionality + responsibility = maturity; Declaration of lips + demonstration with lives = credibility; Focus + consistency = victory; Learn win from within, "Because the Kingdom of God is within you" (Luke 17:20-21)

48. "Trust but verify always" (Acts 17:11) in working with people. Make your promises very carefully, prayerfully and infrequently! Once made, keep your promises, for it is the cornerstone of responsibility which is the defining characteristic of your maturity.

49. The longest distance in life is the one between the talk and the walk, between the idea and the act. Do what you say and say what you do; practice what you preach and preach what you practice (Matthew 23:3), for God loves authenticity and hates hypocrisy! Action is the foundation of victory and prosperity. Therefore go and do likewise, and you will be bountifully blessed in this life and the next to come (Luke 10:37, John 13:15-17). Well done is always much better than well said

(Benjamin Franklin & Matt 25:23).

50. Go make disciples: starting straight locally and finishing strong globally because one can't reproduce globally what he is not locally!

Epilogue

Starting Straight and Finishing Strong:

The Heart Desire of Yang Hong

Acts 20:24: I consider my life worth nothing to me, if only I may finish the race and complete the task the Lord Jesus has given me—the task of testifying to the Gospel of God's grace.

I Timothy 4:12: Do not let anyone look down on you because you are young, but set an example for the believers in speech, in life, in love, in faith and in purity.

II Timothy 4:6-8: For I am already being poured out like a drink offering, and the time has come for my departure. I have fought the good fight, I have finished the race, I have kept the faith. Now there is in store for me the crown of righteousness, which the Lord, the righteous Judge, will award to me on that day—and not only to me, but also to all who have longed for His appearing.

Luke 2:52: And Jesus grew in wisdom and stature, and in favor with God and men.

John 4:34: "My food," said Jesus, "is to do the will of Him who sent me and to finish His work."

John 17: 1, 4: Father, the time has come... I have brought you glory on earth by completing the work you gave me to do.—Jesus

John 19:30: When he had received the drink, Jesus said, "It is finished." With that, He bowed his head and gave up His spirit.

At 30 years of age, one should be well established in life; at 40 years of age, one should have no confusion about life; and at 50 years of age, one should know the will of God concerning his life!—Ancient Chinese Proverb.

Arthur Rubinstein: "I have found that if you love life, life will love you back." (*www.lifequotes.com*)

The Bible declares what God desires.

What really matters the most in life is not how you started but how you finish; not where you came from, but where you are going; not what has happened to you, but what you make out of what happened and how you respond to it. It's your responsibility, your decision and your choice. "If it is to be, it is up to me!" Now, it's up to you!

Remember that the true measure of life, along with its victories and successes, in the final analysis, is not the trophies we take, but the legacy we make. Don't waste any time. Don't waste your life. Ask God to teach you to number your days aright so that you may gain a heart of wisdom (Ps 90:12). Then choose to live your life purposefully, actively, positively and optimistically because your life really matters. Your life matters upward to God; it matters inward to yourself, and it matters outward to countless others over whom you have certain degrees and measures of influence. Live a life that will bring glory and praise to God, a life that will fill you with meaning, purpose, joyful fulfillment and abundant peace, a life that will make a lasting difference in other people's lives! Live a life that will leave a legacy behind.

Life lessons from the Chinese <<E-Jing>>:
The Book of Transitions

Ironically those who may be best equipped to handle the challenges of the present and the uncertainties of the future are also the ones who will delve most profoundly into the proven traditional wisdom of the past. In our contemporary Western society, we have been subconsciously indoctrinated into believing in the Horatio Alger myth—that if you are super smart and work terribly hard, your life will certainly be a steady progression of endless accomplishments and achievements, from having nothing to having it all. This is the so-called "American Dream," "making it" from rags to riches. While admittedly this is an effective managerial strategy of motivation which often works well in stable times of prosperity and success, yet in times of transitions and tensions with numerous cuts and reductions in budgets and personnel, this model causes many of us to question why we who are supposedly pretty smart and do work so hard, nevertheless still have so many things in life spun out of control, leaving us feeling less satisfied and less fulfilled than we should.

However, traditional wisdom from the distant past can have many valuable life lessons to offer us both for our present and for our future. The ancient Chinese model of thinking and reasoning proposed by the famous E-Jing (literally meaning: the Bible on Transitions), provides us with a positive, powerful and thus productive paradigm for self-evaluation, examination and critical reflection, especially in seemingly unpromising times of staleness and stagnation, and even gloom and doom. In this particular model, the world is viewed as an interplay between two opposing forces such as creativity and destruction, expansion and contraction, success and failure, advance and retreat.

Each of these forces are in a constant movement of strengthening and weakening in that when a force gets strong enough, it will eventually peak and turn into its opposites. The cycles of life are continual and inevitable, not subject to any human wills or wishes, constant in change and dynamic in transition, for the only constant one can count on in life is the perpetual change itself.

E-Jing teaches that while there are certain things a person can do to strengthen and temporarily prolong the desired upward mobility of the life cycle, just as useful and productive is the wisdom of learning how to make the most out of the downward aspects without turning inwardly against oneself with self blame and self hate, thus wearing oneself out with a useless resistance against changes. When life is turned upside down as it will be once a while, perhaps it is time for us to learn lessons from the upper side of down.

Standing in stark contrast to the "success syndrome" of our Western philosophies in which we are driven to the very limit (often under the gun) to perform and push through our feelings and circumstances, attempting to impose "successes" on all situations by the sheer force of the human will, human ingenuity, institutional engineering and through methods of controlling and manipulating key environmentally confounding variables, E-Jing emphasizes the traditional Chinese values, virtues and worth of patience, perseverance, endurance, clear self-examination of realistic human limitations, the necessity of internal retreats, surrender, and acceptance. These are the pathway to personal renewal and spiritual revival. It is a time of preparation for the rebuilding of momentum for the upswing of the cycles of life.

In this insightful Chinese philosophy, there is an emphasis on the power of the will to carry through and "get things done." The force of the human will certainly have its purpose when occasions call for it. But the wisdom of always knowing whose you are, and thus who you are, and where you are in life at any given time on your own personal cycle is far more essential and foundational. Indeed, it is the key to authentic power, true success and victorious living. As the wise man once says, there is a time for everything and a season for every activity, a time to birth and a time for death, a time to push through and a time to pull back, a time to leap forward and a time to wait in silence and patience.

When faced with certain losses for instance, it is possible to retreat early in the process with your dignity intact and strength preserved for an alternative approach at a later time, rather than waiting too long and missing your moment. This wisdom teaches people a far more useful and therapeutic concept of life than how to merely resist failures and achieve successes at any costs. It enlightens us on how to fail "successfully," gracefully, nondestructively and unfatally.

E-Jing employs the vivid imagery of water flowing down the stream as an object lesson on how to succeed in a long run. When faced with an obstacle, the water will simply flow around it or over it towards its goal or destiny. In case the obstacle is too big to overflow, the water will pile up patiently on itself, little by little, bit by bit, consistently generating its own new momentum. Eventually, the water flows over the obstacle and continues its progress with its course on the other side. At times, the flow of the water will be forced to change its course in an entirely new and different direction due to the landscape, but ultimately it still reaches its destination in spite of the dead ends and detours, twists and turns. It does not give up its flow until and unless it reaches its goal! That is the resilience we all need indeed!

Several significant life lessons can be learned from this concept or image. If one is not provincially minded or short-sighted, and if one is willing to take a long-term view of things from an eternal perspective, and if one brings along with him patience, consistency, faith and humility to the journey of life, it will become apparent that even obstacles, limitations, stagnation and temporary setbacks have their own constructive purposes for future progresses as preparation for victories and successes! On the other hand, even times of prosperity and victory can be fraught with dangers and snares as well, E-Jing maintains. In times of success, one must learn to be self-controlled and not lose his "cool" while feeling "hot" inside the head with excitements. Times of success have the inherent danger of causing one to become proud and arrogant, aloof from and out of touch with, reality. One can become incautious, complacent, indolent and indulgent with a sense of entitlement and elitism. Moreover, one must know that the very fact of "success" automatically and inevitably draws increased amount of fierce competition, greed, envy, hatred, and other kinds of challenges both physical and psychological. Vice verse, the times of obstacle and crisis are not necessarily destructive either. As a matter of fact, the Chinese words for "crisis" are composed of two profoundly compound characters: "Wei-Ji," meaning respectively and simultaneously, "danger and opportunity". In the midst of dangerous obstacles and oppositions, there are also new found opportunities, opportunities for serious self-examination and evaluation, preparation and edification so as to rise again and launch out into the deep when the appropriate occasion presents itself.

Finally E-Jing helps us to look at changes naturally and learn to manage changes both internal and external, positively and productively. When a person can not change the circumstances, he or she is responsible to check on his attitude, and if necessary, change the attitude towards the circumstances. In life, it is often the small thing that makes the big difference. That small thing is none other than one's attitude, and the big difference is none other than being positive. Therefore our right attitude is the small thing that can and will make the big positive difference. Our inward attitude determines our outward altitude. I have discovered that most of the time, I do not have a problem, for I am the problem, and that problem is often attitudinal in nature. Many of life's crises come as a result of the crisis within us, within our erroneous, irrational and illogical belief and value systems, within our wrong, poor, sour or bad attitudes. Indeed it is true to a large extent that our greatest challenges are not before us, nor behind us, they are in fact within us! Likewise, our greatest resource of resilience resides also within us, even the kingdom of God is "within you" (Luke 17:20-21).

Learning to get along well and live harmoniously with ourselves is an arduous task. With the right faith perspective and the positive life attitude, we will become constructive and not destructive; we will become better and become bitter; we will be the active thermostats, and not the reactive and passive thermometers; we will be victors over our circumstances and not victims of the circumstances. With the same perspective and attitude in life, God will help us to reverse the curse, turn tragedies into triumphs, miseries into melodies, hurts into healings and health, old obstacles into new opportunities if we will focus on Jesus, and draw inspiration and strength and all the other needed resources from the Source. Stumbling blocks will be turned into stepping stones to your success. Crises of life can make us more and more Christ like. The challenges and tragedies will not sink us; instead they will sanctify us inside out, through and through. Truly fulfilling life must be managed and lived from the inside out and not the outside in. The kingdom of God is within you. It is that which is within you that determines that which is without. By balancing the forces of the will with faith in action, with patience, humility and perseverance, we all can experience success, abundance victory and prosperity of life without having to ever lose our cool, the peace of mind and the joy of the heart. All of these are possible, available and are yours to grasp if you will always live your daily life in light of the following four priorities:

Have something bigger, brighter and better than yourself to believe in;

Have someone to love and to be loved by;

Have something meaningful and significant to do here and now;

Have somewhere exciting and eternal to look forward to there and then.

Life Lessons from Moses: Living a life that really matters

Deut 34:7: Moses was a hundred and twenty years old when he died, yet his eyes were not weak nor his strength gone.

What a marvelous commentary on a life well lived, a life that really mattered to literally millions then and perhaps trillions since then! The vision of Moses was not dimmed and his vigor was not abated! What a visionary, vigorous and miraculous man Moses truly was! The life and mission of Moses have several major life lessons to impart to us for our own encouragements and empowerment (Kushner, 2006):

1. In spite of all the searing disappointments and serious ingratitude he experienced, Moses' spiritual greatness is found in his gaze, his forward gaze to the future with the vision of God's people settled in the Promised Land and living with purpose and peace! He always looked forward and upward, and never backward (p.26)!

2. Moses teaches us how to be Our Best Selves even when life does not turn out as we had hoped it would (p.26).

3. Moses teaches us a life lesson on perseverance. Don't give up and don't break up in the face of constant criticism from an ungrateful people he loved and served (p.27).

4. The extraordinary dedication of Moses was born out of keeping his mind constantly focused on the promises and the presence of the God who alone called him (p.27)!

5. Moses was able to keep up the faith with enthusiasm because he always remembered Whom he was working for—not to earn thanks from the Jews, but to please and glorify God (p.37).

6. To learn from Moses, leaders on the one hand are to gain wisdom to recognize the frailty of the human soul: weak, selfish, unreliable, imperfect and easily distracted; on the other hand, they are to keep sight of the goodness in the people, as Moses did, in that he remained aware of the redeeming qualities of the people who have hurt and disappointed him. While we should set high standards for us and for the people, we

must be also simultaneously prepared to see them fall short of those high standards. The key is to pick up the shattered and broken tablets originally made by God alone, carry along with the second set of tablets made by the divine and human joint efforts, and keep on going forward.

7. Another lesson along the same train of thoughts Moses teaches is that if you can not control the behaviors and emotions of others, control your own response to them. Give others room to be themselves while still and always loving them anyways.

8. Moses teaches us to open our hearts to pain and suffering, and then we will heal, not because of suffering itself, but because of opening our hearts to it. The Jewish proverb summaries it succinctly: The world breaks everyone, and afterwards, many are stronger at the broken places (pp.44-45).

9. Moses teaches us to always do the right thing, not for the rewards or applauses of others, but simply because it is the right thing to do (p.48)!

10. We may fail and lose at one thing or at many things, but that does not make us failures or losers. The worth of a person's soul is measured by one's humanity, compassion, and courage to keep on dreaming and keep on trying. True success is being your personal best, and becoming the person you are meant to be (p.53)!

11. When everything has been taken away from you, the last of human freedoms is the individual's right to choose one's attitude in any given set of circumstances. What happened to you, no matter how hurtful or unfair, is ultimately less important than what you do about what happened to you. Concentrate on what you still have left, and not on what you have lost (p.53).

12. Moses also teaches us the importance of keeping our promises (Exodus 13:19) at a time when he could have enriched himself with lots of personal gain. "Keeping promises is the cornerstone of responsibility, and responsibility for one's behavior is the defining characteristic of one's maturity" (p.108).

13. Moses provides us with a life lesson on humility in (Numbers 12:3). Recognize that not everything that happens in your life is all about you. You are not God, and it is not your job to run the world (p. 120).

14. The most enduring and valuable life lesson from Moses, according to Rabbi Kushner is this: face our past with gratitude, and face our future with confidence, in spite of the memories of the dreams that never came true. There are other more attainable dreams waiting for us.

15. The sad but inescapable truth is that very few people in life ever make it to the Promised Land—getting everything they have ever yearned for; nevertheless, at the end of life, like Moses, let us also write a song, or a book, and sing a hymn of praises to God (Deut 32), and bless the people who have quarreled with you for so long (Deut 33). At the end of his life, by choice, and not by chance, Moses clearly articulated pride rather than regrets; gratitude rather than bitterness; and praises rather than envy (p.172), living a life that really mattered, a life with joy and peace, and a life without any regret or remorse!

16. The amazing summary of the life of Moses in Deut 34:7 is that he was just as vigorous and visionary at the end of his life as he was when God first summoned him! Moses had the patience to accept and to live with the shattered tablets of God and the imperfections of the world. He was willing to forgive and refused to allow bitterness in life. He chose to be regenerative and not stagnant as his happy ending for his life (p.135).

Bibliographical References

Anders, Max (1996). *21 Unbreakable Laws of Life: Lessons You Don't Have To Learn The Hard Way*. Nashville: Thomas Nelson Publishers.

Anderson, Neil T (1990). *Victory over the Darkness*. Ventura, CA: Regal Books.

Augsburger, David W (1986). *Pastoral Counseling Across Cultures*. Philadelphia: Westminster Press.

Beason, Fedlyn A (2008). *The Prosperity Gospel and Its Adverse Effect*s. Cleveland TN: Derek Press.

Bennett, William J (1995). *The Moral Compass: Stories for Life's Journey*. NY: Simon & Schuster.

Blanchard, Ken and Mark Miller (2004). *The Secret: What Great Leaders Know and Do*. San Francisco: Berrett-Koehler Publishers, Inc.

Bunyan, John (2003). *The Pilgrim's Progress*. (Chinese translation by Hanchuan Wang).Beijing: China Worker's Publishing House.

Cho, David Yonggi (1987). *Salvation, Health & Prosperity: Our Threefold Blessings in Christ*. Altamonte Springs, Fl: Creation House.

Clinton, J Roberts 1988). *The Making of A Leader: Recognizing the Lessons and the Stages of Leadership Development*. Colorado Springs: NAVPRESS.

Coleman, Robert C (1963). *The Master Plan of Evangelism*. Old Tappan, NJ: Fleming H. Revell Company.

Coleman, Robert C (1990). *"Nothing to Do but to Save Souls:" John Wesley's Charge to His Preachers*. Wilmore KY: Wesley Heritage Press.

Cottrell, David (2002). *Monday Morning Leadership*. Dallas, TX: Corner Stone Leadership Institute.

Covey, Stephen R. (2004). *The 7 Habits of Highly Effective People: Powerful Lessons in Personal Change*. New York: Free Press.

Cunningham, Loren (1991). *Daring to Live on the Edge*. Seattle WA:YWAM Publishing.

Davis, James O. (2009). *Gutenburg To Google: The 20 Indispensable Laws of Communication*. Tulsa, OK: Word & Spirit Resources.

Davis, Ron L (1991). *The Mentoring Strategy of the Master*. Nashville: Thomas Nelson Publishers.

Dewey, John (1933). *How We Think*. Boston: D.C Heath and Company.

Dillon, William P (1993). *People Raising*. Chicago: Moody Press.

Edwards, Gene (1992). *A Tale of Three Kings: A Study in Brokenness*. Wheaton, Il: Tyndale House Publishers, Inc.

Ellis, Albert (1988). *Rational-Emotive Behavior Therapy*. Boston: Allyn and Bacon.

Elmer, Duane (1993). *Cross-cultural; Conflicts: Building Relationships for Effective Ministries*. Downers Grove, Il: InterVarsity Press.

English Dictionary (1992). Edmonds, WA: All Nations

Engstrom, Ted W (1976). *The Making of A Christian Leader*. Grand Rapids: Zondervan Publishing Company.

Foster, Richard J (2009). *Money, Sex and Power: The Challenge of the Disciplined Life*. London: Hodder & Stoughton Ltd.

Foster, Richard J (1988). *Celebration of Discipline*. San Francisco: Harper and Row.

Foster, Richard J (2005). *Freedom of Simplicity*. NY: Harperone.

Frank, Viktor E (1984), *Man's Search for Meaning*. NY: Washington Square Press.

Gladwell, Malcolm (2008). *Outliers: The Story of Success*. NY: Back Bay Books

Gould, William B (1993). *Frank: Life with Meaning*. Pacific Grove, Ca: Brooks/Cole Publishing Company.

Grady, J. Lee (Mar 2001). *"An Abnormal Gospel."* Charisma & Christian Life.

Grady, J. Lee (June 2013). *www.charismamag.com/blogs/fire-in-my-bones*

Graham, Billy (1997). *Just As I Am*. San Francisco: HarperCollins.

Haggai, John (1986). *Lead On!* Dallas: Word Publishing.

Haggai, John (1988). *The Leading Edge*. Dallas: Word Publishing.

Hart, Archibald D (1996). *Habits of the Mind: Ten exercises To Renew Your Thinking*. Dallas: Word Publishing

Hattaway, Paul (2009). *Henan: The Galilee of China*. Carlisle, UK: Piquant.

Hattaway, Paul & Joy (2013). Newsletter #119. *www.asiaharvest.org*

Henry, Lewis C, Ed (1945). *Five Thousands Quotations for All Occasions. Garden City*, NY: Double Day & Company., Inc.

Horne, C. Silvester (1999). *David Livingston: Man of Prayer and Action*. Arlington Heights, Il: Christian Liberty Press.

Hughes, Selwyn, and Thomas Kinkade (1997). *Everyday Light*. Nashville, TN: Broadman & Holman Publishers.

Huijser, Mijnd (2006). The Cultural Advantage: *A New Model for Succeeding with Global Teams*. Boston: Intercultural Press.

Humphrey, Billy (May 13, 2012). *Simplicity of the Gospel: More Lessons from China*. Missions Newsletter on the Internet.

Kreider, Larry and Floyd McClung (2007). *Starting A House Church: A New Model for Living Out Your Faith*. Ventura, Ca: Regal Books.

Kubler-Ross, Elizabeth (1974). *Questions and Answers on Death and Dying*. NY: Macmillan Publishing Co., Inc.

Kushner, Harold S (1981). *When Bad Things Happen to Good People*. NY: Schocken Books.

Kushner, Harold S (1986). *When All You've Ever Wanted Isn't Enough*. NY: Summit Books.

Kushner, Harold J (1989). *Who Needs God*. NY: Summit Books.

Kushner, Harold S (1996). *How Good Do We Have to Be*. NY: Little & Brown Company.

Kushner, Harold S (2001). *Living A Life That Matters*. NY: Alfred A. Knopf.

Kushner, Harold S (2006). *Overcoming Life's Disappointments*. NY: Alfred A. Knopf.

Kushner, Harold S (2009). *Conquering Fear: Living Boldly in An Uncertain World*. NY: Alfred A. Knopf.

Kustenmacher, Tiki (2004). *How To Simplify Your Life*. NY: McGraw-Hill.

Lessin, Roy (2009). *www.meetmeinthemeadow.com/2009/07/ looking-unto-jesus-2*.

Lier, Dan (2006). *The Ten Minute Coach: Daily Strategies for Life Success*. New York: Beaufort Books.

MaHaney, C.J. (2005). *Humility: True Greatness*. Colorado Springs: Multnomah Books.

Martin, Jonathan (2008). *Giving Wisely or Empowering Lasting Transformation?* Sisters, Or: Last Chapter Publishing, LLC.

Maxwell, John C (2007). *The Maxwell Leadership Bible* (NKJV). Nashville: Thomas Nelson.

Menzies, William W & Robert P (2000). *Spirit and Power: Foundations of Pentecostal Experience*. Grand Rapids, MI: Zondervan.

Meyer, Joyce (2007). *100 Ways to Simplify Your Life*. NY: Faith Words.
Mohamed, Arif; Elder, Brett & Grabill, Stephen (editors, 2010 Kingdom Stewardship. Grand Rapids, MI: Christian's Library Press.

Moloney, Francis J (1984). *A Life of Promise: Poverty, Chastity, Obedience*. Wilmington, DL: Michael Glaziers, Inc.

Morgan: Robert J (2010). *100 Bible Verses Everyone Should Know* by Heart. Nashville, TN: B & H Publishing Group.

Munroe, Myles (2005). *The Spirit of Leadership: Cultivating the Attitudes That Influence Human Action*. New Kensington, PA: Whitaker House

Munroe, Myles (2010). *Rediscovering the Kingdom: Ancient Hope for Our 21st Century World*. Shippensburg, PA: Destiny Image Publishers, Inc.

Nee, Watchman (1977). *God's Plan and the Overcomers*. NY: Christian
Fellowship Publishers.

Niebuhr, H. Richard (1951). *Christ and Culture*. NY: Harper and Row,
Publishers, Inc.

NIV Stewardship Study Bible (2010). The Stewardship Council.

Nouwen, Henri, J.M (1989). *In the Name of Jesus: Reflections on Christian
Leadership*. New York: Crossroad Publishing House.

Nouwen, Henri J.M (1994). Here and Now. NY: Crossroad Publishing Company.

Peale, Norman Vincent (1976). *The Positive Principle Today*. NY:
Fawcett Crest Books.

Peale, Norman V (1991). *Thought Conditioners*. Pawling, NY: Peale Center for
Christian Living.

Philipps, Donald T (1992). *Lincoln on Leadership*. NY: Business Plus.

Pipe, John (2007). *Don't Waste Your Life*. Wheaton, Il: Crossway Books.

Ramsey, Dave (2007). *The Total Money Makeover*. Nashville: Thomas Nelson
Publishers.

Rutland, Mark (1987). Launch Out Into The Deep. Wilmore, KY: Bristol Books.

Stowell, Joseph M (1996). Following Christ. Grand Rapids, MI: Zondervan.

Swindoll, Charles R (2001). *Wisdom for the way: Wise Words for Busy People*.
Nashville, TN: J. Countryman.

Taylor, Peter H. (2008). *Sowing in Tears & Reaping with Joy*. Cleveland TN:
Derek Press

Telushkin, Joseph (1994). *Jewish Wisdom*. NY: William Morrow & Company.

The Full Life Study Bible (1992). Grand Rapids, MI: Zondervan Publishing
House.

Vaughan, Roland (2013). "Finishing the Mission," a personal presentation.
Cleveland, TN USA.

Waitley, Denis. (1979). *The Psychology of Winning: Ten Qualities of a Total Winner*. NY: Berkley Books.

Warren, Rick (2002). *The Purpose Driven Life*. Grand Rapids, MI: Zondervan.

Wilkerson, Bruce (2003). *The Dream Giver*. Colorado Springs: Multnomah Books.

Yang, Hong Y (1996). *Cross-Cultural Counseling: A Christ-Centered Approach and Application*. Cleveland TN: Pathway Press.

Yang, Hong Y (1998). *Authority To Overcome: Soaring High On Eagle's Wings*. Cleveland TN: Pathway Press.

Zapico, Jose & Lidia (2010). *Prosperous . . . Who, Me?* Miramar, Fl: JVH Publications